AWARD
of
HER BRITANNIC MAJESTY'S GOVERNMENT

pursuant to the
Agreement for Arbitration (Compromiso)
of a Controversy between the Argentine
Republic and the Republic of Chile
concerning the region of the
Beagle Channel

LONDON
HER MAJESTY'S STATIONERY OFFICE

First published 1977

ISBN 0 11 591649 0*

DECLARATION OF HER MAJESTY QUEEN ELIZABETH II, PURSUANT TO THE AGREEMENT FOR ARBITRATION (COMPROMISO) DETERMINED BY THE GOVERNMENT OF THE UNITED KINGDOM OF GREAT BRITAIN AND NORTHERN IRELAND AND SIGNED ON BEHALF OF THAT GOVERNMENT AND THE GOVERNMENTS OF THE ARGENTINE REPUBLIC AND THE REPUBLIC OF CHILE ON 22 JULY 1971 FOR THE ARBITRATION OF A CONTROVERSY BETWEEN THE ARGENTINE REPUBLIC AND THE REPUBLIC OF CHILE CONCERNING THE REGION OF THE BEAGLE CHANNEL(1)

WHEREAS the Argentine Republic and the Republic of Chile (hereinafter referred to as "the Parties") became parties to a General Treaty of Arbitration signed at Santiago on 28th May 1902(2) (hereinafter referred to as "the Treaty");

AND WHEREAS His Britannic Majesty's Government duly accepted the duty of Arbitrator conferred upon them by the Treaty;

AND WHEREAS a controversy has arisen between the Parties concerning the region of the Beagle Channel;

AND WHEREAS, on this occasion, the Parties concurred with regard to the applicability of the Treaty to this controversy and requested the intervention of Our Government in the United Kingdom of Great Britain and Northern Ireland as Arbitrator;

AND WHEREAS Our Government in the United Kingdom, after hearing the Parties, were satisfied that it would be appropriate for them to act as Arbitrator in the controversy;

AND WHEREAS Our Government in the United Kingdom, in accordance with the Treaty and after consulting the Parties separately, determined the Agreement for Arbitration (Compromiso) which was signed on behalf of Our said Government and the Parties at London on 22nd July 1971(3);

---

(1) In accordance with Article XIII of the Agreement for Abitration (Compromiso), the decision of the Court of Arbitration with this declaration that such decision constitutes the Award in accordance with the General Treaty of Arbitration signed at Santiago on 28th May 1902 was communicated to the Argentine Republic and the Republic of Chile by delivery to the London addresses of the Heads of their Diplomatic Missions on 2 May 1977.

(2) British and Foreign State Papers vol. 95, p. 759.

(3) Miscellaneous No. 23 (1971), Cmnd. 4781.

AND WHEREAS for the purpose of fulfilling their duties as Arbitrator Our Government in the United Kingdom appointed a Court of Arbitration composed of the following members:

Mr. Hardy C. Dillard (United States of America)

Sir Gerald Fitzmaurice (United Kingdom)

Mr. André Gros (France)

Mr. Charles D. Onyeama (Nigeria) and

Mr. Sture Petrén (Sweden);

AND WHEREAS, the Government of the Argentine Republic having on 11th March 1972 denounced the Treaty with effect from 22nd September 1972, both Parties stated their understanding, which was shared by Our Government in the United Kingdom, that this would in no way affect the arbitration proceedings in the present case and that the Treaty and the Agreement for Arbitration (Compromiso) would continue in force with respect to those proceedings until their final conclusion;

AND WHEREAS the Parties have presented to the Court of Arbitration written pleadings and maps and other documents;

AND WHEREAS, having heard representatives of the Parties, the Court of Arbitration, accompanied by the Registrar and representatives of the Parties, visited the Beagle Channel region in March 1976;

AND WHEREAS representatives of the Parties took part in oral hearings before the Court of Arbitration between 7th September and 23rd October 1976;

AND WHEREAS the Court of Arbitration, acting in accordance with the provisions of the Agreement for Arbitration (Compromiso), has considered the questions specified in paragraphs (1) and (2) of Article I of that Agreement, reaching its conclusions in accordance with the principles of international law, and has transmitted to Our Government in the United Kingdom its Decision thereon (a copy of which Decision is annexed to this Declaration), including the drawing of the boundary line on a chart;

AND WHEREAS Our Government in the United Kingdom have fully and carefully studied the Decision of the Court of Arbitration, which decides definitively each point in dispute and states the reasons for the decision on each point;

NOW, in pursuance of Article XIII of the Agreement for Arbitration (Compromiso) and in the name of Our Government in the United Kingdom, WE, ELIZABETH THE SECOND, by the Grace of God of the United Kingdom of Great Britain and Northern Ireland and of Our other Realms and Territories Queen, Head of the Commonwealth, Defender of the Faith, etc., etc., etc. hereby ratify the Decision of the Court of Arbitration and declare that the said Decision constitutes the Award in accordance with the Treaty.

GIVEN in triplicate under Our hand and seal, at Our Court of St. James's this Eighteenth day of April, One thousand Nine hundred and Seventy-seven in the Twenty-sixth year of Our Reign.

ELIZABETH R.

BEAGLE CHANNEL ARBITRATION

between

THE REPUBLIC OF ARGENTINA AND THE REPUBLIC OF CHILE

Report and Decision of the Court of Arbitration

rendered to

Her Britannic Majesty's Government
in the
United Kingdom

182915

Note: This publication reproduces the text of the original signed Report and Decision of the Court, except that, where certain minor typographical or editorial errors have been discovered, these have been corrected.

BEAGLE CHANNEL ARBITRATION

REPORT AND DECISION OF THE COURT

TABLE OF CONTENTS

PART I: REPORT

PART II: DECISION

1. Main Heads

2. Detailed Headings

ANNEXES

MAPS
(in end-pocket)

BEAGLE CHANNEL ARBITRATION
BETWEEN
THE REPUBLIC OF ARGENTINA AND THE REPUBLIC OF CHILE

REPORT AND DECISION OF THE COURT OF ARBITRATION

PART I: REPORT

A. PERSONNEL OF THE CASE

THE COURT:

Members (as appointed on 22 July 1971):

Judge Sir Gerald Fitzmaurice (President)

Judge André Gros

Judge Sture Petrén

Judge Charles Onyeama

Judge Hardy C. Dillard

Registrar:

Professor Philippe Cahier

THE PARTIES:

The Argentine Republic, represented by

As Agents:

His Excellency Señor Ernesto de la Guardia, Ambassador Extraordinary and Plenipotentiary on Special Mission.

His Excellency Señor Julio Barboza, Ambassador Extraordinary and Plenipotentiary on Special Mission.

As Advisers:

His Excellency Señor Luis Maria de Pablo Pardo, Ambassador Extraordinary and Plenipotentiary of the Argentine Republic in the Swiss Confederation, Professor of International Law in the Argentine Catholic University, Buenos Aires.

Rear-Admiral Señor Raul A. Fitte, Argentine Navy.

As Counsel:

Professor Roberto Ago, Professor of International Law in the Faculty of Law of the University of Rome.

Professor Robert Y. Jennings, Q.C., Whewell Professor of International Law in the University of Cambridge.

Professor Paul Reuter, Professor in the University of Law, Economics and Social Sciences of Paris.

Other Advisers, Experts and Secretaries :

Señor Enrique J. A. Candioti, Minister Plenipotentiary, Argentine Agency, Geneva.

Señor Marcelo Delpech, Minister Plenipotentiary, Argentine Agency, Geneva.

Señorita Susana Ruiz Cerutti, First Secretary, Argentine Agency, Geneva.

Señor Federico Mirré, First Secretary, Argentine Embassy, London.

Señorita Graciela Sabá, Second Secretary, Argentine Agency, Geneva.

Señora Luisa E. C. de Lemos, Administrative Officer, Argentine Agency, Geneva.

Señorita Alejandra Robinson, Administrative Officer, Argentine Agency, Geneva.

Señorita Clara Patiño Mayer, Administrative Officer, Argentine Agency, Geneva.

The Republic of Chile, represented by

As Agent :

His Excellency Señor Don José Miguel Barros, Ambassador Extraordinary and Plenipotentiary of Chile to the Netherlands and on Special Mission in the United Kingdom.

As Counsel :

Professor Prosper Weil, Professor in the University of Law, Economics and Social Sciences of Paris.

Professor Ian Brownlie, D.C.L. Professor of International Law in the University of London.

Professor Julio Philippi, Professor of Philosophy of Civil Law in the Catholic University of Santiago.

Other Advisers, Experts and Secretaries :

Señor Don Germán Carrasco, Minister Counsellor, Secretary General to the Chilean Agency, Geneva.

Commander Kenneth Pugh, Chilean Navy.

Señor Don Osvaldo Muñoz, Expert Adviser, Licenciado en Ciencias Juridicas y Sociales de la Universidad de Chile, Chilean Agency, Geneva.

Señor Don Ignacio Cox, Chilean Agency, Geneva.

John Walford, Esq.; Solicitor (Bischoff and Co.).

Jasper Hunt, Esq.; Solicitor (Bischoff and Co.).

B. STEPS PRECEDING THE REFERENCE TO ARBITRATION

On 11 December 1967, the Chilean Ambassador in London, His Excellency Señor Don Victor Santa Cruz delivered on behalf of the Government of the Republic of Chile a Note addressed to Her Majesty's Principal Secretary of State for Foreign Affairs, the Right Honourable George Brown, M.P., in which he referred to a dispute existing between the Republic of Chile and the Republic of Argentina concerning sovereignty over certain islands situated in the region of the Beagle Channel, and mentioned various attempts to reach agreement for the submission of the dispute to adjudication that had come to nothing. He then continued:

> "As it is imperative to find an early solution to this dispute, and having regard to the above-mentioned default of agreement, the Government of Chile has decided to have recourse to Her Majesty's Government as permanent arbitrator under the 1902 General Treaty of Arbitration [sc. between Chile and Argentina], and in this connection to invite them to intervene as Arbiter in the manner provided for in Article 5 of that Treaty."

There followed the formal request, made on the instructions of the Government of Chile, that the necessary proceedings should be initiated by Her Majesty's Government.

On the same day the Chilean Minister for Foreign Affairs sent the Ambassador of the Argentine Republic in Santiago a Note in which, after recalling the negotiations between the two countries, he informed him of the *démarche* made in London.

In a Note of 19 December 1967, addressed to the Argentine Ambassador in London, Her Majesty's Government asked the Argentine Government whether it wished to make any comments in regard to the Chilean request.

The Argentine Ambassador in London replied on 29 December sending copies of two Notes dated 23 December, addressed by the Argentine Foreign Minister to the Chilean Ambassador in Buenos Aires, in which it was stressed that no agreement had been reached between the two countries as to the applicability of the Treaty of 1902 to the extant dispute, and invited the Chilean Government to resume negotiations.

There were no immediate results; but in the end the two Governments, overcoming their differences of view, succeeded in arriving at an agreement for submitting the case to arbitration, and thus it was that, on 22 July 1971, there was signed in London between Her Britannic Majesty's Government, the Government of the Republic of Argentina and the Government of the Republic of Chile, an agreement entitled "Agreement for Arbitration (*Compromiso*) of a controversy between the Argentine Republic and the Republic of Chile concerning the Region of the Beagle Channel", the English and Spanish texts of which, both equally authentic, are set out in the next following section.

C. THE ARBITRATION AGREEMENT OR COMPROMISO

POR CUANTO la República Argentina y la República de Chile (en adelante llamadas " las Partes ", nominadas en orden alfabético en este instrumento) son partes de un Tratado General de Arbitraje (en adelante denominado " el Tratado ") firmado en Santiago de Chile el 28 de mayo de 1902;

POR CUANTO el Gobierno de Su Majestad Británica aceptó debidamente el cargo de Arbitro que le confirió el Tratado;

POR CUANTO entre las Partes ha surgido una controversia en la zona del Canal de Beagle;

POR CUANTO, en esta oportunidad, las Partes han coincidido en la aplicación del Tratado a esta controversia y han requerido la intervención como Arbitro del Gobierno de Su Majestad Británica;

POR CUANTO el Gobierno de Su Majestad Británica, luego de oir a las Partes, se ha convencido de que puede actuar como Arbitro en la controversia;

POR CUANTO para cumplir sus funciones de Arbitro el Gobierno de Su Majestad Británica ha designado una Corte Arbitral integrada por los siguientes miembros:

Sr. Hardy C. Dillard (Estados Unidos de América)

Sir Gerald Fitzmaurice (Reino Unido)

Sr. André Gros (Francia)

Sr. Charles D. Onyeama (Nigeria)

Sr. Sture Petrén (Suecia);

WHEREAS the Argentine Republic and the Republic of Chile (hereinafter referred to as " the Parties ", named in alphabetical order in this instrument) are parties to a General Treaty of Arbitration signed at Santiago on 28th May 1902 (hereinafter referred to as " the Treaty ");

AND WHEREAS His Britannic Majesty's Government duly accepted the duty of Arbitrator conferred upon them by the Treaty;

AND WHEREAS a controversy has arisen between the Parties concerning the region of the Beagle Channel;

AND WHEREAS, on this occasion, the Parties have concurred with regard to the applicability of the Treaty to this controversy, and have requested the intervention of Her Britannic Majesty's Government as Arbitrator;

AND WHEREAS Her Britannic Majesty's Government, after hearing the Parties, are satisfied that it would be appropriate for them to act as Arbitrator in the controversy;

AND WHEREAS for the purpose of fulfilling their duties as Arbitrator, Her Britannic Majesty's Government have appointed a Court of Arbitration composed of the following members:

Mr. Hardy C. Dillard (United States of America)

Sir Gerald Fitzmaurice (United Kingdom)

Mr. André Gros (France)

Mr. Charles D. Onyeama (Nigeria) and

Mr. Sture Petrén (Sweden);

El Gobierno de Su Majestad Británica, de conformidad con el Tratado y luego de consultar separadamente a las Partes, ha fijado el Acuerdo de Arbitraje (Compromiso) como sigue:

Artículo I

1) La República Argentina solicita que el Arbitro determine cuál es la línea del límite entre las respectivas jurisdicciones marítimas de la República Argentina y la República de Chile desde el meridiano 68°36′38.5″W., dentro de la región mencionada en el párrafo 4) de este Artículo y en consecuencia declare que pertenecen a la República Argentina las islas Picton, Nueva y Lennox e islas e islotes adyacentes.

2) La República de Chile solicita que el Arbitro resuelva las cuestiones planteadas en sus notas de 11 de diciembre de 1967 al Gobierno de Su Majestad Británica y al Gobierno de la República Argentina, en cuanto se relacionan con la región a que se refiere el párrafo 4) de este Artículo y que declare que pertenecen a la República de Chile las islas Picton, Lennox y Nueva, islas e islotes adyacentes, como asimismo las demás islas e islotes cuya superficie total se encuentra íntegramente dentro de la zona indicada en el párrafo 4) de este Artículo.

3) Las cuestiones mencionadas en los dos párrafos precedentes constituyen la expresión de la voluntad de las Partes respecto de los puntos controvertidos, sobre los cuales deberá decidir la Corte Arbitral.

4) La región a que se refieren los párrafos 1) y 2) de este Artículo está determinada por seis puntas cuyas coordenadas geográficas son las siguientes:

Her Britannic Majesty's Government, in accordance with the Treaty and after consulting the Parties separately, have determined the Arbitration Agreement (Compromiso) as follows:

Article I

(1) The Argentine Republic requests the Arbitrator to determine what is the boundary-line between the respective maritime jurisdictions of the Argentine Republic and of the Republic of Chile from meridian 68°36′38.5″W., within the region referred to in paragraph (4) of this Article, and in consequence to declare that Picton, Nueva and Lennox Islands and adjacent islands and islets belong to the Argentine Republic.

(2) The Republic of Chile requests the Arbitrator to decide, to the extent that they relate to the region referred to in paragraph (4) of this Article, the questions referred to in her Notes of 11th December 1967 to Her Britannic Majesty's Government and to the Government of the Argentine Republic and to declare that Picton, Lennox and Nueva Islands, the adjacent islands and islets, as well as the other islands and islets whose entire land surface is situated wholly within the region referred to in paragraph (4) of this Article, belong to the Republic of Chile.

(3) The questions specified in the two foregoing paragraphs express the will of the Parties as to the points in dispute which are to be decided by the Court of Arbitration.

(4) The region referred to in paragraphs (1) and (2) of this Article is determined by six points the geographical co-ordinates of which are the following:

	Latitud (S)	Longitud (W)
A	54°45′	68°36′38.5″
B	54°57′	68°36′38.5″
C	54°57′	67°13′
D	55°24′	67°13′
E	55°24′	66°25′
F	54°45′	66°25′

5) El orden en que las preguntas figuran en este Acuerdo de Arbitraje (Compromiso) no implica prelación alguna de una sobre la otra para su consideración por la Corte Arbitral, ni un prejuzgamiento en cuanto al peso de la prueba.

6) Las peticiones que la República Argentina y la República de Chile han formulado en los párrafos 1) y 2) de este Artículo, no constituyen para la otra Parte, ni directa ni indirectamente, una aceptación de las afirmaciones de derecho ni de hecho contenidas en dichas peticiones.

7) La Corte Arbitral deberá decidir de acuerdo con los principios del derecho internacional.

ARTÍCULO II

La Corte Arbitral, de acuerdo con las disposiciones de este Acuerdo de Arbitraje (Compromiso), considerará las cuestiones expresadas en los párrafos 1) y 2) del Artículo I y transmitirá al Gobierno de Su Majestad Británica su decisión al respecto.

ARTÍCULO III

1) La Corte Arbitral elegirá uno de sus Miembros como Presidente. Asimismo designará un Secretario.

2) La Corte Arbitral fijará su sede en un lugar que no merezca observaciones de alguna de las Partes.

	Latitude (S)	Longitude (W)
A	54°45′	68°36′38.5″
B	54°57′	68°36′38.5″
C	54°57′	67°13′
D	55°24′	67°13′
E	55°24′	66°25′
F	54°45′	66°25′

(5) The order in which the questions appear in this Agreement (Compromiso) shall not imply any precedence of the one over the other with regard to their consideration by the Court of Arbitration, and shall be without prejudice to any burden of proof.

(6) The submissions in paragraphs (1) and (2) of this Article which the Argentine Republic and the Republic of Chile respectively have presented shall not constitute for the other Party, either directly or indirectly, acceptance of the assertions of law or fact contained in those submissions.

(7) The Court of Arbitration shall reach its conclusions in accordance with the principles of international law.

ARTICLE II

The Court of Arbitration, acting in accordance with the provisions of this Agreement (Compromiso), shall consider the questions specified in paragraphs (1) and (2) of Article I and transmit to Her Britannic Majesty's Government its decision thereon.

ARTICLE III

(1) The Court of Arbitration shall elect one of its members as President. It shall also appoint a Registrar.

(2) The Court of Arbitration shall establish its seat at a place not objected to by either Party.

ARTÍCULO IV

1) Dentro de un mes a contar de la fecha de la firma del presente Acuerdo de Arbitraje (Compromiso), cada una de las Partes nombrará uno o más Agentes para los efectos del Arbitraje, quienes fijarán un domicilio en la vecindad de la sede de la Corte Arbitral. Las Partes comunicarán al Gobierno de Su Majestad Británica, a la Corte Arbitral y a la otra Parte el nombre y domicilio de esos Agentes.

2) Si cualquiera de las Partes designara más de un Agente, ellos estarán facultados para actuar conjunta o separadamente.

ARTÍCULO V

1) La Corte Arbitral, sujeta a las disposiciones de este Acuerdo de Arbitraje (Compromiso) y luego de consultar a las Partes, fijará sus Reglas de Procedimiento y determinará el orden y fecha de entrega de los alegatos escritos y mapas y todas las demás cuestiones de procedimiento, escrito y oral, que pudieran surgir. La determinación del orden en que deban presentarse estos documentos se hará sin perjuicio de cualquier cuestión relativa al peso de la prueba.

2) El Secretario notificará a las Partes la dirección para la entrega de sus alegatos escritos y otros documentos.

ARTÍCULO VI

La Corte Arbitral podrá nombrar para que la asistan en su tarea los expertos que pueda requerir, a costa de las Partes.

ARTÍCULO VII

Las Partes darán a cualquiera de los Miembros de la Corte Arbitral,

ARTICLE IV

(1) Each of the Parties shall, within one month after the date of the signature of this Agreement (Compromiso), appoint an Agent or Agents for the purposes of the Arbitration, who shall establish an address in the vicinity of the seat of the Court of Arbitration. The Parties shall communicate the names and addresses of their Agents to Her Britannic Majesty's Government, to the Court of Arbitration and to the other Party.

(2) If either of the Parties appoints more than one Agent, they shall be authorised to act jointly or severally.

ARTICLE V

(1) The Court of Arbitration shall, subject to the provisions of this Agreement (Compromiso) and after consultation with the Parties, settle its own Rules of Procedure and determine the order and dates of delivery of written pleadings and maps and all other questions of procedure, written and oral, that may arise. The fixing of the order in which these documents shall be presented shall be without prejudice to any question of any burden of proof.

(2) The Registrar shall notify to the Parties an address for the filing of their written pleadings and other documents.

ARTICLE VI

The Court of Arbitration may, at the expense of the Parties, appoint such experts as it may wish to assist it.

ARTICLE VII

The Parties shall give to any members of the Court of Arbitration

a cualquiera de los miembros de su personal y a los representantes autorizados de cualquiera de las Partes que hayan sido requeridos por la Corte Arbitral para acompañar a Miembros de esa Corte o de su personal, libre acceso a sus territorios, incluso cualquier territorio en disputa, en el entendido de que el otorgamiento de ese acceso no perjudicará en forma alguna los derechos de cualquiera de las Partes al dominio del territorio al cual, en el cual, a través del cual o sobre el cual tal acceso sea otorgado.

ARTÍCULO VIII

En el caso de que las Partes conjuntamente o la Corte Arbitral deseen un reconocimiento y levantamiento, aéreo o de otro tipo, para las finalidades del Arbitraje, este reconocimiento y levantamiento se hará bajo la dirección de la Corte Arbitral y a expensa de las Partes.

ARTÍCULO IX

La Corte Arbitral tendrá competencia para resolver sobre la interpretación y aplicación de este Acuerdo de Arbitraje (Compromiso).

ARTÍCULO X

Cada una de las Partes pagará sus propios gastos y la mitad de los gastos de la Corte Arbitral y de los del Gobierno de Su Majestad Británica, en relación con el Arbitraje.

ARTÍCULO XI

1) En caso de muerte o incapacidad de cualquiera de los miembros de la Corte Arbitral, la vacante no será llenada a menos que las Partes acuerden lo contrario y el proceso continuará como si tal vacante no se hubiera producido.

and to any members of its staff, and to any authorised representatives of either Party who have been requested by the Court of Arbitration to accompany the members of the Court or its staff, free access to their territories, including any disputed territory, on the understanding that the grant of such access shall in no way prejudice the rights of either Party as to the ownership of any territory to, on, through or over which such access is granted.

ARTICLE VIII

In the event of the Parties jointly or the Court of Arbitration desiring a survey, by air or otherwise, for the purposes of the Arbitration, such survey shall be made under the guidance of the Court of Arbitration and at the expense of the Parties.

ARTICLE IX

The Court of Arbitration shall be competent to decide upon the interpretation and application of this Agreement (Compromiso).

ARTICLE X

Each of the Parties shall defray its own expenses and one half of the expenses of the Court of Arbitration and of Her Britannic Majesty's Government in relation to the Arbitration.

ARTICLE XI

(1) Should any member of the Court of Arbitration die or become unable to act, the vacancy shall not be filled unless the Parties agree otherwise, and the proceedings shall continue as if such vacancy had not occurred.

2) En caso de muerte o incapacidad del Secretario, la vacante será llenada por la Corte Arbitral y el proceso continuará como si la vacante no se hubiera producido.

Artículo XII

1) Concluído el proceso ante la Corte Arbitral, ésta transmitirá su decisión al Gobierno de Su Majestad Británica, incluyendo el trazado de la línea del límite en una carta.

2) La decisión resolverá definitivamente cada punto en disputa y establecerá las razones en las cuales se funda para resolverlo.

3) La decisión establecerá por quién, en qué forma y dentro de qué plazo ella será cumplida.

Artículo XIII

1) Si fuera sancionada la decisión a que se refiere el Artículo XII por el Gobierno de Su Majestad Británica, éste la comunicará a las Partes con la declaración de que esta decisión constituye la Sentencia de conformidad con el Tratado, la cual tendrá carácter definitivo de acuerdo con los Artículos XI y XIII de dicho Tratado.

2) La Sentencia será notificada a cada una de las Partes mediante su entrega en el domicilio en Londres de los Jefes de sus respectivas misiones diplomáticas.

Artículo XIV

La Sentencia será legalmente obligatoria para ambas Partes y será inapelable salvo lo dispuesto en el Artículo XIII del Tratado.

(2) Should the Registrar die or become unable to act, the vacancy shall be filled by the Court of Arbitration, and the proceedings shall continue as if such vacancy had not occurred.

Article XII

(1) When the proceedings before the Court of Arbitration have been completed, it shall transmit its decision to Her Britannic Majesty's Government, which shall include the drawing of the boundary-line on a chart.

(2) The decision shall decide definitively each point in dispute and shall state the reasons for the decision on each point.

(3) The decision shall determine by whom, in what manner and within what time limit it shall be executed.

Article XIII

(1) If the decision referred to in Article XII is ratified by Her Britannic Majesty's Government, they shall communicate it to the Parties with a declaration that such decision constitutes the Award in accordance with the Treaty, and that Award shall be final in accordance with Articles XI and XIII of the Treaty.

(2) The Award shall be communicated to each of the Parties by delivery to the London address of the Head of its Diplomatic Mission.

Article XIV

The Award shall be legally binding upon both the Parties and there shall be no appeal from it, except as provided in Article XIII of the Treaty.

182915 B 2

Artículo XV

La Corte Arbitral no cesará en sus funciones hasta que ella haya notificado al Gobierno de Su Majestad Británica que, en opinión de la Corte Arbitral, se ha dado ejecución material y completa a la Sentencia.

Artículo XVI

La nominación de las Partes en orden alfabético empleada en este Acuerdo de Arbitraje (Compromiso), no importa prelación para ningun efecto.

Artículo XVII

Las Partes han informado al Gobierno de Su Majestad Británica que han aceptado el texto de este Acuerdo de Arbitraje (Compromiso).

En fe de lo cual este Acuerdo de Arbitraje (Compromiso) ha sido firmado por representantes debidamente autorizados del Gobierno del Reino Unido de Gran Bretaña e Irlanda del Norte, del Gobierno de la República Argentina y del Gobierno de la República de Chile.

Dado en Londres el día 22 de julio de 1971, en idiomas español e inglés, siendo ambos textos igualmente auténticos, en un solo original que será depositado en los archivos del Gobierno Británico, quien transmitirá copias fieles y certificadas al Gobierno de la República Argentina, al Gobierno de la República de Chile y a la Corte Arbitral.

Por el Gobierno del Reino Unido de Gran Bretaña e Irlanda del Norte:

JOSEPH GODBER

Article XV

The Court of Arbitration shall not be *functus officio* until it has notified Her Britannic Majesty's Government that in the opinion of the Court of Arbitration the Award has been materially and fully executed.

Article XVI

The reference to the Parties in alphabetical order in this Agreement (Compromiso) shall not imply precedence for any purpose whatsoever.

Article XVII

The Parties have informed Her Britannic Majesty's Government that they have accepted the terms of this Agreement (Compromiso).

In witness whereof this Agreement (Compromiso) has been signed by the duly authorised representatives of the Government of the United Kingdom of Great Britain and Northern Ireland, the Government of the Argentine Republic and the Government of the Republic of Chile.

Done at London the 22nd day of July, 1971, in the English and Spanish languages, both texts being equally authoritative, in a single original which shall be deposited in the achives of the Government of the United Kingdom, who shall transmit certified true copies to the Government of the Argentine Republic, to the Government of the Republic of Chile and to the Court of Arbitration.

For the Government of the United Kingdom of Great Britain and Northern Ireland:

JOSEPH GODBER

Por el Gobierno de la República Argentina:

G. MARTINEZ-ZUVIRIA

For the Government of the Argentine Republic:

G. MARTINEZ-ZUVIRIA

Por el Gobierno de la República de Chile:

ALVARO BUNSTER

For the Government of the Republic of Chile:

ALVARO BUNSTER

D. SUMMARY OF THE PROCEEDINGS

Preliminary steps and written proceedings

Shortly after the signature of the *Compromiso*, and in compliance with Article IV (1) thereof, the Parties appointed Agents for the purposes of the Arbitration. The Government of the Argentine Republic appointed as its Agents His Excellency Señor Ernesto de la Guardia and His Excellency Señor Julio Barboza. The Government of the Republic of Chile appointed as its Agents His Excellency Señor Don Alvaro Bunster and His Excellency Señor Don José Miguel Barros, the former of whom resigned in September 1973.

Acting under Article III of the *Compromiso* the Court elected Sir Gerald Fitzmaurice as its President.

At an informal meeting with the Parties held in London at the end of September 1971, various procedural matters were discussed, and it was decided, (*inter alia*) that English would be the language of the case, and that the written pleadings would be submitted in English.

In accordance with Article V of the *Compromiso*, the Court has, after consultation with the Parties, determined all other questions of procedure, written and oral, that have arisen, including the order and dates of the delivery of written pleadings, annexes and maps.

In conformity with Article III of the *Compromiso*, and by courtesy of the Swiss Federal and Geneva Cantonal authorities, the Court established its seat in the city of Geneva by an Order of 10 June 1972. By the same Order it fixed 1 January 1973 for the simultaneous deposit of the Parties' Memorials.

By an Order of 6 October 1972, Professor Philippe Cahier was appointed Registrar of the Court; and at the request of the Parties, the time-limit for the deposit of the Memorials was extended to 2 July 1973. The Memorials were duly delivered as ordered.

On 7 December 1973, the Court issued an Order fixing 2 July 1974 as the date for the deposit of the Counter-Memorials. At the request of the Agent of the Argentine Government, and with the consent of the Agent of the Government of Chile, the Court, by an Order of 22 July 1974, extended the time-limit for the deposit of the Counter-Memorials to 2 October 1974. These also were delivered on the due date.

On 29 November 1974 the Court held a meeting at The Hague with the representatives of the Parties to discuss with them certain procedural matters, —in particular the possibility of the delivery of Replies, and of a visit by the Members of the Court to the Beagle Channel region.

By an Order of 20 December 1974 the Court fixed 1 July 1975 as the date for the delivery of the Replies, and these were forthcoming on that date.

Visit to the disputed region.

At the request of both Parties all the Members of the Court, accompanied by the Registrar and Liaison Officers from both sides, visited the Beagle Channel region during the first fortnight of March 1976, and inspected the islands and waterways concerned, first on the Chilean Naval Transport

Vessel " Aquiles ", and then on the Argentine Naval Transport Vessel " Bahia Aguirre ". Every possible assistance and facility was afforded by the personnel of both Navies and by the individual representatives of the Parties participating in the expedition.

The Court subsequently fixed 7 September 1976 as the date for the opening of the oral proceedings, —and on 29 July the Parties, with the sanction of the Court, deposited a number of additional documents.

The oral proceedings

The formal opening of the oral proceedings took place on 7 September 1976 in the Alabama Room of the Hôtel de Ville, Geneva, by arrangement with the authorities concerned, and was attended by representatives of the Arbitrator Government, the Parties, the Swiss federal and cantonal authorities and of the International Labour Office in whose premises the working meetings were to be held. After a speech of welcome by Mr. Jacques Vernet, Conseiller d'Etat, Head of the Department of Public Works of the Canton of Geneva, the President declared the oral proceedings open and made a general explanatory statement (reproduced as No. 1 in Annex V hereto), which was followed by statements delivered by the Agents of the Parties.

Thereafter, starting on 8 September and finishing on 23 October, the hearings took place in the premises of the International Labour Organisation. During this period two rounds of addresses were presented on behalf of each Party, Chile starting each round (by arrangement between the Parties), and Argentina finishing; with statements by, on behalf of Chile, His Excellency Señor Don José Miguel Barros, as Agent, and Professors Weil and Brownlie, as Counsel, —and on behalf of Argentina, their Excellencies Señor Ernesto de la Guardia and Julio Barboza, as Agents, and Professor Ago, Jennings and Reuter as counsel. Statements were delivered in English or French at the Speaker's choice, a simultaneous translation into English being provided in the latter case.

At the conclusion of the oral hearings the Court requested the Parties to furnish it with further written observations on certain matters dealt with in one of the final statements made on behalf of Argentina. These were deposited, respectively, on 3 November (Chile) and 16 November (Argentina) —the dates specified by the Court.

After a valedictory statement by the President, the text of which is reproduced as No. 2 in Annex V hereto, the oral proceedings were declared closed. As regards the Court's deliberation, see Section F on p. xvii below.

E. FORMAL SUBMISSIONS OF THE PARTIES

In the Memorials

On behalf of the Government of the Argentine Republic

The Argentine Republic

....

concludes and maintains that the boundary line between the respective maritime jurisdictions of the Argentine Republic and of the Republic of Chile from meridian 68°36′38.5″W. of Greenwich runs along the median line of the Beagle Channel, deviating from that line only where inflexions are necessary so that each country may always navigate in waters of its own; and that the line therefore runs equidistant from Islas Bridges and Islote Bartlett, and then equidistant from Islotes Les Eclaireurs and the northern coast of Isla Navarino as far as Banco Herradura where it turns to follow a middle course between Banco Herradura and Banco Gable (thus avoiding obstacles to navigation); thence it continues a middle course through Paso Mackinlay, and then between Isla Martillo and Islotes Gemelos; thereafter, returning to the median line of the Beagle Channel, the boundary continues south-eastwards along the course of the Beagle Channel, with Isla Navarino on one side and the islands and islets Snipe, Solitario, Hermanos and Picton, successively on the opposite side; it continues along the median line of the Beagle Channel between Isla Picton and Isla Navarino, reaching a point equidistant from the eastern coast of Isla Navarino, the southernmost coast of Isla Picton and the northern coast of Isla Lennox, whence it follows along the median line of Paso Goree, to reach the open sea mid-way between Punta Guanaco on Isla Navarino and Punta Maria on Isla Lennox; from there it continues in a generally southerly direction.

Therefore, for all the reasons stated in this Memorial, and for any other reason that the Court might deem relevant to the present case, the Argentine Republic submits that the Court of Arbitration should decide and declare that:

(*a*) the boundary-line between the respective maritime jurisdictions between the Argentine Republic and the Republic of Chile, from meridian 68°36′38.5″W., within the region referred to in paragraph (4) of Article I of the Agreement for Arbitration, is as described above;

(*b*) that in consequence, Picton, Nueva and Lennox Islands and adjacent islands and islets belong to the Argentine Republic.

On behalf of the Government of the Republic of Chile :

Reserving its right to supplement or amend its request, should the need arise in the light of the Argentine pleadings, the Government of Chile accordingly request the Court of Arbitration to decide in favour of Chile the questions referred to in paragraph (2) of Article 1 of the Agreement for Arbitration (Compromiso) dated 22 July 1971 and to make the declarations therein set out.

In the Counter-Memorials

On behalf of the Government of the Argentine Republic :

No further formal Submissions were presented.

On behalf of the Government of the Republic of Chile :

For the reasons set out at length in the Chilean Memorial and this Counter-Memorial, and reserving the right to amend or supplement its request, the Government of Chile formally

(i) renews the request made in paragraph 3 at p. 176 of the Chilean Memorial and

(ii) requests the Court of Arbitration to reject the requests made by the Government of Argentina at p. 446 of its Memorial.

In the Replies

On behalf of the Government of the Argentine Republic :

The Argentine Government maintains the position and submissions as presented in its *Memorial* and *Counter-Memorial* and respectfully asks the Court to reject the Chilean submissions made in p. 151 of its *Counter-Memorial.*

On behalf of the Government of the Republic of Chile :

For the reasons set out at length in the Chilean Memorial and Counter-Memorial, together with this Reply, and reserving the right to amend or supplement its request, the Government of Chile formally confirms the submissions presented at the conclusion of its Memorial and Counter-Memorial, and thus (i) maintains the request made in paragraph 3 at p. 176 of the Chilean Memorial; and (ii) renews the request of the Chilean Counter-Memorial (at p. 151) that the Court of Arbitration reject the requests made by the Government of Argentina at p. 446 of its Memorial and maintained at p. 541 of its Counter-Memorial.

At the end of the oral proceedings

On behalf of the Government of the Argentine Republic :

At the hearing of 23 October 1976:

The Argentine Government concludes and maintains that the boundary line between the respective maritime jurisdictions of the Argentine Republic and of the Republic of Chile, from the intersection of meridian 68°36′38.5″W. of Greenwich with the Beagle Channel is a line which follows that same meridian until the middle of the Beagle Channel and then runs along the median line of the Channel, deviating from that line only where inflections are necessary so that each country may always navigate in waters of its own. The line thus runs equidistant between Isla Grande de Tierra del Fuego and Islas Hoste and Navarino, passes between Islas Bridges and Islote Bartlett, and then runs equidistant from Islotes Les Eclaireurs and the northern coast of Isla Navarino. It continues along the median line of the Channel, as far as the vicinity of Banco Herradura, where it turns to follow the middle of the navigable channel between Banco Herradura and Isla Grande and between Banco Herradura and Banco Gable; thence it continues along the navigable channel through Paso Mackinlay and then returns to the median line passing between Isla Martillo and Islotes Gemelos. Thereafter, the boundary continues along the median line of the Beagle Channel, first between Isla Navarino and Isla Grande and then between Navarino on the one side and the islands and islets of Snipe, Solitario, Hermanos and Picton, successively on the opposite side. The line continues along the median line of the Beagle Channel between Isla Picton and Isla Navarino, and thereafter reaches a point equidistant from the eastern coast of Isla Navarino, the south-westernmost point of Picton and the northern coast of Lennox, whence it follows along the median line of Rada Goree (avoiding obstacles for navigation), to reach the open sea midway between Punta Guanaco on Isla Navarino and Punta María on Isla Lennox. From there it continues in a southerly direction.

Therefore, for all the reasons stated in the Argentine written and oral pleadings, and for any other reason that the Court might deem relevant to the present case, the Argentine Republic submits that the Court of Arbitration should decide and declare that:

(*a*) the boundary line between the respective maritime jurisdictions between the Argentine Republic and the Republic of Chile, from meridian 68°36′38.5″W., within the region referred to in paragraph (4) of Article 1 of the Agreement for Arbitration, is as described above;

(*b*) that in consequence, Picton, Nueva and Lennox Islands and adjacent islands and islets belong to the Argentine Republic.

On behalf of the Government of the Republic of Chile :

At the hearing of 14 October 1976:

In accordance with the *Compromiso* dated 22 July 1971, and in the light of the written and oral argument of the Government of Chile and of the evidence adduced, and in relation to the question submitted to Her Britannic Majesty's Government concerning the interpretation of the Boundary Treaty of 23 July 1881;

The Republic of Chile requests the Court of Arbitration to decide:

First That Picton, Nueva and Lennox Islands, and the islands and islets adjacent to them, belong to the Republic of Chile; and

Second that the other islands and islets included in the list sent to the Registrar with letter No. 131 dated 20 September 1976 and described therein as appurtenant " to the Southern shore ", belong to the Republic of Chile; but, should this second submission not be accepted by the Court, then, as an alternative, that all the other islands and islets whose entire land surface is situated wholly within the region referred to in Article I (4) of the *Compromiso* dated 22 July 1971, belong to the Republic of Chile.

F. THE COURT'S DELIBERATION

The Court started its deliberations soon after the oral hearings were terminated on 23 October 1976.

It wishes in the first place to express its great appreciation for the help it has received from the Parties throughout the proceedings, in the form of written and oral statements, documentation, and cartography that have been in conformity with the highest professional standards.

Secondly, having regard to the sudden and greatly regretted decease of one of its Members, Judge Sture Petrén on 13 December, the Court wishes to state that its deliberation was by then completed on all essential aspects of the case, including the conclusions to be reached; that Judge Petrén had taken part in the whole deliberation up to that date; that he had, like other Members of the Court, already placed his views on record in the form of a written Note and other statements; and had also participated throughout the first reading of the text of the Decision. In addition he took part in the work of preparing the tracing of the eventual boundary-line—see Part II below, paragraphs 103–110.

These facts are set out here having regard to the statement in the *dispositif* of the Decision that it was arrived at by unanimity.

The Decision itself now follows in Part II.

PART II: DECISION OF THE COURT OF ARBITRATION

(*Compromiso*, Article XII (1))

I

SCOPE AND GEOGRAPHY OF THE DISPUTE AND TASK OF THE COURT

1. The dispute between the Republics of Argentina and Chile to which the present decision relates, concerns the territorial and maritime boundaries between them, and the title to certain islands, islets and rocks near the extreme end of the South American continent, in the region of what can conveniently be called in general terms that of the eastern Beagle Channel—a seaway described in paragraph 4 below. For the purposes of the dispute the confines of this region are derived from the co-ordinates specified in Article I (4) of the *Compromiso* set out in Section C of PART I (Report) above, —which are shown by the straight lines joining the six points ABCDEF on the annexed Map A. On account of the resulting shape of the area thus bounded, it has come to be known in the course of the case as the " Hammer ". With respect to territory or waters outside this area the Court has no competence to adjudicate.

2. However, even with reference to what is within the area of the Hammer, the Parties have each framed differently their requests for a decision. These are respectively set out as follows in paragraphs (1) and (2) of the Arbitration Agreement (*Compromiso*) the text of which will be found in Section C of PART I (Report) above:—

> " (1) The Argentine Republic requests the Arbitrator to determine what is the boundary-line between the respective maritime jurisdictions of the Argentine Republic and of the Republic of Chile from meridian 68°36′38.5″W., within the region referred to in paragraph (4) of this Article, and in consequence to declare that Picton, Neuva and Lennox Islands and adjacent islands and islets belong to the Argentine Republic.
>
> (2) The Republic of Chile requests the Arbitrator to decide, to the extent that they relate to the region referred to in paragraph (4) of this Article, the questions referred to in her Notes of 11 December 1967 to Her Britannic Majesty's Government and to the Government of the Argentine Republic and to declare that Picton, Lennox and Nueva Islands, the adjacent islands and islets, as well as the other islands and islets whose entire land surface is situated wholly within the region referred to in paragraph (4) of this Article, belong to the Republic of Chile."

The text of the Notes of 11 December 1967, referred to in the Chilean request above quoted is given in Annex I hereto, except for their annexes lettered B to D which are no longer of any direct relevance. These Notes do not, in any case, appear to the Court substantially to modify the character of the issues it is now called upon to deal with, —a view which was endorsed by the Chilean Agent in the course of the oral pleadings (Verbatim Record, VR/25, p. 3). The meridian 68°36′38.5″W. mentioned in the Argentine request is the meridian constituting the boundary between the respective territories of the Parties on the Isla Grande[1] of Tierra del Fuego (see Map B). This perpendicular boundary, which meets the Beagle Channel at the point near Lapataia marked X on that map, and which ends there, is not, as such, in dispute between the Parties, although in other respects more will be said of it hereafter.

3. The islands of Picton, Nueva and Lennox, specifically indicated in the requests of both Parties, which it will be convenient to designate collectively as the PNL group, or as the disputed (or the three) islands, are situated at the eastern end of the Beagle Channel where it meets the sea. Before it finally does so, however, the presence of these three islands causes it to divide in the manner described in the footnote below[2] (and see also paragraph 4). This has given rise to the question concerning the interpretation to be attributed to such expressions as "south" or "to the south" of the Beagle Channel, which has been one of the principal factors leading to the present dispute. It does not, however, as will be explained later, follow from this that the Court is called upon to define objectively, and in the physical or geographical sense, which of the eastern arms of the Channel is to be considered as being the principal one, or as constituting the so to speak "true" Beagle Channel, although a definition for the purposes of settling the dispute will result from the Court's decision.

4. The Beagle Channel itself, situated near the southern extremity of South America, about 70 miles (112 km.) north of Cape Horn, is named after the British Naval Survey sloop "Beagle", in the course of whose voyages in the period 1831–34 the Channel's existence was first definitely established. It is a narrow seaway, averaging about 3 to 3·5 miles (4·8 to 5·6 km.) in breadth, and with a total length that can variously be estimated as 120–150 miles (192–240 km.) according to the selected starting and finishing points. Connecting ocean with ocean, it begins at its western end with two arms that respectively pass north and south of Isla Gordon and continue eastward after meeting at Point Divide on the eastern point of that island. It then proceeds in a shallow arc (yet in a basically horizontal line) until a point about 4 miles (6·4 km.) short of Picton Island, after which it divides as already mentioned. One arm, considered by Chile to constitute the real prolongation of the Channel to the sea, continues in the same easterly direction but curving towards the east-south-east, and passes north of Picton Island, between it and the Isla Grande south shore[3], past Cape San Pio on that shore, to meet the sea at a line the exact location of which has been a good deal debated in the case but which (within the limits of the "Hammer") could not be put further than the one which would join a point about a mile west of Punta Jesse on the Isla Grande to Punta Oriental at the eastern extremity of Nueva Island. The other arm, considered by Argentina to be the real eastern course of the Channel, departs from the latter's previous general west-east

---

(1) This is the very large island, roughly triangular in shape, the approximate apex points of which consist of Cape Espiritu Santo in the north, at the Atlantic end of the Straits of Magellan; Cape San Diego near Staten Island, in the east; and Peninsula Brecknock on the Pacific side, in the west.

(2) The actual division is at Picton Island. Once abreast of, or past, Picton, there is a choice of courses out of either arm,—passing in the case of the northern arm, either north or south of Nueva Island; or, in the case of the southern arm, either east or west of Lennox Island (see Maps generally).

(3) This shore, from Capes San Diego and Buen Suceso in the east, to Peninsula Brecknock in the west, forms the base of the Isla Grande triangle—see n. (1) above.

direction and describes what gradually grows into almost a right-angled turn, to pass south and west of Picton Island, between it and Navarino Island, and thence between the latter and Lennox Island in what has become a general north-south direction, or even (when abreast of Lennox Island) a south-westerly one, reaching the sea between Punta Maria on that island and Punta Guanaco on Navarino. These details, which can be better appreciated from the annexed Maps A and B, are mentioned so that the geographical situation may be clear.

5. There is, however, a different possible perspective in which the geography of the eastern end of the Beagle Channel can be viewed, according to which its two arms at this end would not be parts of the Channel itself but simply entries to or exits from it, the actual Channel only starting (or stopping) west of Picton Island. This aspect of the matter, for reasons that will become obvious, has not formed part of the case of either Party, and at this stage the Court merely mentions it without, for the moment, making any further comment.

6. The respective requests of the Parties for consideration by the Court, as set out in paragraph 2 above, theoretically represent separate approaches, or a difference in the way each Party views the problem, —but the Court believes that, as regards what it has to decide, no real difference of substance is in practice involved. Both requests raise in terms the question of title to the islands of the PNL group, and both are so framed as to cover the question of title to the smaller islands, islets and rocks which have come to be known in the case as " the small islands in [or within] the Channel ", —that is to say those situated along its course from Point X near Lapataia (*supra*, paragraph 2) to the western extremity of Picton Island, and thereafter in its two eastern branches but still within the " Hammer ". The two different approaches adopted by the Parties, *i.e.* the " maritime " (Argentina) and the " territorial " (Chile), appear to the Court to lead to much the same thing. Title to territory automatically involves jurisdiction over the appurtenant waters and continental shelf and adjacent submarine areas, —to such extent, in such manner, and within such distances from the shore, as may be recognized by the applicable rules of international law. On the other hand, there are no signposts or frontiers in the sea as such, —" maritime jurisdiction " does not exist as a separate concept divorced from dependence on territorial jurisdiction. To draw a boundary between the maritime jurisdiction of States, involves first attributing to them, or recognizing as being theirs, the title over the territories that generate such jurisdiction. But this once done, the maritime jurisdiction will follow from general principles of law which, to save unnecessary complication need not be particularized, but which will enter into the determination of the boundary line that, as part of its decision, the Court is bidden by Article XII (1) of the *Compromiso* to draw on a chart—(*supra*, PART I, Section C).

7. The task of the Court is further defined in a number of ways which are of importance for reaching a correct solution of the questions before it:—

(*a*) under Article I (7) of the *Compromiso* the Court must " reach its conclusions in accordance with the principles of international law ";

(*b*) the Court has no power under the *Compromiso* or otherwise to reach a conclusion *ex aequo et bono*;

(*c*) both Parties, though not perhaps with the same degree of emphasis, regard the PNL group as an indivisible whole for the purpose of determining title to the islands concerned, —and the Court takes note of this attitude without considering itself as necessarily bound by it, should juridical considerations otherwise require;

(*d*) it was common ground between the Parties, though subject to certain different shades of interpretation:—

(i) that their rights in respect of the disputed area, and in particular of the PNL group, are governed exclusively by the Boundary Treaty ("*Tratado de Límites*") signed between them on 23 July 1881 (the 1881 Treaty)—the text of which is given in paragraph 15 below—according to its correct interpretation in the light of the principles now enshrined in Articles 31–33 of the Vienna Convention of 1969 on the Law of Treaties;

(ii) that the Boundary Treaty of 1881 was intended to provide, and must be taken as constituting, a complete, definitive and final settlement of all territorial questions still outstanding at that time, so that nothing thereafter remained intentionally unallocated, even if detailed demarcations of boundaries on the ground were left over to be carried out later, or particular differences of interpretation might still require to be resolved;

(iii) that in consequence, the régime created by the 1881 Treaty, whatever it was, superseded and replaced all previous territorial arrangements or understandings between the Parties, together with any former principles governing territorial allocation in Spanish-America, —subject (at least in the opinion of one of the Parties) to the continuing relevance of those arrangements, understandings or principles for purposes of interpreting the 1881 régime, —see *infra*, paragraph 21.

8. With regard to the last three of the above-stated propositions—those numbered (i), (ii) and (iii) respectively—the Court would observe that, while it has taken note of the Parties' wish to avoid any failure of allocation, it must also, if it deems it necessary for the exercise of its judicial function of deciding in accordance with international law, be entitled to have recourse to any valid and relevant juridical considerations lying outside the Treaty, in order duly to accomplish its mandate of responding to the requests of the Parties as set out in Article I, paragraphs (1) and (2) of the *Compromiso*—(*supra*, paragraph 2).

II

PRELIMINARY HISTORICAL CONSIDERATIONS

9. Before coming to the Treaty of 1881, the Court thinks it necessary to refer to certain of the pre-1881 historical elements that serve to explain the structure of the Treaty and may be relevant to its interpretation. Speaking in very general terms, it appears to the Court that, previous to 1881, and subject to wide divergencies of interpretation and application, the Parties were agreed in principle that their rights in the matter of claims or title to territory were governed *prima facie* (and if no recognized basis of derogation existed) by the doctrine of the *uti possidetis juris* of 1810. This doctrine—possibly, at least at first, a political tenet rather than a true rule of law—is

peculiar to the field of the Spanish-American States whose territories were formerly under the rule of the Spanish Crown, —and even if both the scope and applicability of the doctrine were somewhat uncertain, particularly in such far-distant regions of the continent as are those in issue in the present case, it undoubtedly constituted an important element in the inter-relationships of the continent.

10. As the Court understands the matter, the doctrine has two main aspects. First, all territory in Spanish-America, however remote or inhospitable, is deemed to have been part of one of the former administrative divisions of Spanish colonial rule (vice-royalties, captaincies-general, etc.). Hence there is no territory in Spanish-America that has the status of *res nullius* open to an acquisition of title by occupation. *Secondly*, the title to any given locality is deemed to have become automatically vested in whatever Spanish-American State inherited or took over the former Spanish administrative division in which the locality concerned was situated (*uti possidetis, ita possideatis*, —the full formula). Looked at in another way, *uti possidetis* was a convenient method of establishing the boundaries of the young Spanish-American States on the same basis as those of the old Spanish administrative divisions, except that the latter were themselves often uncertain or ill-defined or, in the less accessible regions, not factually established at all, —or again underwent various changes.

11. However, the Court considers that it is no part of its task to pronounce on what would have been the rights of the Parties on the basis of the *uti possidetis juris* of 1810 because, in the first place, these rights—whatever they may have been—are supposed to have been overtaken and transcended by the regime deriving from the 1881 Treaty, —see paragraph 7 (*d*) (iii) above. But secondly, it seems that, previous to this date, each of the Parties was, by virtue of *uti possidetis*, claiming, or had at various times claimed, most of the continent south of the Rio Negro and east of the Andes, down to the far south, —except that, as was only to be expected, the main emphasis of these claims was placed, by Argentina, on the Atlantic seaboard, and by Chile on the Pacific seaboard in the southern regions where the Cordillera of the Andes died away and no longer provided a natural boundary. Thus was adumbrated the so-called " Oceanic " principle, which itself—so it was claimed—derived from *uti possidetis*. At the same time both Parties also laid claims of sorts to, or in, large areas of the interior, —that is to say continental Patagonia, the Magellanic region, Tierra del Fuego and the Fuegian islands. As will appear later, the Court does not think it necessary to attempt to evaluate the respective merits of these claims, as they stood at that time.

12. The unsatisfactory or at least indeterminate nature of claims based on *uti possidetis*, given the existence of rival claims, similarly based, seems to have been tacitly recognized by both the Parties themselves, —for in 1855 after various incidents and controversies, they decided in effect to " freeze " their respective claims by means of a special territorial clause in what was otherwise mainly a commercial treaty—the Treaty of Peace, Friendship, Commerce and Navigation signed between them in Santiago on 30 August of that year. By Article 39 of this Treaty, the Parties, while recognizing

> " as the boundaries of their respective territories those existing at the time when they broke away from Spanish dominion in the year 1810 ",

made no attempt to define what those boundaries were, but instead agreed

> "to defer the questions that have arisen or *may arise* regarding this matter [stress added] in order to discuss them later . . . and in case of not being able to reach a complete agreement, to submit the decision to the arbitration of a friendly nation."

The next following provision of this Treaty, Article 40, in effect "entrenched" its Article 39 by providing a right of denunciation to be exercisable only in respect of those clauses that related to commerce and navigation. It is in consequence of this that Article 39 of the Treaty has never been formally denounced, —but its requirements in respect of boundaries became satisfied when the agreement it referred to was reached on the basis of the Treaty of 1881, so that, within the limits of the Treaty area, it was thenceforth an executed, and no longer an executory provision. Moreover, in so far as Article 39 involved an obligation to negotiate, this was replaced by Article VI of the 1881 Treaty—(for text, see paragraph 15 below).

13. Until the discussions, starting in 1876, that resulted in the Treaty of 1881, all attempts to implement the intention of Article 39 of the 1855 Treaty in respect of boundaries had come to nothing. Negotiations for a boundaries agreement, such as those that took place in 1865, and again in 1872–1873, proved abortive, as also did proposals for settlement by arbitration considered in 1874. Throughout, both countries maintained (at least on paper) their claims from the Rio Negro down to the far south. But in about 1874–1875, incidents[4] leading to conflicting claims to exercise jurisdiction, and mutual accusations of violation of the *status quo* established by Article 39 of the 1855 Treaty, seem to have given the two Governments pause, for it was in the following year, 1876, that negotiations of a more serious character, ending eventually in success, were embarked upon and led to the Treaty of 1881.

14. The Court will, so far as necessary, consider the 1876–1881 negotiations in connexion with the 1881 Treaty that resulted from them, —for these negotiations are naturally of significance mainly if not wholly for the light they may shed on the meaning of the text of the Treaty itself. However, before setting out this text, to which the Court is now coming, it will be helpful to state what were the four main regions concerning which the claims of the Parties were in conflict prior to 1881, but were supposed to be settled, by the Treaty of that year. These regions were (1) that part of Patagonia (bounded on the west by the main chain of the Andes) that stretched from the Rio Negro down to a (then) undetermined line north of the Straits of Magellan; (2) the Magellanic area, *i.e.* the Straits of Magellan and the territory and islands bordering these immediately to the north and south; (3) the rest of the Isla Grande of Tierra del Fuego, with Staten Island (Isla de los Estados) off its extreme south-eastern end; and finally (4), the Fuegian islands or archipelago, sometimes known as the Cape Horn archipelago, to the south, south-west and west of the Isla Grande.

([4]) See Chilean Annexes 16–19; and also pp. 11, 24 *et seq.*, 107, and 109–110 of the text described in n. 60 below of the speech of Señor Irigoyen, the Argentine Foreign Minister, made at the date of the conclusion of the 1881 Treaty—(see *infra*, paragraph 113). There were incidents relating to the Straits of Magellan and the Rivers Gallegos and Santa Cruz, —Argentine and Chilean warships were involved, —a lighthouse, —and also foreign ships, the "Devonshire" (American), "Jeanne-Amélie" (French), and "Elgiva" (British).

III

THE TREATY OF 1881

A. PRELIMINARY MATTERS

(1) General considerations

15. In accordance with the traditional canons of treaty interpretation now enshrined in the Vienna Convention on the Law of Treaties, which (see paragraph 7 (*d*) (i) above) both the Parties have accepted as governing the matter, the Court will next proceed to consider what is the effect of the Treaty of 1881, interpreted "in good faith" and "in accordance with the ordinary meaning to be given to [its] terms . . . in their context and in the light of its object and purpose"—(Vienna Convention, Article 31). This involves in the first place an analysis of the text of the Treaty, which was entitled "*Tratado de Límites*" (Boundary Treaty). This is set out in full below, the English translation side by side with the Spanish original, because the latter is the only authentic version and also because doubts have arisen here and there as to what exactly should be considered the correct English rendering(5):

TRATADO DE LIMITES	BOUNDARY TREATY
(23 July 1881)	
En nombre de Dios Todopoderoso. Animados los Gobiernos de la Républica de Chile y de la República Argentina del propósito de resolver amistosa y dignamente la controversia de límites que ha existido entre ambos países, y dando cumplimiento al articulo 39 del Tratado de Abril del año 1856, han resuelto celebrar un Tratado de límites y nombrado a este efecto sus Plenipotenciarios, a saber:	In the name of Almighty God. The Governments of the Republic of Chile and of the Argentine Republic, desirous of terminating in a friendly and dignified manner the boundary controversy existing between the two countries, and giving effect to Article XXXIX of the Treaty of April, 1856, have decided to conclude a Boundary Treaty, and have for this purpose named their Plenipotentiaries as follows:
S.E. el Presidente de la República de Chile, a Don Francisco de B. Echeverría, Cónsul General de aquella República.	His Excellency the President of the Republic of Chile, Don Francisco de B. Echeverria, Consul-General of that Republic;
S.E. el Presidente de la República Argentina, al Doctor Don Bernardo de Irigoyen, Ministro Secretario de Estado en el Departamento de Relaciones Exteriores.	His Excellency the President of the Argentine Republic, Dr. Don Bernardo de Irigoyen, Secretary of State for Foreign Affairs.

(5) Each side has furnished its own English version, and these do not always quite correspond. The Chilean is used here because it was supplied to the Court in a convenient, self-contained form,—but where material differences of translation exist in relevant contexts, these are commented upon in the appropriate place.

Quienes, después de haberse manifestado sus plenos poderes y encontrándolos bastantes para celebrar este acto, han convenido en los artículos siguientes:

Artículo I

El límite entre Chile y la República Argentina es de Norte a Sur, hasta el paralelo cincuenta y dos de latitud, la Cordillera de los Andes. La línea fronteriza correrá en esa extensión por las cumbres más elevadas de dichas Cordilleras que dividan las aguas y pasará por entre las vertientes que se desprenden a un lado y otro; las dificultades que pudieran suscitarse por la existencia de ciertos valles formados por la bifurcación de la Cordillera y en que no sea clara la línea divisoria de las aguas, serán resueltas amistosamente por dos peritos nombrados uno de cada parte. En caso de no arribar éstos a un acuerdo, será llamado a decidirlas un tercer perito designado por ambos Gobiernos. De las operaciones que practiquen se levantará un acta en doble ejemplar, firmada por los dos peritos, en los puntos en que hubieren estado de acuerdo y además por el tercer perito en los puntos resueltos por éste. Esta acta producirá pleno efecto desde que estuviere suscrita por ellos y se considerará firme y valedera sin necesidad de otras formalidades o trámites. Un ejemplar del acta será elevado a cada uno de los Gobiernos.

Artículo II

En la parte Austral del Continente y al Norte del Estrecho de Magallanes, el límite entre los dos países será una línea que, partiendo de Punta Dungeness, se prolongue por tierra hasta Monte Dinero; de aquí continuará hacia el Oeste, siguiendo

These Representatives, after exchanging their full powers, and finding the same sufficient for the purpose of this act, have agreed upon the following Articles:

Article I

The boundary between Chile and the Argentine Republic is from north to south, as far as the 52nd parallel of latitude, the Cordillera de los Andes. The boundary-line shall run in that extent over the highest summits of the said Cordilleras which divide the waters, and shall pass between the sources (of streams) flowing down to either side. The difficulties that might arise owing to the existence of certain valleys formed by the bifurcation of the Cordillera, and where the water divide should not be clear, shall be amicably solved by two Experts, appointed one by each party. Should these fail to agree, a third Expert, selected by both Governments, will be called in to decide them. A Minute of their proceedings shall be drawn up in duplicate, signed by the two Experts on those points upon which they should be in accord, and also by the third Expert on the points decided by the latter. This Minute shall have full force from the moment it is signed by the Experts, and it shall be considered stable and valid without the necessity of further formalities or proceedings. A copy of such Minute shall be forwarded to each of the Governments.

Article II

In the southern part of the Continent, and to the north of the Straits of Magellan, the boundary between the two countries shall be a line which, starting from Point Dungeness, shall be prolonged by land as far as Monte Dinero; from this point

182915 C 2

las mayores elevaciones de la cadena de colinas que allí existen, hasta tocar en la altura del Monte Aymond. De este punto se prolongará la línea hasta la intersección del meridiano setenta con el paralelo cincuenta y dos de latitud y de aquí seguirá hacia el Oeste coincidiendo con este último paralelo hasta el *divortia aquarum* de los Andes. Los territorios que quedan al Norte de dicha línea pertenecerán a la República Argentina; y a Chile los que se extiendan al Sur, sin perjuicio de lo que dispone respecto de la Tierra del Fuego e islas adyacentes el artículo tercero.

Artículo III

En la Tierra del Fuego se trazará una línea que, partiendo del punto denominado Cabo del Espíritu Santo en la latitud cincuenta y dos grados cuarenta minutos, se prolongará hacia el Sur, coincidiendo con el meridiano occidental de Greenwich, sesenta y ocho grados treinta y cuatro minutos hasta tocar en el canal " Beagle ". La Tierra del Fuego, dividida de esta manera, será Chilena en la parte occidental y Argentina en la parte oriental. En cuanto a las islas, pertenecerán a la República Argentina la isla de los Estados, los islotes próximamente inmediatos a ésta y las demás islas que haya sobre el Atlántico al Oriente de la Tierra del Fuego y costas orientales de la Patagonia; y pertenecerán a Chile todas las islas al Sur del canal " Beagle " hasta el Cabo de Hornos y las que haya al occidente de la Tierra del Fuego.

Artículo IV

Los mismos peritos a que se refiere el artículo primero fijarán en el terreno las líneas indicadas en los dos

it shall continue to the west, following the greatest altitudes of the range of hillocks existing there, until it touches the hill-top of Mount Aymond. From this point the line shall be prolonged up to the intersection of the 70th meridian with the 52nd parallel of latitude, and thence it shall continue to the west coinciding with this latter parallel, as far as the divortia aquarum of the Andes. The territories to the north of such a line shall belong to the Argentine Republic, and to Chile those extending to the south of it, without prejudice to what is provided in Article III, respecting Tierra del Fuego and adjacent islands.

Article III

In Tierra del Fuego a line shall be drawn, which starting from the point called Cape Espiritu Santo, in parallel 52° 40′, shall be prolonged to the south along the meridian 68° 34′ west of Greenwich until it touches Beagle Channel. Tierra del Fuego, divided in this manner, shall be Chilean on the western side and Argentine on the eastern. As for the islands, to the Argentine Republic shall belong Staten Island, the small islands next to it, and the other islands there may be on the Atlantic to the east of Tierra del Fuego and of the eastern coast of Patagonia; and to Chile shall belong all the islands to the south of Beagle Channel up to Cape Horn, and those there may be to the west of Tierra del Fuego.

Article IV

The Experts referred to in Article I shall mark out on the ground the lines indicated in the two preceding

artículos anteriores y procederán en la misma forma que allí se determina.

Artículo V

El Estrecho de Magallanes queda neutralizado a perpetuidad y asegurada su libre navegación para las banderas de todas las naciones. En el interés de asegurar esta libertad y neutralidad no se construirán en las costas fortificaciones ni defensas militares que puedan contrariar ese propósito.

Artículo VI

Los Gobiernos de Chile y de la República Argentina ejercerán pleno dominio y a perpetuidad sobre los territorios que respectivamente les pertenecen según el presente arreglo. Toda cuestión que, por desgracia, surgiere entre ambos países, ya sea con motivo de esta transacción ya sea de cualquiera otra causa, será sometida al fallo de una Potencia amiga, quedando en todo caso como límite inconmovible entre las dos Repúblicas el que se expresa en el presente arreglo.

Artículo VII

Las ratificaciones de este Tratado serán canjeadas en el término de sesenta días, o antes si fuese posible, y el canje tendrá lugar en la ciudad de Buenos Aires o la de Santiago de Chile.

En fé de lo cual los Plenipotenciarios de la República de Chile y de la República Argentina firmaron y sellaron con sus respectivos sellos y por duplicado el presente Tratado en

Articles, and shall proceed in the manner therein indicated.

Article V

The Straits of Magellan shall be neutralized for ever, and free navigation assured to the flags of all nations. In order to assure this freedom and neutrality, no fortifications or military defences shall be constructed on the coasts that might be contrary to this purpose.

Article VI

The Governments of Chile and the Argentine Republic shall perpetually exercise full dominion over the territories which respectively belong to them according to the present arrangement.

Any question which may unhappily arise between the two countries, be it on account of the present Arrangement, or be it from any other cause whatsoever, shall be submitted to the decision of a friendly Power; but, in any case, the boundary specified in the present Agreement will remain as the immovable one between the two countries.

Article VII

The ratifications of the present Treaty shall be exchanged within the period of sixty days, or sooner if possible, and such exchange shall take place in the city of Buenos Ayres or in that of Santiago de Chile.

In testimony of which the Plenipotentiaries of the Republic of Chile and of the Argentine Republic have signed and sealed with their respective seals, and in duplicate, the

la ciudad de Buenos Aires a los veintitrés días del mes de Julio del año de Nuestro Señor mil ochocíentos ochenta y uno.

FRANCISCO DE B.
ECHEVERRIA (L.S.)

BERNARDO DE IRIGOYEN (L.S.)

present Treaty, in the city of Buenos Ayres, on the 23rd day of the month of July, in the year of our Lord 1881.

FRANCISCO DE B.
ECHEVERRIA (L.S.)

BERNARDO DE IRIGOYEN (L.S.)

* * *

16. There is one general consideration of major importance affecting the interpretation of the Treaty of 1881 as a whole, particularly as regards its structure, to which attention should be drawn at the outset. Like most treaties, it represented a compromise between the different and often directly conflicting claims of the Parties. Neither Party obtained all it wanted, but each obtained what it wanted most, at the sacrifice of something (to it) less important. That this was so, and that the Treaty was to be seen in this light, has been more or less common ground between the Parties, although they have differed in their views concerning the nature of the compromise and what was to be deemed to enter into it. This will be further discussed in the context of the provisions of the Treaty now to be considered.

17. For this purpose the Court will begin by indicating the particular clause in the above reproduced text of the Treaty that specifically deals with the disposition of the various categories of islands that include the PNL group,—namely the second (*i.e.* last) sentence of Article III (the " Islands clause "), beginning with the words " As for the islands " (" En cuanto a las islas "). It attributes certain categories of islands to Argentina, and others to Chile. In the latter attribution there figure " all the islands to the south of the Beagle Channel up to Cape Horn " (" y pertenecerán a Chile todas las islas al Sur del canal ' Beagle ' hasta el Cabo de Hornos "). It is this attribution that raises the issues involved by the division of the Channel into its two eastern arms, passing respectively north of Picton Island and south-west of it, the geography of which has been described in paragraphs 3 and 4 above. With this preliminary mention of the Islands clause, it will now be convenient to take the provisions of the Treaty in the order in which they occur.

(2) The title of the Treaty

18. " *Tratado de Límites* "—of limits—Boundary Treaty. This title suggests the spirit and intention of the Treaty as a whole,—for a limit, a boundary, across which the jurisdictions of the respective bordering States may not pass, implies definitiveness and permanence. As the International Court of Justice said in the *Temple of Préah Vihéar* case (1962 Reports, at p. 34), " when two countries establish a frontier between them, one of the primary objects is to achieve stability and finality ". It is true that, in the present case, the only one amongst the provisions of the 1881 Treaty having effect as allocations of territory, or as recognitions of existing title, that fails to draw or define a specific boundary, is the one just mentioned in paragraph 17 above, in which the Fuegian Islands are dealt with. A boundary nonetheless resulted from the attributions made, as will become clear in due course.

(3) **The Preamble**

19. Although Preambles to treaties do not usually—nor are they intended to—contain provisions or dispositions of substance—(in short they are not operative clauses)—it is nevertheless generally accepted that they may be relevant and important as guides to the manner in which the Treaty should be interpreted, and in order, as it were, to "situate" it in respect of its object and purpose. As the Vienna Convention says (Article 31, paragraph 2),

> "The context for the purpose of the interpretation of a treaty shall comprise, in addition to its text, *including its* preamble and annexes . . ." [stress added].

The Preamble to the Treaty of 1881 cannot be any exception in this respect. *First,* it evidences the intention of the Parties of "resolving" (Spanish "resolver"(6)) their previous or existing boundary controversies,—from which it is legitimate to deduce the consequences stated in paragraph 7 (*d*) (i) and (ii) above, namely that the regime set up by the Treaty, and no other, was meant thenceforth to govern the question of boundaries and title to territory, and that it was meant to be definitive, final and complete, leaving no boundary undefined, or territory then in dispute unallocated or, it might be added, left over for some future allocation. This view is confirmed by the terms of the final phrase of the second paragraph of Article VI of the Treaty which, after specifying that any differences that might "unhappily arise" on account of the Treaty, or "from any other cause whatsoever", were to be "submitted to the decision of a friendly Power", then proceeded to add:

> "the boundary specified in the present settlement ["arreglo"] remaining in any case ["quedando en todo caso"] as the immovable limit ["límite inconmovible"] between the two countries."(7)

This provision, already mentioned in paragraph 12 above, is discussed again in a later context—see paragraphs 173 and 174 below.

20. *Secondly,* the Preamble of the 1881 Treaty also emphasizes the Treaty's terminal and final character by, in effect, contrasting it with the provisional character of "Article 39 of the Treaty of April 1856"—(signed in 1855 but ratified the following year) by which—see paragraph 12 *supra*—the Parties deferred the settlement of boundary questions for further discussions and agreement or, failing the latter, for reference to arbitration, and for the time being recognized as the boundaries of their respective territories those existing in 1810—(the *uti possidetis juris*). This was clearly intended as a temporary régime only, to last until the future settlement by agreement or arbitration that was evidently contemplated,—and it seems to the Court that the object, or one of the objects, of the Preamble to the 1881 Treaty was to make it clear that the Treaty constituted precisely the contemplated settlement, duly reached by agreement, since it stated that the Parties were desirous of "giving effect" to Article 39 of the 1855–6 Treaty (Spanish "dando cumplimiento",—literally "giving completion" or "fulfilment" to(8)).

(6) The English "terminating", in the text in paragraph 15 above, does not, in the context, give quite the right effect.

(7) The translation given here is closer to the Spanish original than that of the English text of Article VI in paragraph 15 above.

(8) This is another instance of a not quite adequate English rendering—see previous two footnotes.

21. Up to this point there would not be much difference of view between the Parties, so that the deduction figuring as subparagraph (iii) of paragraph 7(*d*) above would, subject to the reservation there specified, be legitimate, as well as those indicated in subparagraphs (i) and (ii) already mentioned in connexion with this Preamble. But beyond this, the Parties' views diverge in one important respect. The Chilean view appears to be that for all practical purposes the 1881 Treaty erases or eliminates all applicability or relevance of the former *uti possidetis juris*, which was thenceforth replaced entirely by the Treaty. The contrary, Argentinean, view does not go so far as to maintain that *uti possidetis* overrides the Treaty settlement whenever the latter conflicts with it,—for that would be to transform the settlement into a work of supererogation. What Argentina does maintain is that *uti possidetis* survives as a traditional and respected principle, in the light of which the whole Treaty must be read, and which must prevail in the event of any irresolvable conflict or doubt as to its meaning or intention. Without pronouncing on this contention, considered as a general proposition that might be applicable in the case of other Latin-American treaties, the Court must point out that, in the particular case of the 1881 Treaty, no useful purpose would be served by attempting to resolve doubts or conflicts regarding the Treaty, merely by referring to the very same principle or doctrine, the uncertain effect of which in the territorial relations between the Parties, had itself caused the Treaty to be entered into, as constituting the only (and intendedly final) means of resolving this uncertainty. To proceed in such a manner would merely be to enter a *circulus inextricabilis*.

22. There is, however, one aspect of the matter that requires further consideration. It is evident that the main reason why Argentina seeks to maintain *uti possidetis* as being at least a latent element of the 1881 settlement, is that this would, or might, lend assistance to her views about what has been called in the course of the case (*supra*, paragraph 11), the " Oceanic ", or sometimes the " Atlantic-Pacific " principle or doctrine, according to which each Party had a sort of primordial or *a priori* right to the whole of—and to anything situated on—in the case of Argentina, the Atlantic coasts and seaboard of the continent, and in the case of Chile the Pacific,—the counterpart of this naturally being the renunciation of all rights in respect of the opposite coasts or seaboard. It seems however that the Parties, while willing to profit by the positive aspects of this doctrine, were less willing to abide by its concomitant negatives. There is evidence that both sides sought, or were prepared, when they could, to establish themselves at available points on the reverse shores of the continent(9). Be that as it may, the " Oceanic " doctrine was itself based on, or a resultant of, what the Parties claimed to be the position under *uti possidetis*, and no more than the latter can it be regarded as governing *a priori* the interpretation of the 1881 Treaty. In this connexion the remarks made in paragraph 21 above are equally applicable.

(9) Chile's claim to the whole of Patagonia, south of the Rio Negro was itself an example of this, as was also her claim to the Atlantic end of the Straits of Magellan. As regards Argentina, although it is difficult to be sure of what was being referred to, Pacific aspirations certainly seem to be reflected in the following passage from the speech of Señor Irigoyen, the Argentine Foreign Minister (at p. 137), mentioned in n. 4 to paragraph 13 above, in which he said—quoting Dr. Moreno with approval (see paragraphs 135 and 158 below)—that " since we are talking of ports, I would say that, while I am certain that by the July settlement, we did not give away any ports on the Atlantic, I believe it probable that the Republic [*i.e.* Argentina] does acquire them in waters which flow into the Pacific . . ."

23. Nevertheless, the Court realizes that this does not entirely dispose of the matter. The doctrine, even though it has to be rejected as a principle having binding or interpretative force generally, may yet be relevant and have a part to play in particular contexts; —but it will be convenient to postpone discussion of that aspect of the matter until those contexts come to be considered. All that the Court is saying here is that the doctrine does not have the status of a sort of *jus cogens* of the whole Treaty.

B. THE TERRITORIAL PROVISIONS

(Articles I–III)

(1) **General structure of the territorial settlement**

24. It is evident that if the Treaty was to accomplish its purpose, it had to deal with, or cover, each of the four main regions or categories described in paragraph 14 above. This it did, as regards region (1)—Patagonia (" north of the line "(10), —by defining a north-south boundary down the Andes as far as the 52nd parallel (Article I), and a west-east one following that parallel to the 70th meridian, and thence by an *ad hoc* line to Cape Dungeness on the Atlantic (the " Dungeness-Andes " line of Article II). The area east and north of these two lines was to be Argentinean, —west and south, Chilean. As regards region (2)—the Straits of Magellan and the Magellanic area—this went to Chile (Articles II and half of III). In region (3), namely the Isla Grande of Tierra del Fuego, the eastern part went to Argentina and the western to Chile—(this was by virtue of Article III, first half, the " Isla Grande clause "). Finally, in region (4)—the islands—some of these went to Argentina and some to Chile (under the second half of Article III, the " Islands clause ").

25. A few years previous to the conclusion of the 1881 Treaty when, as mentioned in paragraph 13 above, negotiations for a definitive boundary treaty were seriously embarked upon after some preliminary interchanges in the period 1872–5, there emerged in July 1876 what became known as the " Bases of Negotiations " of that year, or the " Bases of 1876 ". These, which encompassed the territorial provisions of the proposed settlement, emanated from the Argentine Government, being put forward by Señor Bernado de Irigoyen, the then Foreign Minister of Argentina. They were not at the time accepted by Chile, and the negotiations for a treaty were temporarily set aside in favour of renewed attempts to agree upon terms for settling the boundary question by arbitration, which occupied the years 1877–9. These, too, came to nothing, and new Argentine proposals made

(10) For present purposes Patagonia is most easily thought of as the region east of the Andes and south of the Rio Negro as far as the Dungeness–Andes line described in the text above. It can conveniently be called " Patagonia proper ". Together with the region south of that line down to the Straits of Magellan (also geographically, included in the notion of Patagonia), it was sometimes called " continental " Patagonia. But this latter region, *i.e.* west and north of the Straits up to the Dungeness–Andes line, is perhaps best thought of as " Magellanic " Patagonia. Other candidates for the appellation—as depicted in older writings and maps—would be the Isla Grande of Tierra del Fuego (" Fuegian " Patagonia) and the islands (" archipelagonian " Patagonia)—which could however also include the Isla Grande, just as could " Magellanic " Patagonia. The relevance of these complexities will appear later.

in 1879 were rejected as being much less favourable to Chile than Señor Irigoyen's "Bases of 1876". There matters rested until, late in 1880, a fresh initiative led to the good offices of the United States Ministers in Buenos Aires and Santiago being invoked. Both these happened to be named Thomas Osborn, being distinguished only by their middle initials. Thenceforward exchanges were carried on through them, and led to the conclusion of the Treaty in July 1881. The Court does not, however, think it necessary to describe these negotiations, except as regards one or two particular matters that will be considered in due course later. What did recover all its importance at this point and largely upon Señor Irigoyen's insistence—were his own proposals of 1876, viz. the "Bases" of that year, on the foundation of which the concluding negotiations (of 1881) were carried on, and which, as will be seen, entered with very little change into the eventual Treaty. The first of these Bases (*Base Primera*) was reflected generally in Article II of the Treaty; the second (*Base Segunda*) in the first half of Article III; and the third (*Base Tercera*) in the second half of that Article—the Islands clause. There were two structural differences, however. The Treaty supplemented the 1876 *Base Primera* by an Article I dealing with the boundary down the Andes; and it combined the two remaining Bases (*Segunda and Tercera*) into a single provision, as Article III. Because of their importance, and because it will be necessary to refer to them again, the Spanish and English texts of these Bases, as made available by Argentina, are set out below:

BASE PRIMERA

PUNTO DE DIVISION SOBRE EL ESTRECHO: "MONTE DINERO" A 52° 19′

"La línea partiría de ese punto, siguiendo las mayores elevaciones de la cadena de colinas que se estiende hacia el Oeste, hasta la altura denominada "Monte Aymond" a 52° 10′.

De este punto se trazará une línea que, coincidiendo con el círculo 52° 10′ llegue hasta la Cordillera de los Andes. Esta línea será la division entre la República Argentina que quedará al Norte y la República Chilena al Sud.

BASIS ONE

PLACE OF DIVISION ON THE STRAIT: MONTE DINERO AT 52° 19′

The line would start from that point following the highest peaks in the range of hills which extends towards the west as far as the peak named "Monte Aymond" at 52°10′.

From this point a line shall be traced which, coinciding with latitude 52°10′, reaches as far as the Cordillera of the Andes. This line shall be the division between the Argentine Republic which will lie to the north and the Chilean Republic to the south.

BASE SEGUNDA

DIVISION DE LA TIERRA DEL FUEGO

"Del punto denominado 'Cabo del Espíritu Santo' y en la latitud 52° 40′ se trazará una línea hacia el Sud que coincida con el meridiano (de

BASIS TWO

DIVISION OF TIERRA DEL FUEGO

From the point named "Cabo del Espíritu Santo" and in latitude 52°40′ a line shall be traced towards the south which follows the meridian

Greenwich) 68° 34′ cuya línea se prolongará hasta el ' Canal Beagle '. La Tierra del Fuego dividida de este manera será argentina en su parte Oriental—chilean en la parte Occidental.

(of Greenwich) 68°34′ which line will extend as far as the " Canal Beagle ". Tierra del Fuego thus divided shall be Argentine in its eastern part—Chilean in the western part.

BASE TERCERA

ISLAS

" Pertenecerán a la República Argentina la Isla de los Estados, los islotes próximamente inmediatos a ésta y las demás islas que haya sobre el Atlántico al Oriente de la Tierra del Fuego y costas Orientales de la Patagonia y pertenecerán a Chile todas las otras islas al Sud del Canal de Beagle hasta el Cabo de Hornos y las que se hallan al Occidente de la Tierra del Fuego."

BASIS THREE

ISLANDS

There shall belong to the Argentine Republic Isla de los Estados, the islets in close proximity to it and such remaining islands as are on the Atlantic to the east of Tierra del Fuego and eastern coasts of Patagonia and there shall belong to Chile all the other islands to the south of the Beagle Channel as far as Cape Horn and those which are to the west of Tierra del Fuego.

(2) **Patagonia and the nature of the " Compromise " (Articles I and II)**

26. While both the Parties subscribed to the view (*supra*, paragraph 16) that the Treaty represented a compromise between their rival claims to the same territories, they differed as to the character of this compromise; as to what territorial claims were covered by it; and as to the effect of it on the interpretation of the whole territorial settlement brought about by the Treaty. Consequently, although it is the Islands clause of Article III with which the Court will in due course be particularly concerned, it is necessary first to review the other territorial provisions that preceded it. At the outset the Court observes that the Parties do not agree on the way the three territorial articles are related *inter-se*. According to Argentina there is no link between them except that they follow in sequence. Each article is intended to apply to a predetermined sector to the exclusion of any other, and each sector is to be determined by one article and one only. Each article is, so to speak, autonomous. Thus Argentina claims that the geographic scope of Article II in the north must necessarily stop at the latitude to which the effects of Article I extend southwards; and to the south, the scope of the same Article II must stop where the effects of Article III begin. In contrast, Chile claims that the Treaty must be viewed as an integrated or organic whole, and that the geographic scope of the three articles cannot be fully understood without reference to the compromise which conditioned their field of application. Thus Article II cannot be understood without reference to the provisions of Article I, nor can it be understood without reference to Article III. This view appears to the Court to be the correct one.

27. With regard to the character of the " compromise "; —to put the matter in its simplest terms, Chile contends that the essential aspect of it was a renunciation by her of her claim to " Patagonia proper " (see footnote

10 above), and a recognition on her part of Argentina's title to that considerable area, —in return for an Argentinean renunciation of all Magellanic claims, and a corresponding recognition of Chile's right of exclusive control over the Straits of Magellan and all the bordering territory and islands south of the Dungeness–Andes line, as far, in principle, as Cape Horn, excepting only such territory or islands as other provisions of the Treaty might specifically attribute to Argentina or deny to Chile.

28. On the Argentine side, this view of the compromise was totally rejected. It was contended that Chile never had any valid claim to Patagonia proper, and that the definitions—(contained in Article I and II)—of the Patagonian boundary lines—(north–south along the Andes down to the meeting with the Andes–Dungeness line, and then west–east along that line to the Atlantic)—operated merely as recognitions of the validity of Argentina's already acquired title, not as new attributions of territory to her.(11) Patagonia proper consequently never entered into the compromise, which only started with the attribution to Chile of the Magellanic area. The true basis of the compromise or bargain was not therefore Patagonia *versus* the Straits and bordering areas, but the latter *versus* a recognition in Argentina's favour of the " Atlantic " principle. It was because of this latter recognition that Argentina was, under Article III of the Treaty, allocated the eastern (Atlantic) half of the Isla Grande of Tierra del Fuego, Staten Island off the south-eastern toe of the continent and, as Argentina contends, all those Atlantic islands that fringe the Fuegian archipelago on its eastern side, down to Cape Horn, including the PNL group.

29. Without pronouncing as yet on the " Atlantic " aspect of the matter, the Court is unable to accept the view that Patagonia proper (by a very great deal the largest area involved in the Treaty settlement) has to be regarded as excluded from the reciprocal concessions underlying that settlement. This could only be so if the claim of one or other Party to the Patagonian interior was so manifestly valid as to admit of no serious question. No doubt, as Argentina herself stresses, Article I of the Treaty was, in form, a boundary-defining, rather than a territory-attributing provision. But to assume that this was so because the issue of title was no longer in dispute would be unrealistic, —and if Article I did not in terms attribute territory, Article II clearly did so. This was the Article under which the status of Patagonia as Argentinean was really determined,—for having first defined its southern, cross-continent, boundary by means of the Dungeness–Andes line, it then went on to provide in terms that " the territories to the north of the said line shall belong to the Argentine Republic "—" Los territorios que quedan al Norte de dicha línea pertenecerán a la República Argentina ". This was a definite attribution of territory.

30. In connexion with this attribution the Court is unable to accept the contention—(predicated presumably on the view that Patagonia proper was always, and already, Argentine)—according to which the attribution to Argentina effected by Article II must be regarded as relating only to the

(11) Argentina did seem to concede that it was by *attribution* that she obtained the small triangle of territory bounded by the eastern end of the 52nd parallel, the Atlantic, and that part of the Dungeness–Andes line that meets the 52nd parallel at meridian 70°. This triangle is coloured red on Map B, —and see paragraph 30 below.

triangle of territory (shown in red on Map B) created by the prolongation eastwards of the line of that parallel from its intersection with the 70th meridian at the Cono Grande, until it reaches the Atlantic coast; and consisting of the area south of that prolongation and lying between it and the eastern (*i.e.* Cono Grande–Cape Dungeness) portion of the Dungeness–Andes line. The attribution made by Article II cannot be thus confined, because it is quite explicit and unqualified; —the territories " north of the said line " (" de dicha línea ")—*i.e.* of the whole Dungeness–Andes line—" shall belong " (" pertenecerán ")—not " do belong " (" pertenecen ') to the Argentine Republic "; —and " the said line " is carefully defined east–west from its starting-point at Cape Dungeness to where it meets the 52nd parallel at the 70th meridian and, continuing thence, runs " to the west, coinciding with this latter parallel as far as the *divortia aquarum* [watershed] of the Andes ".(12) This was an attribution of the whole of Patagonia north of the Dungeness–Andes line up to its generally recognized northern boundary, say at the Rio Negro.

31. In these circumstances the Court finds it unnecessary to consider whether Chile's claim to Patagonia proper, previous to the conclusion of the Treaty, was good or bad, or strong or weak. It was certainly sustainable, even if only as a bargaining or negotiating counter, and had been strenuously maintained for many years in earlier discussions, and in those that led up to the Treaty. Indeed, so far was the principle of a division of some kind from being in issue, that these discussions seem to have been centred almost exclusively on the question of how far down the continent from the Rio Negro the southern boundary should be drawn. Chile at different times claimed various boundaries considerably to the north of the Dungeness–Andes line, Argentina declining successively to accept them, —and the agreement eventually arrived at, which gave Chile nothing north of this line(13), was the price she had to pay for obtaining in return the exclusive control of the Straits and of the whole Magellanic region, which was her chief desideratum throughout, —just as Argentina's was the definitive recognition of her exclusive title to all of Patagonia except that small part of it that lay south of the Dungeness–Andes line as far as the Straits. This was what Chile conceded by giving up a claim that still had enough vitality and content, at least politically, to make its final abandonment of primary importance to Argentina. It is on this basis, as well as on the actual attribution of Patagonian territory to Argentina effected by Article II of the Treaty, that the Court reaches the conclusion that it was the antithesis Patagonia/Magellan, rather than Magellan/Atlantic which constituted the fundamental element of the Treaty settlement. The rest, notwithstanding its importance, was secondary to that. It does not however follow from this conclusion that no " Atlantic " element at all entered into the framework of the Treaty;—the real question is to determine what precise scope it had in that respect, and this will more conveniently be considered at a later stage.

(12) As a matter of pure wording, the Treaty text of Article I differed in certain respects from the *Base Primera* of 1876 (*supra*, paragraph 25), but the effect is substantially the same, —and the proposal was fundamentally that of the Argentine Government.

(13) But south of it she obtained much of what, according to other concepts of it, could be called " Magellanic " or other forms of Patagonia—see n. 10 above.

(3) The Magellanic area and Chile's attribution under Article II

32. Chile's attribution under Article II of the Treaty appears at first sight to be perfectly straightforward; but in fact involves a point of considerable difficulty, having, possibly, a direct bearing on the question of the title to the PNL group. Just as, in accordance with what has been described above, Argentina was, by this Article, attributed the territories north of the Dungeness–Andes line, so also was it provided that " to Chile [shall] belong those [territories] extending to the south of it ", —" y a Chile los que se extiendan al Sur [de dicha línea] ". This attribution was, by definition, limited in the north by the Dungeness–Andes line itself, but was not assigned any specific southern limit. It was qualified only by the clause figuring at the end of Article II, which stipulates that Chile's allocation of the territories south of the Dungeness–Andes line would be " without prejudice to what is provided in Article III respecting Tierra del Fuego and adjacent islands "—(" sin perjuicio de lo que dispone respecto de la Tierra del Fuego e islas adyacentes el artículo tercero "). The exact significance of this clause will be considered in a moment, —but the ensuing situation is claimed by Chile to be that, *in principle*, and subject only to the effects of this one qualifying clause, the result of Article II was to attribute to her all the territory and islands to the south of the Dungeness–Andes line as far as Cape Horn.

33. Argentina rejects this view, and contends, in the first place, that a further qualification, additional to that involved by the " without prejudice " clause at the end of Article II, results from the expression that occurs right at the start of the Article, viz. " In the southern part of the Continent,(14) and to the north of the Straits of Magellan, the boundary between the two countries shall be a line which, . . .", etc. —(" En la parte Austral del Continente y al Norte del Estrecho de Magallanes, el límite entre los dos paises será una línea que . . ."). According to Argentina the effect of this, and particularly of the words " and to the north of the Straits of Magellan ", was to confine the application of the whole Article, so far as Chile's allocation under it was concerned, to the area north of the Straits and between these and the Dungeness–Andes line. Chile, however, contends that the phrase in question was designed only to indicate the particular region in which the *dividing line* between the blocs of territory respectively allocated to each country was to be drawn, and did not in itself have the result of limiting the ultimate extent (north and south of that line) of those allocations, or of excluding *a priori* from Chile's allocation all territory south of the Straits. In other words, Chile contends that the legal effect of the specified line is governed by the division indicated in the first half of the last sentence of Article II (immediately before the " without prejudice " clause), —whereas the opening sentence of the Article is merely intended to locate the actual area through which the boundary would run and bring about the division. The Court considers this view to be broadly correct as a matter of textual interpretation. The Argentine allocation, though north of the Straits, was also north of the Dungeness–Andes line and therefore had nothing to do with the area betwen that line and the Straits, —while in respect of Chile's allocation, no southern terminal was specified,

(14) The comma here does not figure in the Spanish text, but this does not seem to affect the sense.

and the mention of " Tierra del Fuego and adjacent islands " in the " without prejudice " clause[15] must tend to indicate or imply a potential extension to, and inclusion of those regions in her allocation, —subject of course to what might be attributed to Argentina or denied to Chile by Article III, —thus negativing any limitation of the Article to exclusively " continental " territory in the manner Argentina has contended for—(vide *supra*).

34. This conclusion is borne out by the relevant part of the Treaty terms, as proposed by Argentina herself in 1876 through Señor Irigoyen, the Argentine Foreign Minister, and chief negotiator for his country. These terms, or " Bases ", of 1876 (*supra*, paragraph 25) were reported to the Government of Chile by the chief Chilean negotiator at the time, Señor Diego Barros Arana, Chilean Minister in Buenos Aires. Having, in a telegram of 5 July 1876[16], informed his Government that, following " four long conferences and many discussions, Señor Irigoyen . . . *has presented me* [stress added] with the following terms for a friendly settlement . . .", Señor Barros Arana then confirmed and elaborated these in a despatch dated a few days later (10 July)[17], the accuracy of which the Court sees no reason to doubt. After giving an account of his conferences and discussions with Señor Irigoyen, Señor Barros Arana went on: " I must inform you that *I am copying the text* [stress added] of the conditions drawn up during our conference and that these are, with minor differences in words, what I informed you of in my cable dated 5 instant." He then continued as in the *Base Primera* set out at the end of paragraph 25 above: [18]

> " 'Point of division on the Strait', Monte Dinero, latitude 52°19′. The line would start from that point [and] . . . [here came a description of the line] . . . would be the dividing line *between the Republic of Argentina which would lie to the north and the Republic of Chile to the south*" [stress added].

35. The objection that can be made to the conclusion stated at the end of paragraph 33 above, and fortified in paragraph 34—a conclusion which would otherwise seem to be incontrovertibly correct—is that Article III proceeds to make allocations of territories and islands south of the Straits of Magellan, not only to Argentina, but also to Chile. If it confined itself to doing the former alone—allocating terrotorities and islands to Argentina—there would be no difficulty. Such allocations would thereby be taken out of Chile's global allocation under Article II and would go to Argentina, while all areas not specifically so allocated would automatically remain Chilean by virtue of Article II. The moment, however, that Article III proceeds (as is the fact) to make allocations to Chile, as well as to Argentina, of localities south of the Straits, it merely does all over again what (according to the Chilean contention) is supposed already to have been done globally under Article II. In other words, if Chile's view of Article II is correct, the attributions made to her under Article III would appear to be redundant and unnecessary.

---

[15] This clause, which constitutes one of the very few differences—of substance at least—between the Treaty Article II and the *Base Primera* of 1886, was incorporated at a late stage, on the proposal of Señor Melquiades Valderrama, the then Chilean Foreign Minister.

[16] Chilean Annex No. 21, p. 42 of the Volume.

[17] *ibid.*, No. 22.

[18] At the end of p. 43.

36. Chile invokes the integrative approach (*supra*, paragraph 26) to counter the above interpretation that seems to lead to a double attribution to her of the western part of Tierra del Fuego and the islands south of the Beagle Channel as a result of Articles II and III. Thus she correctly asserts that Article II does not specify what part of Tierra del Fuego and what islands fall respectively to Argentina and Chile. This is left for Article III. It follows that while the two articles deal with the same territories, they do not duplicate each other, and thus the alleged redundancy is, at best, only a partial or seeming one. Chile denies that Article III is merely a subtraction from or exception to Article II. The two are linked through the " without prejudice " clause so that, while Article II sets out in principle a general allocation, Article III fulfils or implements it in detail. Argentina could reply to this that if the Chilean view were correct, it would only have been the details of *Argentina's* attributions that needed spelling out. Once these were known, those of Chile would result automatically from Article II, and would not need any spelling out. But this is not necessarily conclusive—see paragraph 38 below.

37. It might be argued that, so far, the objection stated above, in paragraph 36, is one of form rather than substance, —that the redundancy (whatever the reason for the method of drafting which caused it) does not matter so long as, whether on the one basis or the other, the Parties obtain what they were respectively intended to obtain and no more, —that provided Argentina obtains what is attributed to her under Article III, it makes no difference whether Chile, with respect to what is *not* attributed to Argentina, obtains it as a result of the global effect of Article II, subject to the " without prejudice " clause, or does not obtain anything more under Article II than the region between the Dungeness-Andes line and the Straits of Magellan, and has to look to Article III for her attributions south of the Straits. As regards the *waters* of the Straits, since an attribution to Chile of both shores would give her these waters, it makes no difference, except as a matter of presentation, whether she receives the two shores at once under Article II, or receives one under that Article, and the other under Article III.

38. But in fact, the redundancy involved may perhaps be not merely formal in kind, devoid of material content: it may lead to definite anomalies and even to possible contradictions. This can be seen in the context of the very question the Court has principally to decide in the present case, —the title to the PNL group. Under Article III this group goes to Chile if it lies " to the south of the Beagle Channel ", as that designation is to be interpreted for the purposes of the Treaty, —but *only* if it does so—(since it clearly does not come under the one other head of Chile's Article III attribution, viz. of being " to the west of Tierra del Fuego "). However, according to the Chilean global view of Article *II*, Chile obtains the group simply by reason of its being south of the Dungeness-Andes line, and but for the " without prejudice " clause, would do so irrespective of its situation in relation to the Beagle Channel. Moreover, if it appeared that the group was *not* south of the Channel, it would not go to Chile under Article III, but might still (arguably at least, despite the " without prejudice " clause) do so under Article II, unless the mere fact of it not being Chilean under Article III made it Argentinean under that Article—which does not necessarily follow.

39. To this it can be replied that even ignoring the " without prejudice " clause, all conflicts or anomalies can be disposed of by applying the rule *generalia specialibus non derogant*, on which basis Article II (*generalia*) would give way to Article III (*specialia*), the latter prevailing; and hence that no logical objection can be made to an Article II allocation to Chile of, *in principle*, everything south of the Dungeness-Andes line.

40. Argentina, for her part, contends that even if these difficulties can be thus resolved, it should not be necessary to do so, since Article II can be interpreted in such a way as to avoid all redundancies, duplications and possible conflicts (which it cannot have been the intention of the negotiators of the Treaty deliberately to create) simply by deeming Chile's allocation under it to be confined to what lies between the Dungeness-Andes line and the Straits of Magellan; any attributions south of the Straits depending exclusively on the effect of Article III: only in this way could it be made certain that the clear intention of Article III to limit Chile's allocations in respect of Tierra del Fuego and the islands to those specifically provided for by it, would be carried out and not nullified through the operation of the otherwise engulfing and " catch-all " effects of Article II.

41. To the Argentine contentions and other objections mentioned above, Chile opposes two further main considerations. *The first* of these is that to deny the global effect, *in principle*, of Article II would be to render pointless the important " without prejudice " clause figuring at the end of it, and to deprive that clause of all meaning and object although, at a certain stage of the negotiations for the 1881 Treaty, it was specifically proposed from the Chilean side and accepted without demur on the Argentine—(see footnote 15 above). If, however, the Argentine view of the effect of Article II is correct, and Chile received nothing south of the Straits of Magellan under this Article, her allocations in that area depending entirely on Article III, then a " without prejudice " clause potentially qualifying Chile's Article II allocation in respect of that area would not in any case have given Chile anything south of the Straits. Furthermore, as has already been mentioned (*supra*, end of paragraph 33), the specific indication of " Tierra del Fuego and adjacent islands " in the " without prejudice " clause shows that the allocation which this clause was directed to qualifying, and which otherwise would have been without limit south of the Dungeness-Andes line, was one that did in principle extend to and comprise all of Tierra del Fuego and the islands, except of course in so far as Article III might make specific allocations in those regions to Argentina, or limit those of Chile.

42. In this last connexion, the Court is unable to follow the Argentine contention whereby the " without prejudice " clause, by pointing ahead to Article III, implies that the Chilean allocation under Article II does not trespass on the sphere of Article III, —and therefore that the reach of Article II does not extend beyond the Straits of Magellan. Rather does it seem to the Court that it was because of the danger, arising precisely from its generality, that Article II might conflict with Article III, that the addition of the " without prejudice " clause was required.

43. The Chilean argument stated in paragraph 41 above, is, it will be observed, balanced by the Argentine contention that, if the Chilean view is

the right one, all those parts of Article III that make attributions to Chile are rendered pointless and redundant because they already result from Article II. Chile however advances, as *a second* main consideration, certain further elements of a different order: namely that, historically (see paragraph 31 above), the question that really divided the two countries during the years of long and arduous discussion preceding agreement on Article II of the 1881 Treaty, was essentially the *situs* of the east-west line that would separate their main spheres of influence south of the Rio Negro, and not the *principle* that this line, once drawn, and whatever its basic latitude might be, would thenceforth have an ordinating or regulative, and not merely a boundary-fixing effect, —that is to say that subject to the frontier along the Andes, and to any special attributions of particular pieces of territory, Argentina would be installed north of this line, without northward limit, and Chile south of it, without southward limit other than the sea. It was contended that the general attitude of the Parties showed the existence of a tacit understanding that somewhere north of the Straits of Magellan a horizontal line would be drawn that would distinguish their respective areas of control and sovereignty. The difficulties that arose were over the fixing of this line, not the determination of its legal consequences. Hence, when the Dungeness-Andes line was finally agreed upon, this understanding took effect and received formal expression in Article II of the Treaty, —the territories north of the line to Argentina, and those south of it to Chile, subject only to the " without prejudice " clause. This view is strongly supported by the account of the 1876 Irigoyen-Barros Arana negotiations given in paragraph 34 above.

44. The point discussed in the preceding paragraph is of course a completely different one from that involved by the fact that the difficulty in fixing the horizontal boundary-line north of the Straits of Magellan arose from the Argentine insistence on this being done in such a way that Chile would obtain no port or piece of coast on the Atlantic. Here the Court recalls what it said in paragraphs 23 and end of 31 above, and will revert to the matter later.

45. Chile also supports her contention described above in paragraph 43 by historical material which was conveniently summarised in the course of the oral hearings before the Court.(19) But even if this material could be matched by counter-material from the other side, which might cancel it out (as to which see paragraphs 47 and 48 below), the Argentine counter-argument has really functioned on an essentially different plane, namely that of the part played by the Patagonian question in the " transacción "—(" accommodation ")—involved by the Treaty settlement. On the assumption that Patagonia was excluded from this as being already Argentinean, it would not be an unreasonable hypothesis that, under Article II, all that Argentina really received *de novo* was the small triangle of Patagonian territory north of the Dungeness-Andes line at its eastern end, described in footnote 11 and paragraph 30 above (the rest of Patagonia being hers already)—and that to balance this, Chile received no more under Article II than the region between that line and the Straits of Magellan. But, as has already been seen (paragraphs 29 and 30), the Court feels unable to accept

(19) Oral Proceedings, VR/2, pp. numbered " 141–151 ".

the Argentine view of the Patagonian question. At the risk of repetition, this view was to the effect that Article I, by defining a north-south boundary down the Andes, simply *recognized* Patagonia north of the 52nd parallel as being (already) Argentinean, so that it was inadmissible to suppose that this whole territory would have been attributed to her, as if *de novo,* by Article II. Thus Article I merely defined a boundary but made no actual attribution. This was true, so far as concerned Article I, but ignored the attribution unqualifiedly made by Article II,—*supra,* paragraph 29.

46. If therefore, as the Court thinks, Argentina, by the combined effect of Articles I and II, obtained the whole of Patagonia north of the Dungeness-Andes line and east of the Cordillera of the Andes, it does not seem unreasonable to regard Chile as receiving *in principle* under Article II the much smaller area between that line and Cape Horn, subject always to the effect of the " without prejudice " clause and the provisions of Article III. This would also be consistent with the view, stressed by Chile, that, it being a primary object of the Treaty to give her the exclusive *control* of the Straits, it would be natural to do this by means of a single provision (Article II) under which she would simultaneously receive both shores of the Straits, and not merely one.

47. On the Argentine side, some stress was laid on a despatch of October 1876 from the then Chilean Minister for Foreign Affairs, Señor Alfonso, to his representative in Buenos Aires (Señor Barros Arana), where the negotiations for the eventual Treaty of 1881 were taking place. In this despatch(20) reference was made to the 1876 " Bases of negotiation ", and it was stated with regard to the Dungeness-Andes line, that the " territories to the north of this line would be Argentinean and those to the south, up to the Strait (" hasta el Estrecho "), would be Chilean ". Yet this limitation " hasta el Estrecho " did not appear in the corresponding 1876 Bases of negotiation (*supra,* paragraph 25, *Base Primera*) and had not appeared in the reports from the Chilean representative in Buenos Aires dated July of the same year (see *ante,* paragraph 34), to which the October despatch of the Chilean Foreign Minister was the reply. The latter moreover, in an earlier despatch of May 1876, again referring to what was to become the Dungeness-Andes line, had said just the opposite, namely that " *All the territories* situated to the south of [the] said line, *including the Straits and the Tierra del Fuego* [stress added] would, therefore, be acknowledged as an integral part of the Chilean territory "(21). After receipt of the Irigoyen Bases, this was repeated by the same writer in August 1876, when he instructed his representative in Buenos Aires that any settlement would be unacceptable which did not " ensure for Chile the full and complete possession *of all the Strait with the area of territory adjacent* " [*scilicet,* as to both shores] " required to guarantee and make effective such possession . . . " [stress added].(22) On the Argentine side of the negotiation (and it was from this side that the 1876 Bases had been put forward), no limitation " hasta el Estrecho " seems ever to have been proposed, and none figured in the final, 1881, text of Article II which, however, had had added to it precisely the " without prejudice " clause that clearly implied the extension, *in principle,* of Chilean territory south of the Dungeness-Andes line, and south of the Straits, to Tierra del Fuego and the islands.

(20) Chilean Annex No. 24.
(21) *ibid.,* No. 20 at p. 41.
(22) *ibid.,* No. 23.

182915

48. The Court has thought it desirable to go into the details of the interchanges just described, not because the matter is to be regarded as in any way decisive in itself, but because it affords a good illustration of two general features that figure prominently in the present case,—namely how alleged intentions which would have lent themselves to the simplest kind of expression in the text, are not reflected there, and sometimes something quite different is,—and secondly, the considerable difficulty that must exist in drawing firm conclusions from statements and declarations the real effect of which (quite understandably, given the circumstances of the time and of the negotiation) may well be uncertain and even contradictory.

49. Normally, the Court would now endeavour to reach a conclusion about the extent of the Chilean allocation effected by Article II, considered in itself. But it has been seen that the rival theses are closely balanced, even if the balance seems to tilt somewhat in favour of the Chilean view, though perhaps not with complete finality. In these circumstances the Court proposes not to reach any definite conclusion on the matter at this stage, but to defer it, and return to it if necessary when other aspects of the case have been examined. In fact, this would be necessary only if it ultimately appeared that there were areas that would not be allocated at all under the Treaty unless they were caught by the residuary effect of Article II.

(4) The Isla Grande clause of Article III

50. For convenience of reference the Spanish and English texts of this clause are set out again below:

ARTÍCULO III

En la Tierra del Fuego se trazará una línea que, partiendo del punto denominado Cabo del Espíritu Santo en la latitud cincuenta y dos grados cuarenta minutos, se prolongará hacia el Sur, coincidiendo con el meridiano occidental de Greenwich, sesenta y ocho grados treinta y cuatro minutos hasta tocar en el canal "Beagle". La Tierra del Fuego, dividida de esta manera, será Chilena en la parte occidental y Argentina en la parte oriental.

ARTICLE III

In Tierra del Fuego a line shall be drawn, which starting from the point called Cape Espiritu Santo, in parallel 52° 40′, shall be prolonged to the south along the meridian 68° 34′ west of Greenwich until it touches Beagle Channel. Tierra del Fuego, divided in this manner, shall be Chilean on the western side and Argentine on the eastern.

There is no dispute between the Parties about the meaning and effect of the above-cited text of the first half of Article III of the Treaty, according to which the Isla Grande of Tierra del Fuego was divided between the two countries,—and there is no point on which the Court need pronounce in relation to this provision as such, although the interpretation to be given to some of its phraseology will be considered in connexion with the second half of the Article—the Islands clause. There was, however, one important geographical consequence of the Isla Grande clause that should be mentioned now. In effecting a division of the Isla by means of the perpendicular drawn from Cape Espiritu Santo to Point X near Lapataia on the Beagle Channel (see Map B), the clause created, very roughly, two back-to-back right-angled triangles with one common side (the perpendicular), —the western triangle going to Chile and the eastern to Argentina. Thus, proceeding northwards from the base of the perpendicular at Point X, the western limit of Argentina's allocation was defined by this perpendicular, while the other two sides *needed no defining*, being already self-evident, —on the eastern side, the Atlantic coast from Cape Espiritu Santo to Capes San Diego and Buen Suceso near Staten Island, —and, on the remaining (southern) side, the south shore of the Isla Grande from Cape Buen Suceso westwards to Cape San Pio, about 7 miles (say 11 km.) due north of Nueva Island in the PNL group; and onwards back to the base of the perpendicular at Point X near Lapataia on the Beagle Channel, —thus completing the circuit of the Argentinean triangle. From this it is evident that it was the south shore of the Isla Grande from Cape Buen Suceso to Point X on the Beagle Channel, and its appurtenant waters, *that constituted, in principle, the southern limit of Argentina's attributions under the Treaty*, —except of course in so far as particular islands or groups of islands situated beyond that limit might be allocated to her under the second half of Article III (the Islands clause).

51. In the case of Chile, her Isla Grande " triangle " consisted automatically of the southern and eastern shores and hinterland of the Straits of Magellan, —already, accordingly to the Chilean contention, hers by virtue of Article II (*vide supra*, paragraphs 32 *et seq.*), but in any case becoming so under the first half of Article III, —while (again in so far as not already attributed by virtue of Article II) the whole south shore of the Beagle Channel, from west of Isla Gordon to the north-eastern end of Navarino Island, was to become allocated to her under the second half of Article III—the Islands clause—(" all the islands to the south of the Beagle Channel ")[23]. This left the PNL islands situated roughly mid-way between the south shore of the Isla Grande (Argentinean) and the north-eastern and eastern coast of Navarino (Chilean). Chile contends that they are hers because they too are " south of the Beagle Channel ". Argentina claims them equally, on the ground (*inter alia*) that they are not " south " of the Channel which, in her view, flows in this locality between Navarino Island on the west, and Picton and Lennox Islands on the north-east and east. This brings the Court to the next stage of the case; but before passing on from this (the Isla Grande) clause of Article III to the " Islands clause " of the same Article, it should be mentioned that the implications for the " Atlantic " question of the way the Cape Espiritu Santo–Beagle Channel line was drawn, will be considered in connexion with this latter (Islands) clause—see paragraph 76.

(5) The " Islands clause " of Article III

(i) *Preliminary questions*

52. *The first* preliminary question that arises is whether the Court must necessarily go into both the sets of attributions effected by the Islands clause—the Argentine and the Chilean, —that is to say whether, if it should be found that the PNL group falls within one (*i.e.* either) of these attributions, it would be necessary also to establish that it does *not* fall within the other. Such a process, which must of course imply that the group could fall under

[23] An Argentine contention that certain *western* islands failed to get allocated to Chile, if Chile's interpretation of the " Islands clause " of the Treaty is correct, is considered hereafter in paragraphs 63, and 100–102.

both attributions, ought, in principle, to be excluded *a priori*: for if the group falls within the one attribution, this should automatically eliminate the possibility that it falls within the other, since it must be axiomatic that the negotiators cannot have intended a double attribution of the same islands to both Parties. Thus a definite finding in the one sense, not only ought to preclude a finding in the other, but also to act as a bar, *in limine,* even to the examination of it. However, the Court does not propose to proceed in that way, if only because it may not be possible to reach a sufficiently definite conclusion in favour of the one attribution without also considering the other. The difficulties mentioned in paragraph 38 above may equally be relevant here. The Court must therefore investigate both sets of attributions in some detail.

53. *The second* preliminary question that arises is whether, having regard to the different ways in which the Parties have framed their respective requests (see *supra*, paragraph 2), the Court, in resolving the question of the PNL group, should proceed by the method of drawing a line in the Beagle Channel which would place the group either north or south of it—or place part of it north and part south—or should adopt an attributive method, from which a line would result. The Court has in any case to draw a line on a chart (Article XII (1) of the *Compromiso—supra*, end of paragraph 6); but such a line could either give rise to attributions or be a resultant of these. Thus an enquiry conducted from both points of view seems called for. On the other hand the Court does not consider it to be any part of its task (for which it would also not be qualified) to determine what, as a matter of physical topography, is the "true" course of the "authentic" Beagle Channel at its eastern extremity. What the Court has to decide, whether directly or as a matter of necessary inference, is what that course is, *or must be deemed to be, for the purposes of the Treaty of 1881.*

54. There are also a number of questions, in a sense preliminary, but difficult to deal with as such,—for instance whether the PNL group must be allocated as a whole or could and should be divided,—whether the Beagle Channel should be viewed as running neither north nor south of the islands of the group, but as stopping short of them—and with what effect. These are all matters best left for later consideration.

(ii) *Analysis of the Argentine attribution under the "Islands clause" of Article III—Contentions of the Parties*

55. For convenience of reference the "Islands clause" of Article III of the 1881 Treaty is set out below in the Spanish and English texts:—

En cuanto a las islas, pertenecerán a la República Argentina la isla de los Estados, los islotes próximamente inmediatos a ésta y las demás islas que haya sobre el Atlántico al Oriente de la Tierra del Fuego y costas orientales de la Patagonia; y pertenecerán a Chile todas las islas al Sur del canal "Beagle" hasta el Cabo de Hornos y las que haya al occidente de la Tierra del Fuego.

As for the islands, to the Argentine Republic shall belong Staten Island, the small islands next to it, and the other islands there may be on the Atlantic to the east of Tierra del Fuego and of the eastern coast of Patagonia; and to Chile shall belong all the islands to the south of Beagle Channel up to Cape Horn, and those there may be to the west of Tierra del Fuego.

For the interpretation of this text there are two principal points of departure:

(*1*) The Argentine attribution is divided into three (or according to another view, that may well be correct, only two) categories, viz. (*a*) Staten Island and neighbouring (immediately proximate) islets; (*b*) the " remaining island (*i.e.* other than Staten and islets) that there may be " (" que haya "), and which are *both* " on the Atlantic " *and* " to the east of Tierra del Fuego "; and (*c*) those there may be (equally on the Atlantic) *and* " to the east . . . of the eastern coast [" costas " in the Spanish[23a]] of Patagonia ". But according to a different reading of (*b*) and (*c*), fusing them into one category, the requirement is that the island or islands concerned should be both " on the Atlantic " and, simultaneously, " to the east " *both* of Tierra del Fuego *and* " of the eastern coasts of Patagonia "; —in short, it would not be enough for an island (being on the Atlantic) to be to the east of Tierra del Fuego, —it would also have to be to the east of the " eastern coasts " of Patagonia; and *vice-versa.* It therefore springs to the eye that these categories—apart from that comprising Staten Island—however they may be read, are not crystal clear as to what they comprise.

(*2*) As will appear in more detail presently, Argentina concedes (or does not deny) the self-evident point that the PNL group does not lie east of Tierra del Fuego if that term is confined to the Isla Grande. It is for this reason that she insists that the term, as it appears in the Islands clause of Article III, was meant to embrace both the Isla Grande and the rest of the Fuegian archipelago. Chile maintains that the reference to Tierra del Fuego in that clause was confined to the Isla Grande, but that in any event the PNL group is not covered by any part of the Argentine attribution under that clause.

56. *Meaning of " Tierra del Fuego " (Chile's view)*—Three points are made:

(*1*) Appealing to those parts of the 1881 Treaty, other than the " Islands clause ", in which the term " Tierra del Fuego " appears, Chile claims that, in each such part, this term obviously refers only to the Isla Grande of Tierra del Fuego, and not (or not also) to the rest of the Fuegian archipelago. It must therefore mean the same thing in the Islands clause, since no change of meaning is there indicated. Thus the " without prejudice " clause at the end of Article II specifies " Tierra del Fuego *and* adjacent islands "—[stress added]; consequently it does not include the islands in the term " Tierra del Fuego ". Again, Article III (first half) starts with the words " In Tierra del Fuego a line shall be drawn ", but this line is the perpendicular from Cape Espiritu Santo to the Beagle Channel, and it is in the Isla Grande alone, that it is drawn. A little lower down, the clause continues " Tierra del Fuego divided in this manner ", *i.e.* by the perpendicular; and again, it is only the Isla Grande that is so divided. Chile accordingly contends that when (without any indication of a change of meaning) the Islands clause of Article III says " to the Argentine

[23a] This is another place where the Spanish and English texts do not correspond—see nn. 5 and 6–8 above. The Spanish being the authentic text, the word " coasts " has been used for the English of this expression wherever it occurs after this point.

Republic shall belong . . . the other islands there may be . . . to the east of Tierra del Fuego ", this must mean islands to the east of the *Isla Grande* of Tierra del Fuego (other than Staten Island and neighbours), —whereas the PNL islands are manifestly to the south of the Isla Grande, not east of it. Also, the separate attribution of Staten Island tends to confirm the view that the expression " Tierra del Fuego ", as used in the Argentine attribution under the Islands clause, signifies the Isla Grande, of which Staten Island is not a part.

(*2*) Chile further points out that while certain maps show " Tierra del Fuego " as including the archipelago, nevertheless most of those that, by a great majority, show this appellation, do so in such a way so to indicate the Isla Grande only, —and these maps are not solely Chilean by origin: a number are Argentine([24]).

(*3*) Señor Irigoyen, the Argentine negotiator, himself said in the speech he made to his National Chamber of Deputies after the conclusion of the Treaty, that the broader sense of " Tierra del Fuego "—to include the archipelago—was " its less correct one "—(this speech is more fully considered hereafter—see paragraphs 113–116 *infra*).

57. *The Argentine view as to the meaning of " Tierra del Fuego "*—As previously noted in paragraph 55 (*2*), Argentina maintains that in the Islands clause (which is the clause, and the only one, in which attributions of islands are made, and which opens with the words " As for the islands "—" En cuanto a las islas "), the signification of the expression " Tierra del Fuego " cannot be limited to the Isla Grande of Tierra del Fuego but must also include the Fuegian archipelago. It may have been a drafting oversight that caused the failure to indicate this in terms, but Argentina contends that the intention is clear, and also appears clearly from the " without prejudice " clause of Article II (see text in paragraph 15 *supra*) where, as already noted, it is stated that Chile's allocation under that Article shall be " without prejudice to what is provided in Article III respecting Tierra del Fuego and adjacent islands ". The islands adjacent to Tierra del Fuego could only be the Fuegian islands, —*i.e.* the archipelago. Therefore, even if the term " Tierra del Fuego " itself, as used in the " without prejudice " clause of Article II, meant the Isla Grande, this clause must obviously indicate that Article III, in its " islands " portion, was intended to deal with the islands that were adjacent to the Isla Grande. Accordingly the term " Tierra del Fuego " in that part of the Islands clause that contained the Argentine attribution must be interpreted as if it read " the Isla Grande of Tierra del Fuego and the Fuegian archipelago ".

58. *Meaning of " Patagonia "*—As to the expression containing the appellation " Patagonia ", interpretation is made difficult by the uncertainty, already noted (*supra*, paragraph 24 and footnote 10), attendant upon the identity of the geographical entity thus named. As there indicated, it could denote Patagonia north of the Dungeness–Andes line (" Patagonia proper "); it could mean Patagonia south of that line and north of the Straits of Magellan; and it could mean Patagonia south of the Straits and co-terminous

([24]) See for instance Plate No. 16 to the Argentine Memorial, Nos. 9–11 to the Reply, and No. 7 in the Argentine " Additional Maps and Charts ". See also Chilean Plates 7 and 52 for maps of English and French origin.

with the Isla Grande. Both these last-mentioned regions would come within the concept of "Magellanic Patagonia". Or again Patagonia could be synonymous with Tierra del Fuego including the archipelago ("Fuegian Patagonia"). All these identifications seem to have been used in maps of earlier date, travellers' descriptions and accounts; and even as late as 1904, a map drawn by Sir Thomas Holdich (see *infra* footnote 44 to paragraph 89) and published by the Royal Geographical Society, London (Plate No. 11 in the Argentine Additional Charts and Maps), entitled 'Sketch Map of Patagonia', comprised the whole territory south of the Rio Santa Cruz—some 140 miles (224 km.) north of the Dungeness–Andes line—as far as Cape Horn. The question for the Court, however, is what did "Patagonia" mean in the Islands clause of the Treaty? The following views were expressed:

(*1*) *Argentina*—Just as Argentina maintains that the expression Tierra del Fuego in the Islands clause is not confined to the Isla Grande, but must also extend to the rest of the archipelago, because that clause was clearly intended to deal with the Fuegian islands—(and she refers in support of this view to the "without prejudice" clause at the end of Article II, which speaks of Tierra del Fuego "and" the "adjacent islands", which can therefore only mean Fuegian islands),—so also does she maintain that the islands contemplated in the Islands clause must be exclusively Fuegian ones and cannot comprise non-Fuegian islands (other than Staten Island). In consequence, the notion of islands off the "eastern coasts of Patagonia" could not, for the purposes of the Islands clause, relate to any Patagonian islands that did not at the same time have a Fuegian character. This, however, entailed that the description of Patagonia itself, given by Argentina, must necessarily be one that, for the purposes of the Islands clause, virtually equated that region with Tierra del Fuego([25]), including the archipelago, and excluded any idea of Patagonia north of the Straits of Magellan, let alone north of the Dungeness–Andes line. (From this identification of Patagonia with Tierra del Fuego it would follow that whatever was east of the latter would also, *ipso facto*, be "east of the eastern coasts" of the former.) In any case, whatever the precise meaning of the term Patagonia, it could not in the context (so Argentina maintained) be held to refer to areas that could not possibly come within the notion of "Tierra del Fuego and adjacent islands".

(*2*) *Chile* rejects this view on a number of grounds. In the first place, as has been seen in paragraph 56 (*1*) above, she contends that the very process by which the "without prejudice" clause of Article II of the Treaty, in pointing to Article III, mentions the islands separately from Tierra del Fuego, shows that the latter expression was, in that Article—*i.e.* in the Islands clause—intended to be read as meaning the Isla Grande only. *Secondly*, Chile draws attention to the dilemma

([25]) See Argentine Counter-Memorial, n. 36 on pp. 98–99 generally, where it is stated, *inter alia*, that in the *Base Tercera* of 1876 (the equivalent of the Islands clause of the 1881 Treaty) "the eastern coasts of Patagonia mean the coasts of Southern Patagonia, located between the Strait of Magellan and Cape Horn. For all practical purposes, the term Patagonia is *more or less equivalent, here, to the term Tierra del Fuego*, next to which [*i.e.* in the Islands clause] it is located"—[stress added].

created for Argentina by the reference to Patagonia in the Islands clause, and suggests that the reason for this—the reason why Argentina seeks to, as it were, project the notion of Patagonia southwards so as to overlap the Isla Grande—is to be found in her overall concept of the Treaty structure, according to which each Article of the Treaty is autonomous—confined to its own limited area of application (see paragraph 26 above). Thus if it were to be conceded that the Islands clause of Article III makes Argentina any attribution of islands north of the Straits, this major thesis would be contradicted if that clause were given any application to islands the situs of which was not Fuegian(26). The projection southward of Patagonia was therefore necessary in order to avoid the clear implication that Article III could apply to areas north of the Dungeness–Andes line, or even of the Straits of Magellan(27).

(3) *Chile's view* was consequently the reverse of Argentina's, and was to the effect that it could not be correct simply to equate the notion of Patagonia with that of Tierra del Fuego. This could only give rise to unacceptable redundancies and confusions. What in that event would be the point of specifying the two sets of requirements—namely of being " east of Tierra del Fuego ", and " east of . . . the eastern coasts of Patagonia ", if the notions of Tierra del Fuego and Patagonia were broadly interchangeable?—and which criterion would prevail, that of being " east of " or that of being " east of . . . the eastern coasts of "? Patagonia must therefore denote something other than Tierra del Fuego,—and here Chile rejected as inadequate or unconvincing the Argentine explanation (footnote 26 above) that if there was duplication it had been effected *ex abundanti cautela* to make sure of covering the whole region, including the archipelago, whatever appellation it was given,—for in that case why two different criteria (" east of " and " east of eastern coasts of ") for the same locality? All this, in Chile's view, pointed to a Patagonia outside Tierra del Fuego, and in any case north of the Straits of Magellan. In support of this, Chile cited one of the only two or three maps which it seemed to be agreed were taken account of by the negotiators of the Treaty (for the others see paragraphs 61 (*3*) and 90 below). This was the Admiralty Chart No. 554 of the Magellanic region (Map 13 to the Argentine Memorial), founded on the charts of the early explorers, and available in editions ranging from 1832 to 1875, on which the appellation " Patagonia " is confined to the area north of the Straits, while the area south of these is either not given any name or, in the Beagle Channel vicinity (but north of it, not in the archipelago), is called " Tierra del Fuego ".

(*4*) But Chile did not have to show exactly what Patagonia meant,—only that, whatever it meant, the PNL islands did not, relative to it,

(26) In her Memorial (pp. 375–377), and repeated in her Counter-Memorial (p. 98), Argentina explains that the mention of the eastern coasts of Patagonia in the third Basis of 1876, and again in Article III of the Treaty, " could only have been made out of abundant caution in order to avoid any doubt which may arise on the multiplicity of the meanings of the terms used ".

(27) Since the Court has rejected the Argentinean " autonomous " theory, it follows that islands off coasts north of the Straits of Magellan or of the Dungeness–Andes line, are not excluded *a priori* on this ground from falling under the Argentine attribution under Article III.

satisfy the criteria that would bring them within the Argentine attribution under the Islands clause. The use of the term " coasts ", in the plural, " las costas orientales de la Patagonia ", suggested that more than one " Patagonia " could have been contemplated,—Fuegian, Magellanic, or even further north. But be that as it may, the essential ingredient of Chile's position about Argentina's attribution, and of the difference between that position and Argentina's, to which the Court now comes, goes beyond the question of the localization of " Patagonia ".

59. *The expressions " . . . to the east of . . . ", and " . . . to the east of . . . the eastern coasts of . . . "—The Chilean view*—With regard to the former of these expressions, Chile, as previously indicated, insists that the effect of the words " to the east of " in relation to Tierra del Fuego was confined to the Isla Grande; —but that even if that appellation was taken to cover the archipelago, it would still remain the case that the PNL group—being in the archipelago—could not be regarded as lying " to the east of " it, *since a group cannot lie to the east of an entity of which it is itself an integral part.* Still less of course could it be considered to lie " to the east of . . . the eastern coasts of Patagonia ", whatever interpretation might be given to that expression.

60. *The same—the Argentine view*—With the Argentine reply to the Chilean contention just stated, *the heart of the Argentine case is reached.* The Argentine view is that the expressions " to the east of " etc. cannot be read literally, but must be applied in a more generalized form so as to admit of the notion of " in the eastern part of ", " on the eastern side of ", or " towards the eastern confines (or ' fringes ') of . . . ", —the point being, naturally, that the PNL group does in fact lie in the eastern part, or on the eastern side of the archipelago. In support of this contention Argentina puts forward the following principal considerations:—

(*1*) A literal reading of the text would empty the Argentina attribution under the Islands clause of all worth-while content—apart from Staten Island and its neighbouring islets; for, according to Argentina, there are no islands in the Atlantic east of the Isla Grande or Patagonia except possibly for a few worthless islets and rocks. Since the 1876 Bases of negotiation, which ultimately figured in the text of the 1881 Treaty almost verbatim, stemmed from an Argentine, not a Chilean, proposal (*supra*, paragraph 25), it cannot be supposed that a statesman of the calibre of Señor Irigoyen, the then Argentine Foreign Minister, who was also the chief negotiator on that side, could have intended to bring about the voluntary handing over of the whole Fuegian archipelago to Chile in return for only Staten Island and a few barren rocks, when Chile was already being given the exclusive control of the Straits of Magellan, and the whole Magellanic area apart from Argentina's Isla Grande triangle. (Here it has to be remembered that Argentina does not admit the vast Patagonian territory north of the Dungeness–Andes line as being a compensating factor: this, according to her view, was, if not outside the Treaty text, outside the Treaty " deal "; —but the Court has not been able to accept this view—paragraph 29 above.)

(*2*) It is not only in the context of the north-south Andean, and east-west Dungeness–Andes boundaries, but also in that of the Islands clause that Argentina invokes the " Oceanic ", or, here, " Atlantic " principle which, for this purpose, is given concrete form as a " Cape Horn " or " meridian of Cape Horn " principle, on the basis that the Atlantic and Pacific oceans must be regarded as meeting at Cape Horn, and that the territorial claims of the Parties have (in the Argentine view) always been governed by the oceanic doctrine. Therefore, the claims of each side " hasta el Cabo de Hornos " (" as far as Cape Horn ") can be satisfied if each receives the islands situated on its own side of the Cape Horn meridian. Argentina discounts the difficulty caused by the fact that this meridian cuts across and divides certain islands (including Cape Horn Island itself, and the island of Navarino) that form an important (and undisputed) part of the south (Chilean) shore of the Beagle Channel, on the ground that she claims only undivided islands wholly situated east of the Cape Horn meridian. (This, it may noticed, already involves a certain retreat from the strict " meridian " contention.) Accordingly, Argentina maintains that the expression " to the east of Tierra del Fuego " (or " east of the eastern coasts of Patagonia ") in the Islands clause must be read as denoting, or including, all " whole " islands fringing the archipelago on its eastern (Atlantic) side, east of the Cape Horn meridian. This would cover the PNL group. It would also cover a number of other islands not actually in dispute in the present proceedings, the title to which it is not within the competence of the Court to pronounce upon. Yet they must be named, because it is not otherwise possible to understand the precise nature of the Argentine " Atlantic " contention, and what is meant by the claim that all the islands fringing the Cape Horn meridian on its eastern side were assigned to Argentina under the Islands clause. These islands (all of them, as the Court understands it, actually in Chilean physical possession) are, reading from north to south, those of Terhalten and Sesambre, some 6–7 miles (say 9 km.) south of Lennox Island; the Evout isles some distance further south towards Cape Horn; the Barnevelt isles, perhaps 8 miles (12 km.) east of the Wollaston group containing Cape Horn Island, and in that group, Deceit and Freycinet Islands (see Map B).

(*3*) *Argentina* also invokes the words in the Islands clause: " on the Atlantic " (" las demás islas sobre el Atlántico "). It is of course evident that the satisfying of this test alone would not be sufficient: the islands claimed must also be " to the east of . . . " etc. Nevertheless, Argentina contends that these words have a certain autonomous effect as indicative of the underlying intention of the Argentine attribution: Argentina was, in principle, to have any islands that were on the Atlantic, as she contends that the PNL islands are.

61. *The Chilean replies* to the above described Argentine contentions must now be indicated. As regards that stated in sub-paragraph (*1*) of paragraph 60, Chile asserts as follows:

(*1*) In fact, there are islands in the Atlantic east of the Isla Grande and off the Patagonian coasts further north—see *infra*, sub-paragraph (*3*); —but Chile points in any event to the language of the Islands clause

(" the remaining islands that there may be"—Spanish " las demás islas que haya ") as lacking in positive assertion on the subject—(the Argentine rendering of this passage into English, " *such* [stress added] remaining islands as are . . . to the east ", etc., involves the same element of uncertainty differently expressed,—but this is a matter to which the Court will return).

(*2*) Furthermore, Chile argues, since Argentina received under the Treaty the whole Patagonian coast from the Rio Negro downwards, and again the whole eastern coast of the Isla Grande, it was to be expected that she would also receive any islands that there were off those coasts, and this was that what the Islands clause brought about in Argentina's favour. To Argentina's contention that islands off mainland or quasi-mainland coasts automatically go with the mainland and do not require separate attribution, Chile's view was that in a Treaty such as that of 1881, a principal aim of which was finality and completeness, it would be entirely natural to deal separately and specifically with any islands off the coasts of the mainland territories it attributes. This was the object of the separate mention of Patagonia in the Islands clause, —and the argument that, in the context of that clause, Patagonia must be equated with Tierra del Fuego because, otherwise, non-Fuegian islands would be brought in, simply begs the question, besides being open to the objections indicated in paragraph 58 (*3*) above.

(*3*) " *las demás islas* "—It seems desirable to explain this point a little more fully. Argentina's contention that if Tierra del Fuego is deemed to be synonymous with the Isla Grande, then no islands other than the separately attributed Staten Island lie to the east of it, is categorically denied by Chile. The latter brings to bear as witness several maps, including the Colton and Martin de Moussy maps (Chilean Additional Evidences, Maps Nos. 207, 208, 209 and, especially, 210), which clearly show the Aurora, Wallis, New Georgia and Clarigos Islands lying east of Staten Island. In the course of the oral proceedings Chile claimed that the authority of the de Moussy map was all the more impressive in that Señor Irigoyen stated that it was one that he had consulted (speech referred to in footnotes 4 and 9 *supra*, at pp. 91 and 133)([28]). Chile also points to a number of other islands as qualifying under the Islands clause of Article III, such as the Malvinas (Falklands), the New Year and Dampier Islands, Observatorio Island, etc. Argentina denies that these are Fuegian islands within the meaning of Article III, and makes the further point noted in the footnote below([29]). With respect to any islands lying off " the eastern coasts of Patagonia ", Argentina not only asserts that they would in any event be Argentinean by virtue of her attribution of " Patagonia ", but she also supplied a map (Argentine Counter-Memorial Map No. 84) designed to show that any such islands were merely barren reefs or " toy " islands of no consequence. Chile denies

([28]) Oral Proceedings, VR/3, the page numbered " 92/113 ".

([29]) Argentina makes the point that it could not possibly have been the intention, in a purely Argentine-Chilean Treaty, to make attributions of islands the title to which might be the subject of disputes with third countries.

that the size of the islands concerned is relevant, and calls attention to the incidents involving the "Jeanne-Amélie" and the "Devonshire" (see footnote 4 *supra*) to show that Argentina had an interest in certain islands owing to the presence of guano. Chile's object, in short, is to show that notwithstanding the lack of any positive affirmation in the Islands clause as to the existence of islands east of Tierra del Fuego, etc., the Argentine contention that there are in fact none that could reasonably qualify, is wrong.

62. *As to the "Atlantic" principle* (sub-paragraphs (*2*) and (*3*) of paragraph 60), *Chile* makes the following points:

(*a*) She denies the existence of any such principle, and in any case its applicability to the Islands clause. She does not argue that the Treaty is devoid of any "Atlantic" *aspect*, but maintains that, within the Treaty area, its scope is confined to the concave arc comprising the eastern coast-line of the continent from the mouth of the Rio Negro to Cape San Diego and Staten Island[30]. She also maintains that, to the extent to which it is applicable, the principle is essentially a coastal, and not, as such, an oceanic one. The coasts concerned are involved *because they face east*, not because the ocean that washes them happens to be called the Atlantic. Chile denies the applicability of the principle to any islands *south* of the Isla Grande, or to coasts other than mainland coasts, or to oceans as opposed to coasts (and certain particular coasts, at that). Chile has also pointed out that (see paragraphs 26 and 58(*2*) above) it is precisely Argentina that has insisted on the self-contained and non-overlapping character of each provision of the Treaty. Hence the existence of an underlying Atlantic element in one Article of the Treaty would not imply a "carry-over" of it to another. Any such element would have to exist independently, for each provision alleged to be governed by it. The way in which the Dungeness–Andes and Espiritu Santo/Beagle Channel lines were drawn, particularly in the vicinity of the Atlantic end of the Straits of Magellan, no doubt reflected an Argentine desideratum of keeping Chile removed from the eastern, mainland, coast of the continent; and the same consideration would have motivated the allocation to Argentina of the eastern half of the Isla Grande; — but there was nothing to suggest the application of the same element in the case of island coasts situated south of the continent, such as those of the PNL group which in any case rank only dubiously as being "on the Atlantic" ("sobre el Atlántico")—see further, paragraphs 65 (*e*) and (*f*) below.

(*b*) Chile asks why, if Argentina's view of her entitlement to all the islands fringing the archipelago on its eastern side down to Cape Horn is correct, the same words ("as far as Cape Horn") do not appear in her (Argentina's) attribution, as they do in Chile's, of "all the islands to the south of the Beagle Channel up to Cape Horn"? The expression "to the south of the Beagle Channel" was almost enough in itself to imply Cape Horn, only some 70–80 miles (112–128

(30) See further as to this, *infra*, paragraph 66(*2*)(*b*) and n. 37.

km.) to the south, even without the mention of it,—or at least to point in that direction,—whereas " to the east of Tierra del Fuego " pointed in quite a different direction, and really did need a specific mention of Cape Horn in order to convey the idea suggested on the Argentine side. It might also be asked why if the Argentine " Atlantic " view is correct, the Chilean attribution of all islands south of the Beagle Channel was not limited to those lying to the west of the Cape Horn meridian, special provision being made for those that were cut by that meridian.

(*c*) In short (Chile argues), Argentina is really seeking to do two things here. First, she is attempting to introduce a vertical, meridian, principle of division, despite the fact that any such notion is wholly foreign to the Islands clause which proceeds by attribution, the vertical process having been deliberately abandoned when the Isla Grande perpendicular was stopped at Point X on the Beagle Channel, and a horizontal one having been implied in the attribution to Chile of all islands to the south of the Channel. Secondly, Argentina is attempting to establish as the real underlying principle of her attribution, the notion (see paragraph 60 (*3*) above) that this attribution can be read as if it stopped at the words " on the Atlantic ", and as if the requirement of also being " to the east of Tierra del Fuego ", etc., did not exist. This, however, could not be correct, for the expression " the other islands there may be on the Atlantic " would be meaningless if not completed by an indication of where in the Atlantic they may be. The words " [that] there may be " required such an indication since the Atlantic constitutes an extensive area([31]). The designation of east of Tierra del Fuego etc., is therefore an indispensable part of the attribution.

(*d*) Finally, if there was any " Atlantic " factor implicit in the Islands clause, it was satisfied by Argentina being attributed Staten Island and the other islands there might be " to the east "—(as Chile maintains)—of the Isla Grande and of " the eastern coasts " of Patagonia north of the Straits of Magellan.

63. *The allegedly unallocated western islands*—There was one further point that should receive mention here, although it will be convenient to postpone consideration of it until Chile's attribution under the Islands clause comes to be dealt with. This was an Argentine argument to the effect that unless the words " Tierra del Fuego " were construed as covering not merely the Isla Grande but the archipelago also, and unless the expression " to the east of Tierra del Fuego " was interpreted as meaning, or as including, the notion of " in the eastern part " or " at the eastern side " or " on the eastern fringe on . . . ", it would be found that Chile's attribution of the islands " to the west of Tierra del Fuego " left certain western islands, though unquestionably Chilean, unallocated under the Treaty, and this could not have been intended. Hence the Argentine interpretation must be allowed,—and if in the west, then also in the east. This contention is considered in paragraphs 100–102 below.

([31]) In connexion with the cartography of the case, Chile has also pointed to the existence of some evidence of an Argentine aspiration to interpret her attribution as if it specified islands south, rather than east, of Tierra del Fuego,—see as to this paragraph 157(*b*) *infra*.

(iii) *The Court's view of the Argentine attribution*

64. It can be seen from the foregoing statement of the Parties' contentions that the interpretation of the Argentine attribution under the Islands clause of the Treaty is not a simple matter. The Chilean version, although not itself entirely free from difficulty, is the more normal and natural on the basis of the actual language of the text. It amounts to this, —that the PNL group does not come within the Argentine attribution because, whether or not it is " on the Atlantic ", and whether or not the Atlantic, in the context, means the ocean that washes the southern shores of the continent, the PNL group is not situated " to the east of Tierra del Fuego "—*i.e.* of the Isla Grande; —and even if Tierra del Fuego should here be regarded as comprising the archipelago, the group is part of the archipelago and not situated east of it. This interpretation is certainly not manifestly incorrect: it is the one that would in principle prevail, unless displaced by very persuasive considerations.

65. On the other hand, while it cannot by any means be said that the Argentine interpretation is wholly implausible, or that it could not possibly be correct having regard to all the circumstances, it is attended by many and serious difficulties, most of which have already been brought out above in the course of stating the Chilean view of the matter. The Argentine interpretation depends on subjecting the text to a process, not exactly of amendment, but of what is known as emendation, *i.e.* adjustment to accommodate a different outlook. This is in no way an illegitimate proceeding as such,—but its acceptability in any given case must depend on how compelling are the reasons that operate to support it, and also on the degree of adjustment entailed. The following are the adaptations that would be required:

(*a*) Starting with the major points, there is first the need to read the expression Tierra del Fuego—denoting, in the context of all the other territorial provisions of the Treaty, the Isla Grande only—as meaning, or including, in the particular context of the Islands clause, the archipelago south of the Isla Grande. This is not *per se* an unreasonable notion, —still, a definite adjustment that imposes a strain on the text has to be made. Next, and much more difficult, the words " to the east of " have to be understood as if they were " in the eastern part of ". Thus an entire phrase, the actual wording of which is " to the east of Tierra del Fuego " has to be taken as if it read " in the eastern part [or " on the eastern fringe "] of the archipelago of Tierra del Fuego ", —which is, on the face of it, a very different thing: it converts something that, whatever its exact effect, certainly does not include the PNL group, into something that could do so; but at the same time it gives the impression of having been especially formulated to achieve that end, —in short it represents what is sometimes known as a " self-serving " process, —the result causes the cause, instead of deriving from it. Even allowing for the possibility that the Spanish expression " al Oriente de " may be capable of some such meaning as " towards the east of ", the interpretation involved is not the natural one. It must also be asked what, according to that interpretation, the point of reference for determining the " eastern part " would be. How far east of centre, and where would the centre be?

(*b*) Next, there is the problem of " Patagonia ". If the Argentine view is correct, and Patagonia north of the Straits of Magellan has to be excluded on *a priori* grounds, then it would seem that, here, Patagonia is to be equated with Tierra del Fuego, either with or without the southern archipelago, depending on what " Tierra del Fuego " must be taken to cover; —but with this difference, that the relevant qualification is " to the east of . . . the eastern coasts of " Patagonia / Tierra del Fuego, or, to transpose it into Argentinian terms " in the eastern part . . . of the eastern coasts of " Patagonia / Tierra del Fuego (" en la parte oriental . . . de las costas orientales de la Patagonia / Tierra del Fuego "). This hardly even makes sense, and certainly does not lend itself to any precise interpretation. It seems a curious notion, or at any rate a tautologous one, that an island should be both east of a locality, and also east of the eastern coasts of the same locality. The actual phrase " to the east of . . . the eastern coasts of ", though clumsy, and at least concealing a redundancy, is intelligible on the assumption that the Patagonia referred to is the region of Patagonia lying between the Dungeness–Andes line and the Straits of Magellan, for this has not only eastern but western (Pacific) coasts as well. If this is not the Patagonia referred to, then the difficulty would remain that Patagonia would be doing double duty for Tierra del Fuego. This difficulty disappears if the Chilean view is correct that Patagonia, in the context, includes areas north of the Straits. In either case, however, an obvious dilemma for Argentina persists, the nature of which has been stated in paragraph 58 (*2*) above.

(*c*) The term " coasts " is also not free from difficulty. The expressions " coasts " and " the eastern coasts of " suggest something in the nature, more or less, of continuous coastlines, such as those of a mainland or major island territory. These notions are inappropriate and hard to apply in the case of an archipelago with small scattered units separated by considerable stretches of sea.

(*d*) The Argentine interpretation involves other uncertainties which, though they may be speculative, are nevertheless real. The expression " the other " (or " remaining ") islands (" las demás islas "), coming as it does immediately after the attribution of Staten Island and neighbouring islets, coupled with the rather insistent indications of an eastern orientation, suggests—at least as the initial idea to which the mind is directed—the notion of something in the same general direction as Staten Island, and not something in the quite different direction of the PNL group. The " que haya " qualifying the " y las demás islas " enhances this impression—although Argentina argues that her attribution, beginning with Staten Island, then works back *westwards* and southwards to the PNL group and the islands near Cape Horn. But this view is not easy to reconcile with the " que haya " because, while there might have been doubt about the presence of pertinent islands east or north of Staten Island, there could have been none regarding the existence of those of the PNL group and the other islands between them and Cape Horn. The expression " que haya " was therefore quite an inappropriate one to use if it was this group and these islands that were intended to be denoted.

182915 E

(*e*) In the same category of inappropriate or inapt expressions when used in connexion with the PNL group, is that of being " on the Atlantic " (" sobre el Atlántico "). In the first place, the Court has received the strong impression that what the spokesmen and negotiators of the Parties in the past had chiefly in mind when they referred to, and when they were discussing, the question of a Chilean presence, or non-presence, on the Atlantic, were those areas of the ocean that lay along the eastern mainland seaboard of the continent, and not what was often known loosely to mariners at that time, and still figures in some geographical dictionaries, as the " Southern Ocean "—a belt of sea circling the globe almost continuously at about the level of parallels 50°–60°, and absolutely so at the level of the parallel of Cape Horn (about 56°). The idea is exemplified in Chilean Plate No. 34—(and the map itself is a quasi-official Argentine one(32))—where the ocean south of the Isla Grande is described as " Oceano Antartico ". It is also well-described in paragraph 101 (in Chapter I) of the Chilean written Reply (pp. 70–71) which reads as follows:

> " First of all it is necessary to call attention to the fact that on the maps of the 18th and 19th centuries the term " Atlantic Ocean " was commonly applied only to the sea washing the coasts on the northern sector of the arc of a circle described above (see the cartography cited in " Further Remarks . . .", pp. 78–9) [33]. The oldest maps distinguish between the Atlantic Ocean, to the north of this arc of circle, and the sea area washing the southern islands, to which a variety of names are applied: 'Novum Mare Australe', 'Mare Magellanicum', 'Nouvelle Mer du Sud' (Chilean Plates 141, 143, 144, 149, 152)[34]. This distinction was to persist for the better part of the 19th century. For example, it has been seen that in 1878 the map illustrating the Fierro-Sarratea Treaty of 6 December 1878 shows that by the expression " Sea and coasts of the Atlantic Ocean and the adjacent islands " the Parties did not have in mind the regions situated to the south of Tierra del Fuego and of Staten Island (Ch. Plate 11; Ch. C.M. p. 47, para. 22). Again the map of Julio Popper illustrating a lecture given to the Argentine Geographic Institute in 1891—ten years after the conclusion of the Treaty of 1881—was to produce the new name " Argentine Sea " for what the author himself described as " the *unnamed maritime extension* which bathes the southern extreme of the Republic and which extends from Staten Island to Cape Horn and from the Beagle Channel to the Atlantic Ocean " (Ch. Plate 55; " *Some Remarks* . . .", [35] p. 46). This map produced by Popper is all the more significant because it emanated from an author who was particularly favourable to the Argentine claims in this region (cf. Ch.

(32) Published in 1885 (see further, paragraphs 148 and 157(*d*) below) by the Argentine National Geographical Institute " under the auspices of the . . . Honourable National Government ". It shows the PNL group as Chilean.

[33] The square bracketed numbers for this and the three succeeding notes indicate explanations not given in the original text. The reference here is to the Chilean volume of " Further Remarks concerning the Cartographical Evidence ".

[34] Note in the Chilean written Reply: "For the views of the navigators in the 18th century, see Further Remarks . . ., p. 78."

[35] The reference is to the *first* of the special Chilean volumes on cartography.

Mem. p. 85, para. 2). The name "Mar Argentino", distinct from that of "Oceano Atlántico" is also to be found on another official Argentine map of the 19th century (Ch. Plate 125)" [36].

Accordingly, Chile, while disclaiming any intention of drawing a conclusion about the geographic limits of the Atlantic Ocean, suggests that the facts cited confirm the view that when the Argentine Government laid claim to the "Atlantic coast", that claim related to the seaboard in the shape of an arc of a circle formed by that of Patagonia, the east coast and south-eastern extremity of Tierra del Fuego, and Staten Island, as mentioned in para. 62(*a*) above.

(*f*) Still, since these matters are speculative, let it be assumed that it is the Atlantic—at least in the sense of not being the Pacific—that washes the southern shore of the Isla Grande, east of the Cape Horn meridian. Nevertheless the word "on", in the concept of being "on the Atlantic" is imprecise, and capable of more than one interpretation. It must therefore remain a matter for doubt whether this description (which suggests something of which the primary geographical characteristic would be that of being so situated) is really one that would immediately direct the mind to the islands of the PNL group. These are much more readily thought of as being akin in this respect to islands in a river mouth or in the outflow of an estuary or delta. The description "sobre el Atlantico" is particularly inapt with regard to Picton Island, which is the one that, by dividing the eastern Beagle Channel into two arms, creates the problem of what its eastern course is to be deemed to be, and which is partly screened from open Atlantic waters by Lennox and Nueva Islands. If Picton is "on the Atlantic", it could with almost equal plausibility be said that some islands even further up the Channel are so (or are "on the Pacific" if west of the Cape Horn meridian), since it is sea water that surrounds them, and it comes from the Atlantic or Pacific as the case may be. In short, considering that the group of three islands is to be treated as a unit, its components seem to present themselves far more as islands appertaining to the Channel than as being "on the Atlantic".

66. The above-described difficulties and obscurities, no one of which might be actually decisive in itself, must constitute, cumulatively, a serious obstacle to the positive acceptance of the Argentine thesis, even if not necessarily calling for its complete rejection. The Court will now review the considerations, already partly referred to, that have been advanced from the Argentine side as grounds for ignoring this obstacle. These seem to fall into three main categories.

(*1*) *Weaknesses of the Chilean interpretation of the Argentine attribution*—Briefly, there is the question of what islands there are, actually present east of the Isla Grande or of the eastern coasts of Patagonia and of what kind: there is the question described in paragraph 63 above, of the effect of Chile's allocation of the islands "to the west of Tierra del Fuego" if no gloss is placed on that expression, and, if one is, what repercussions

[36] With regard to the "Popper" and other maps here mentioned, see hereafter, paragraph 157(*d*), and n. 118.

that would have for the corresponding " to the east of . . ." (this question is further considered in paragraphs 100–102 *infra*): there is the fact that the PNL islands can, from one point of view, be said to be " on the Atlantic ", though this does not suffice of itself to bring them within the Argentine attribution: there is the fact that islands do have coasts; —and so on. Finally, the Chilean interpretation does not wholly dispose of the problem of the identity of " Patagonia ", —but this arises chiefly from the way the clause is drafted, although the Argentinean interpretation of the expressions " Tierra del Fuego " and " to the east of " aggravates the problem. But, when all is said and done, it remains the case that the Chilean interpretation, though leaving certain things not fully explained, gives rise to far fewer and less serious difficulties, especially cumulatively, than the Argentine. At least it provides a reasonable basis for affirming that, whatever else does or does not come within the Argentine attribution, the PNL group does not.

(2) *The Atlantic principle*—The following points are material:

(*a*) It is evident that the validity of the Argentine view of the Islands clause depends on, and largely stands or falls by the applicability to that clause of the Atlantic principle, —and even so, it would be no easy matter for the interpretative process to absorb the textual adjustments—almost transformations—that would be required in order to give effect to it. This is because the Argentine view comes very close to turning the presence of an island on the Atlantic into a condition sufficient in itself, if the island is east of the Cape Horn meridian, —see paragraph 60(*2*) and 62(*c*) *supra*.

(*b*) It has already been indicated (*supra*, paragraph 22) that there is no real ground for postulating the existence of an accepted " Oceanic " principle (ultimately deriving from the very *uti possidetis* which, as such, the Treaty was intended to supersede) figuring as something that must *a priori* govern the interpretation of the Treaty as a whole. Particular parts of it, such as those relating to the boundary-lines defined in Articles II and III were clearly based on Argentine *desiderata* relating to the Atlantic coast in those particular localities([37]);—but since the underlying balance of the Treaty as a whole was (see paragraphs 29–31 above) the polarity Patagonia/Magellanic area and control of the Straits, any " Atlantic " motivations are, the Court thinks, to be given effect to only in respect of the individual Articles that clearly show this intention by reason of their method of drafting or content. This must especially be the case on the basis of the Argentine non-overlapping view of the Treaty (*supra*, paragraphs 26, 58(*1*) and 62(*a*)). The Islands clause of Article III does not exhibit this element, —or if it does, seems to do so only by the attribution to Argentina of Staten Island and the other islands east

([37]) Thus when, on the same occasion as that described in paragraph 34 above, Señor Irigoyen told Señor Barros Arana that " he could not accept that Chile's dominion should extend to any point on the Atlantic *coast* " [stress added], it was clear from the context that this was in connection with the boundary at the Atlantic end of the Straits of Magellan, which was almost exclusively the subject of this very long and full report (Chilean Annex No. 22), —and it contains no record of any *discussion* about the islands question. This also seems to emerge clearly from the reports made to their Government by the Chilean representatives in Buenos Aires (Señores Lira and Barros Arana) in 1875 and 1877, that figure as Chilean Additional Annexes 532–536; —and see further, n. 42 below.

of Tierra del Fuego (whether the Isla Grande or the archipelago) and east of "Patagonia"; —while the attribution to Chile of "*all* [stress added] the islands south of the Beagle Channel" seems positively to exclude the east of Cape Horn/west of Cape Horn principle of division, by attributing to Chile all those islands that in fact are situated south of the Beagle Channel "as far as Cape Horn", irrespective of whether they lie east or west of the Horn.

(*c*) A good deal of stress has been laid by Argentina on an alternative proposal for submitting to arbitration the question of the title to most of the Isla Grande and the archipelago, that was put forward from the Argentine side in May 1881, at a time when it seemed doubtful whether agreement on the eventual Treaty of July 23 would be reached, and which was taken up again temporarily after the signature of the Treaty in case it should fail to be ratified. From the fact that the area thus to go to arbitration included (but only with much else besides) the eastern archipelago islands—except Staten Island—down to Cape Horn, the deduction contended for was that Argentina was then still claiming those islands, and that this claim must therefore be regarded as having been given effect to in her attribution under the Treaty. The Court is unable to follow the logic of this reasoning. A map displayed at the oral hearing in order to illustrate the point, showed quite clearly that, had the matter been referred to arbitration, virtually the whole area ultimately covered by Article III of the Treaty would have been thrown open to mutual claims by each Party, to territories and islands both east and west of Cape Horn, subject only to one of the conditions of the proposed arbitration, namely the one that read "Tierra del Fuego and the islands will be divided between the two Republics, in accordance with the terms agreed upon by the respective Chilean and Argentine negotiators—Señores Barros Arana and Irigoyen—in July 1876"—(Chilean Annex 36(D), on p. 81). But (*vide supra*, paragraph 25) this was the very same "*Base Tercera*" that was finally embodied, virtually without change, in Article III of the 1881 Treaty. Consequently, the arbitration proposal put forward to meet the possible non-signature or non-ratification of the Treaty, left the islands question exactly where it already stood, and was still to stand when, in due course, the signature and ratification of the Treaty did come about; —and thus it can provide no useful indication whatever as to the interpretation to be given to the Argentine attribution under the Treaty. What it does suggest on the other hand, is that no *a priori*, or strict, "Oceanic" principle governed the Parties' respective attributions; —otherwise there would have been nothing, or very little, to arbitrate about.

(*3*) *Contemporary or subsequent official statements or declarations*—Argentina pleads various statements and declarations of statesmen and others, tending to show an intention to obtain for Argentina the Atlantic-side islands down to Cape Horn, or a belief that the 1881 Treaty had the effect of allocating her these. Certain such statements or declarations will be considered later, but the Court has already, in paragraph 48 above, given a preliminary indication of its general attitude to this kind of evidence, particularly when it is confused or contradictory, and yet, if relied on, would have the result of putting on a text quite a different construction from that which it apparently bears on the face of it. Especially must this be so where the alleged meaning is one that could so easily have been expressed in terms, if really desired and intended. That understandable motivations, political or other, may have prevented this, or rendered it difficult, can serve to explain, but hardly to cure, the insufficiency. A single example will be enough at this stage to illustrate the kind of difficulty the Court finds. In his long address to the Argentine Chamber which the Foreign Minister, Señor Irigoyen, gave in explanation of the 1881 Treaty, about a week or ten days after its signature, one remark that he made, amongst others to be noticed later (see paragraphs 113–116 below), was the following:

> "We bore in mind the political consideration of maintaining our jurisdiction over the Atlantic coasts, and we have achieved this. These coasts extend for approximately 1,500 miles . . . and they will remain under the exclusive jurisdiction of this Republic, whose flag will be the only one flying as a symbol of sovereignty, from Rio Negro down to the Strait and Cape Horn."

Yet only a few weeks later, on 18 September 1881, the Chilean Foreign Minister, Señor Valderrama, equally giving an explanation of the Treaty to his Chamber, spoke as follows:

> "The Treaty ensures for Chile dominion of the Straits of Magellan, the major part of Tierra del Fuego and all the islands to the south of the Beagle Channel . . . in other words, the Straits and all the territories extending to the south, with the exception of a section of Tierra del Fuego bathed by the Atlantic and the island of los Estados, belong to Chile."

It is clear that these two statements, in so far as they relate to the islands, are not only incompatible, but say almost diametrically opposed things. Since there can be no question but that both were made in perfect good faith and represented the genuine conviction of the speakers, the Court can only regard them as cancelling each other out, so that it would be difficult to draw any certain deduction from either.

(iv) *The "Valderrama proposal"*

67. By way of addendum, mention must be made of an episode in the negotiations for the Treaty of 1881, the importance of which was much insisted upon by Argentina, namely the affair of the "Valderrama proposal". The story is long and involved; but briefly, in the course of the negotiations for the Treaty taking place in the period May–July 1881, the Chilean Foreign Minister, Señor Valderrama, on 3 June, proposed an amendment of the Islands clause of the draft treaty (the *Base Tercera* of 1876—see *supra* paragraph 25) which, had it been accepted by Señor Irigoyen—and it was not—would (according to Argentina) have had the effect, either of making it quite clear that the PNL group of islands (or the category of islands to which these belonged) did *not* come within the Argentine attribution; —or else (but the practical result is much the same) of removing the group, or the category concerned, from that attribution. Argentina has contended that this was a sort of last minute attempt by Chile to so to speak bring herself on to the Atlantic by taking certain Atlantic islands out of Argentina's attribution and transferring them to her own. (But here at least, a *non-*

sequitur is involved; for so far as the PNL islands are concerned, mere removal from the Argentine attribution (if such had been the effect), would still not, of itself, have placed them in the category of being south of the Beagle Channel.)

68. Chile contended that, in fact, the effect of the Valderrama amendment, even had it been adopted, would not have been as Argentina maintains, and that the Argentine attribution (as it stood in the Bases of 1876, and was to remain in the Treaty as signed) would not have undergone any alteration of substance as a result of the proposed amendment, —because (*inter alia*) the Spanish text of the proposed amendment did not materially differ from the original 1876 Basis. *Prima facie* it seems to the Court that this view is probably correct, since the comparison of the three texts concerned (1876 Basis, Valderrama proposal, and Treaty text that appears on pp. 158–9 and 172–3 of the Argentine Counter-Memorial, seems to show that the only real difference was that, for the concept of " demás islas que haya sobre el Atlántico al Oriente de la Tierra del Fuego " etc., there was substituted that of " demás [*islotes*] que haya sobre . . ." etc.—islets or small islands. The Court is unable to see that this change implies that those *other* (" demás ") islets or small islands were also to be confined to the category mentioned just before, of islets or small islands immediately proximate to Staten Island, so as to exclude from Argentina's attribution any other Atlantic islands, amongst which she numbers the PNL group. This would merely have been to make the same allocation of the islets or small islands near Staten Island twice over, and also to deprive the words " to the east of Tierra del Fuego and eastern coasts of Patagonia " of any independent signification. Clearly, whether the case was one of islands, small islands, or islets, the word " other " implied some category additional to, and different from, that of those in the near vicinity of Staten Island.

69. However, let it be assumed for immediate present purposes that this view is wrong, and that the Valderrama amendment, if adopted, would have had the effect Argentina contends for. On that basis then, Argentina puts forward an argument which the Court has not found it easy to follow, but which seems to amount to this—namely, that because an amendment under which—so Argentina contends—the PNL group would have failed to come within her allocation, was *not* accepted, and the original text was restored, *therefore* it follows, or it must be assumed, that this original text (Basis of 1876) did place the group within the Argentine allocation, and consequently that the Treaty attribution, the wording of which was identical with that of the 1876 Basis, did so too.

70. The Court is unable to admit the logic of this argument which seems to involve another *non-sequitur*, or at least an inference of such an uncertain nature that it could not possibly prevail over the considerations that lead the Court to hold the attribution of the PNL group to Argentina under the Islands clause of the Treaty, not to be established. To put the matter in another way, —if it appears not to be established that the Treaty, as it stands, gives Argentina the group, the fact that a previous, rejected version would *even less* have done so, becomes irrelevant and without interest. It simply means that according to neither version was Argentina allocated the group: it certainly cannot be argued that because the one did not, the other necessarily did.

71. The Court has thought it right to go into this matter in some detail because the Argentine contention has been made the foundation of a challenge to the probative value of certain Chilean maps and documents to which the Court will come later. These are said to be based on the rejected Valderrama amendment, not the final Treaty text, —the underlying implication being that the former did not give Argentina the PNL group, whereas the latter did. Hence the evidential value of these maps and documents is said to be nil. The fallacy involved is the same: if in any event the correct (Treaty) text does not establish the group as Argentinean, then a map or document that equally does not do so, cannot be invalidated in that particular respect merely because it was based on a version of the Treaty that was not accurate, —for even if it had accurately reflected the Treaty text, the latter itself failed to establish the group as Argentinean. If analysed, Argentina's contention seems to amount to this, —that because, in her view, the Treaty should be read as allocating the PNL group to her, any map or document that does not designate the PNL group as Argentinean cannot be consonant with the Treaty, or must be based on an earlier incorrect version of it. Leaving aside for later consideration the question whether the maps and documents in question really were so based, the underlying postulate involved in this argument, namely that the correct text gave Argentina the PNL group, is one which, of course, assumes exactly what has to be proved, and what the Court thinks has not been.

72. The Court realizes that the whole purpose of this Argentine contention is, precisely, to show by inference, that this in fact was what the Treaty did, —but the Court is not convinced that there is a sufficient difference between the two texts concerned (see paragraph 68 above), or that the inference is sufficiently clear, to warrant this conclusion. What might be called the Valderrama argument could never be enough by itself to establish the Argentine case, —and even regarded as a contributory factor, with others, it is inadequate to overcome the powerful considerations operating *contra* that the Court has drawn attention to earlier.

(v) *The Protocol of 1893*

73. Finally, before leaving the question of the Argentine attribution under the 1881 Treaty, the Court must deal with something which, though it falls outside the Treaty as such, both in date and content, has been much insisted upon by Argentina as allegedly throwing a strong light on an important point affecting the interpretation of the Treaty generally, and the Islands clause of it in particular.

74. In support of her contention that the entire Treaty of 1881 must be regarded as governed by an under-lying "Oceanic" principle which, prevailing over all else, must cause each of its provisions to be read subject to an implied rule of "Atlantic coasts and islands to Argentina, Pacific ones to Chile", Argentina has attributed great prominence to the Protocol signed on 1 May 1893 between the two countries (the text of which is given in Chilean Annex 62, pp. 189–191). It specifies the bases and procedural details for carrying out the two demarcations on the ground contemplated by the Protocol, —namely those along the Cordillera of the Andes (Article I of the Treaty) and the perpendicular dividing the Isla Grande of Tierra del Fuego (first half of Article III). The Treaty did not contemplate any demarcation along the Beagle Channel or in the region of the islands south

of the Isla Grande. But notwithstanding these facts, and the further fact that, accordingly, the Protocol of 1893 was confined entirely to the two demarcations just mentioned (Andes and Isla Grande)(38), Argentina has argued that the Protocol embodied a general confirmation of a comprehensive "Oceanic" principle obtaining between the Parties and operating, as Chile has put it, as a sort of *jus cogens* of the 1881 Treaty. This argument Argentina derives from the terms of Article II of the Protocol, which came after an Article I that consisted partly of a verbatim recital of the first sentence of Article I of the 1881 Treaty (Andes boundary) and partly of a detailed spelling-out of the effect of this sentence relative to the division along "the line of the highest peaks of the Cordillera of the Andes". Then came Article II of the Protocol, which read:

> "The undersigned declare that, in the opinion of their respective Governments, and according to the spirit of the Boundary Treaty, the Argentine Republic retains her dominion and sovereignty over all the territory that extends from the East of the principal chain of the Andes as far as the Atlantic coasts, just as the Republic of Chile over the Western territory as far as the Pacific coasts; *it being understood that, by the provisions of the said Treaty, the sovereignty of each state over the respective coastline is absolute, in such a manner that Chile cannot lay claim to any point towards the Atlantic, just as the Argentine Republic can lay no claim to any toward the Pacific* [stress added]. If in the peninsular part in the South, approaching parallel 52° South, the Cordillera should be found penetrating among the channels of the Pacific there existing, the Experts shall undertake a survey of the ground in order to fix a dividing line leaving to Chile the shores of these channels, as a result of which surveys both Governments shall determine the line amicably."

It is in the words italicised in this passage that Argentina sees both the affirmation and the confirmation of the "Oceanic" principle as having to be read into all "the provisions of the said Treaty".

75. There is some force in this view. Yet the Court feels unable to give so wide and general a scope to a phrase that is so evidently set in a particular and limited context, —that of the Andes Boundary, as appears quite clearly both from the Article which preceded that phrase (*i.e.* Article I of the Protocol, described above), and also from the sentence that immediately follows the one in Article II that has been italicised, which equally related to the Andes boundary. The same applies to the opening part of the passage quoted, in which the reference to "the spirit of the Boundary Treaty" is confined to the consequences of the Andes boundary (Article I of the 1881 Treaty). Especially would an extension to the islands be unwarranted, given that the Protocol nowhere mentions these, and has no reference to them at all.

76. Indeed the Court thinks that the way the Protocol is arranged tends, rather, to confirm the conclusion it reached earlier, namely that the 1881 Treaty did not embody any all-embracing "Oceanic" principle, but simply ensured an Atlantic-Pacific *outcome* in particular localities, namely in the Andes, the Atlantic end of the Straits of Magellan, the eastern coast of the Isla Grande, and Staten Island. In this connexion, it is noticeable that

(38) That this was so even according to the account given by Argentina herself, can clearly be seen from paragraph 26 on p. 287 of the Argentine Counter-Memorial.

Article IV of the Protocol, which provided for the demarcation in the Isla Grande of the perpendicular from Cape Espiritu Santo to the Beagle Channel, made no actual mention of any oceanic basis of division, presumably because this resulted *de facto* and automatically from the wording of the first half of Article III of the Treaty, which provided that the Isla Grande, divided by this perpendicular, should be " Chilean on the western side and Argentine on the eastern ". Consequently, so as not to bring Chile on to the Eastern—*i.e.* Atlantic—side in the Bahia San Sebastian (see Map B), Article IV of the Protocol, by taking as the northern starting point of the perpendicular the middle one of three hillocks visible from the sea at Cape Espiritu Santo, simply effected a displacement of the line by about one mile to the west. But in the Andes it was necessary to be more precise, because of the way in which certain valleys and inlets of the Pacific cut across the north–south line of the peaks and *divortia aquarum* of the Cordillera. However, to balance the modification made in favour of Argentina over the Isla Grande coast at the Bahia San Sebastian (*vide supra*), Article II of the Protocol effects a modification in favour of Chile by means of the passage beginning " If in the peninsular part in the South . . ." as above quoted. For its part, the Court does not see in these (agreed) modifications anything that could bring about a change in the basic character of the 1881 Treaty.

77. Argentina has nevertheless laid stress upon them in another context. The Protocol of 1893, signed on May 1 of that year, was preceded by another instrument, dated 10 March, drawn up by the boundary commissioners who were to carry out the actual demarcation. This was entitled the " Act of the Experts "on which the Protocol itself was evidently based, there being virtually no differences of substance, and few of wording except that there are one or two clauses which the Protocol expands or elaborates. This " Act of the Experts " could in fact, in practice, have constituted the basis for the demarcation. But according to Argentina, what she regarded as being only an informal document, was not sufficient, or was inappropriate, for bringing about modifications in a Treaty that had been ratified by the National Congresses of both Parties. Hence the " Act " of March became the " Protocol " of 1 May. Again the Court is at a loss to perceive the significance of this, seeing that the " modifications " in the Treaty resulting from both Act and Protocol were the same, and in neither case were such as to affect the character of the Treaty or to import into it an oceanic principle to any greater extent than was already evident in respect of particular localities in certain parts of the Treaty, and no further. One small difference between the " Act " and the Protocol calls for mention. At the start of the passage underlined* in the quotation given in paragraph 74 above, the Act reads " it being understood that by the provisions of this *covenant* ", *i.e.* of the Act itself, instead of, as in the Protocol, " by the provisions of the said *Treaty* "—[stress added in both phrases]. The latter version is clearly more favourable to the Argentine thesis, but in the Court's opinion does not produce any real change in the resulting position.

78. It is possible that the Argentine contentions that have been under consideration above are really part of a more general theory to the effect that when a boundary Treaty provides for a demarcation on the ground it cannot (or the boundary definitions it contains cannot) be regarded as final and conclusive until the demarcation has been carried out. The Court will state

* Italicised in this publication.

elsewhere (see paragraph 169(*b*) below) why it cannot agree with this view, at least in the form in which it has been put forward in the present case. But in any event it can have no application in respect of the attributions made in the Islands clause of the 1881 Treaty, since no demarcation was provided for in respect of these, or for the Beagle Channel itself.

(vi) *Conclusion regarding the Argentine attribution*

79. The Court can therefore only conclude from the aggregate of the considerations set out above, that it has not been established that the PNL group was attributed to Argentina under the Islands clause of the Treaty. Accordingly, the Court will now turn to the question of whether the group falls within the Chilean attribution under that clause.

(vii) *The Chilean attribution under the " Islands clause "—Preliminary points*

" . . . all the islands to the south of the Beagle Channel "

80. The Chilean attribution under the " Islands clause " reads " and to Chile shall belong all the islands to the South of the Beagle Channel [al Sur del Canal Beagle] as far as Cape Horn [hasta el Cabo de Hornos], and those there may be [que haya] to the west of [al Occidente de la] Tierra del Fuego ". Since the islands of the PNL group, whether or not to the south of the Beagle Channel, are certainly not " to the west of Tierra del Fuego " (including or not including the archipelago), it is exclusively on their situation relative to the Beagle Channel that the question of their attribution to Chile depends. As has already been indicated, it is the fact that these islands lie beween the two arms into which the Beagle Channel divides at its eastern end, that gives rise to the problem of their relationship to the Channel, since either of these arms could, in the purely topographical sense, be regarded as the " true " continuation of the Channel eastwards to the open sea. Whether the islands lie " to the south of " the Channel, depends therefore on which arm is deemed to provide the test of that. For reasons that will be stated in a moment, the Court does not think it possible to determine this matter on the basis of such differences as there may be between the physical characteristics of the two arms. The solution must be sought in the 1881 Treaty itself. But before coming to that, the Court will consider another possible aspect of the matter.

81. It is evident that the difficulty caused by the existence of the two arms could, in a certain sense, be at least avoided if the Channel proper, or as such, were regarded as stopping just before it divides at Picton Island or, if looking westwards, as only starting there, the two arms constituting simply entrances or exits, —and some colour is lent to this idea by the number of maps that show the words " Beagle Channel " placed so as to finish before Picton(39). But suppose this were a legitimate process, it would ultimately solve nothing. It would by no means with absolute certainty take the islands outside all possibility of being regarded as coming within Chile's attribution (depending on the interpretation given to the expression " to the south

(39) Included are some of the earliest—see Chilean Plate 1 (Fitzroy, Stokes and Murray) and Admiralty Chart 1373, 1st edn., 1841 (Chilean Plate 4). But there is an evident distinction between a toponymic, and a course reference—and to insert an appellation in a waterway is not necessarily to indicate the whole extent of its course—see further, paragraph 90 below. It may be otherwise where a line is shown, either instead of, or additionally to the appellation, —see for instance the Nordenskjöld map of 1898, and a Belgian map of 1901 (Argentine Counter-Memorial Plates 36 and 41), both of which trace a line from Point X eastwards that stops short of Picton Island.

of "), —but even if it did, they would not thereby necessarily become part of Argentina's, since all the difficulties attendant upon that, which have already been noticed, would remain. It might indeed be easier to view them as islands "on the Atlantic" (though again not as regards Picton), rather than as appurtenant to the Channel (see paragraph 65(*f*) above), but they would still not be situated "to the east of" Tierra del Fuego or Patagonia, however these appellations were interpreted (see paragraphs 58 and 65(*b*) above). The final result would thus be that the group would emerge as not definitively attributed to either Party—a result that certainly could never have been intended.

82. But in any case, the Court does not believe there would be any warrant for the process of deeming the Channel to end (or only to start) just west of Picton Island, merely in order to take the PNL group out of it and avoid the problem created by its two eastern arms. At its western end also, the Channel, where divided by the presence of Isla Gordon, has two arms, respectively known as the *Brazo Nordoeste,* and the *Brazo Sudoeste*. Both are regarded as being Beagle Channel. This configuration is repeated at the eastern end with, as the only real differences, that the eastern arms are somewhat broader and are divided by the presence of three islands instead of one.

83. The Court has also considered whether there is any ground upon which it could and should divide the group. Since its terms of reference require it to decide in accordance with international law, a division would have to be based on a difference of a juridical character between the situation of one of the islands as compared with that of the other two. The Court cannot find any such difference. Even if one of the islands can be regarded as being more evidently "on the Atlantic" than the others, this would not suffice of itself; all three islands must be either north or south of the Beagle Channel unless the latter were to be regarded (whether flowing north or south of Picton Island) as then passing between Nueva and Lennox Islands—as depicted for instance on the Argentine map of 1893 reproduced as Chilean Plate No. 63([40]). For this the Court can see no warrant either.

(viii) *The Chilean attribution—Geography of the two arms of the Beagle Channel*

84. Although without strict accuracy as a matter of the points of the compass, it will be convenient to call the two eastern arms the "northern" and the "southern" respectively—the one flowing between the Isla Grande and Picton and Nueva Islands; the other, between Picton and Lennox Islands on the east, and Navarino Island on the west. With regard to the physical characteristics of these two arms (apart from the different directions in which they proceed, as described earlier in paragraph 4), the Court notes the following resemblances and dissimilarities. Both are navigable, though the southern arm is the deeper off Picton Island. Both are used, —the choice depending—apart from weather and tides—on the direction of approach or destination; but in the days of sail, the southern was the more sheltered. In the case of both, one side is not continuous: in the northern arm there is a gap between Picton and Nueva Islands, and, in the southern, between

([40]) This map is one of those discussed hereafter in the section on cartography—see paragraph 157(*d*).

Picton and Lennox. The former is a gap of some 8–9 miles (12·8 to 14·5 km.), the latter of some 6 miles (9·6 km.). The breadth of the northern arm varies from about 3·5 miles (5·6 km.) to some 7 or 8 miles (12·8 km. at most), —the southern arm is narrower, varying from about 2·5 to 6 miles (4 to 9·6 km.), and is more continuously narrow than the northern which broadens out considerably past the mid-point (Punta Nordeste) of Picton, whereas the southern arm, after broadening in much the same way when past Picton, narrows again abreast of Lennox Island.

85. The Court does not consider these differences as being more than differences of small degree, or as being in any way decisive in themselves, in the sense of differentiating the two arms into waterways of distinct categories, one being a channel (or part of one), the other not. In particular, the criterion of breadth or narrowness is not *per se* a test of channel-like quality, as witness such cases as those cited in the footnote below(41). In fact, in general, the world's narrowest waterways are called Straits rather than Channels. A strait has been defined as " A narrow stretch of sea connecting two extensive areas of sea ", whereas the same source defines a channel as " A *relatively* [stress added] narrow stretch of sea between two land masses, and connecting two more extensive areas of sea "—(W. G. Moore, *A Dictionary of Geography*). The latter definition suggests that the length of the " land masses " bordering a channel, as compared with the very short extension of many straits, though by no means all, may be a relevant factor. But maps and terminology vary greatly, —the point is that no one of these elements is in itself determinant. Nor equally is the fact of a lack of continuity in one, or even both, shores of a channel, or of its being partly indistinguishable from open sea. A glance at the geography of the North Eastern and North Western Providence Channels in the Bahamas shows them to have, on both sides, only the most exiguous and discontinuous of coast-lines, —the English, St. George's, Sicilian and Malta Channels virtually consist of open sea, —and often it is not possible to say at what point a Channel ceases to be such and becomes open sea. But it is certainly not possible to say it has so ceased, as long as, like both arms of the Beagle Channel, it has a continuous coast-line on one side, and island coasts on the other which, though non-continuous, are separated by only a few miles, and lie only a short distance from the *medium filum aquae*.

86. The conclusion the Court reaches therefore is, that from the point of view of what has to be decided for the purposes of the present dispute, there is only one difference of substance between the two arms of the Beagle Channel, namely that which arises from their different directions of travel. If the northern arm, which travels in a general west–east direction, though with a dip to the south east, is to be considered as being the Channel contemplated by the 1881 Treaty, then the PNL group lies to the south of it and comes within Chile's attribution. But if it is the " southern " arm,

(41) For instance the northern Canada and Greenland Channels, named Robeson, Kennedy, Sverdrup, Peary and McClintock, varying between 30 and 70 miles (48–112 km.) wide; the Yucatan Channel (120 miles, 192 km.); the N.W. Providence (Bahamas) Channel—average breadth 40–80 miles (64–128 km.); the St. George's Channel (Ireland–Wales), 50–70 miles (80–112 km.); the English Channel (Manche) 80–100 miles—mostly more (128–160 km.); the Sicilian Channel (Cape Bon/Marsala or Cape Granikoia), 100 miles (160 km.); the Malta Channel, south of Sicily (60 miles, 96 km.); and the Mozambique Channel, 300 miles (480 km.) at shortest distance over to Madagascar.

travelling in a general north–south direction that has to be so considered, then the group lies east of it, and does not fall within the ambit of the expression " to the south of the Beagle Channel ". Accordingly, the Court will now consider which is the arm that has to be deemed to be the one contemplated by the Treaty.

(ix) *Which arm of the Channel is the " Treaty " arm?*

87. *Difficulties of interpretation*—In endeavouring to carry out this task, the Court has found itself confronted by three major obstacles:

First, the Treaty itself furnishes no *express* indication at all as to what may have been thought of as being the course of the Beagle Channel: it simply says " to the south of the Beagle Channel " without definition or description of the Channel itself.

Yet, *secondly*, the Court has been unable to discover, in all the years of negotiation that preceded the conclusion of the Treaty, the least discussion as to what was the course of the Channel. Nor, for that matter, was this gone into for many years subsequent to the conclusion of the Treaty(42). Since it has to be assumed that the negotiators were neither ignorant of, nor indifferent to, the geography of the region, it can only be supposed that they regarded the Channel's course as too evident to need discussion or definition. The Court considers this to be a legitimate, and also a highly significant deduction, to which it will return in due course.

Thirdly, the sole putatively reliable sources of outside information presumed to have been, at any rate known to, and available for the negotiators (whether in fact they made use of them or not), namely the statements, writings and maps of the early discoverers or explorers of the Beagle Channel, tend to be doubtful or conflicting, —and in the opinion of the Court they afford little certain guidance. These sources were extensively relied upon by both Parties, and both put forward highly plausible and (but for the contrary arguments of the other side) seemingly convincing reasons in support of the view that what the early discoverers and explorers of the Channel saw, or regarded as being its true course, was either the northern arm, or else the southern, as the case might be.

88. The truth seems to be that the descriptions given by the early explorers depended very much, as might be expected, on their direction of approach or destination, and the nature of the particular activity being conducted at the moment. Regarded as a whole, these descriptions, and their related maps and charts, are inconclusive; and this view is borne out, at least *prima facie*, by the reply dated 4 May 1896 given by the British

(42) This is strikingly borne out by the reports and interchanges concerning the Argentine–Chilean Boundary Commission, *circa* 1890—see Chilean Annexes 53–58. Even when the question of delimiting the " centre-line " of the Beagle Channel—*i.e.* of, in effect, attributing the " small islands within the Channel "—was under consideration in 1904, the matter of the two eastern arms does not seem to have been specifically brought in—see Chilean Annexes 69–71; and see, earlier, Annex 58 at p. 178 of the volume. But, as might be expected, the Director of the Chilean Boundary Demarcation Office in 1904, Señor Alejandro Bertrand, had in fact no doubt that the Channel flowed along the northern arm between Tierra del Fuego and Picton Island—see Chilean Annex 72, at p. 207.

Admiralty to an official Argentine enquiry as to the opinion of Captain R. Fitzroy, commander of the Beagle, and a chief actor in these events. This (as given in Chilean Annex 365)(43) was to the effect that

> "The Lords Commissioners [*i.e.* of the Admiralty] do not find that Captain Fitzroy ever strictly defined the course and limits of the Beagle Channel nor is there anything to show which of the arms passing by Picton Island he considered to be the principal one."

In this connexion it has also to be borne in mind that the early explorers were concerned with the Channel only in the geographic sense, and not as forming an element in a future (general and political) territorial settlement, of which they could know nothing.

89. *Some other sources of information*—In these circumstances the Court has sought for some independent investigation and assessment of the available evidence. Two such are afforded by (*a*) the long and carefully written Memorandum prepared in the Hydrographic Department of the British Admiralty, dated 28 December 1918, based on an earlier one of 6 July (reproduced in Chilean Annex No. 353); and (*b*)—expressing a rather different opinion—a statement by Sir Thomas Holdich(44) writing from the Royal Geographical Society, London, on 30 September 1918, to which the Admiralty Memorandum of December 1918 was, in some sort, a reply. Both these documents were drawn-up at the request of the Foreign Office in London at a time when it seemed that the Beagle Channel question might be submitted to British arbitration. Both, together with related correspondence, are annexed hereto as part of Annex II. But because the Court will quote mainly from the Admiralty Memorandum, it also annexes, as Annex II A, certain paragraphs from the Argentine written Reply in the case, as a balancing factor.

(*a*) The Admiralty Memorandum (No. 9 in Annex II) shows that subsequent to 1896 (see paragraph 88 above) the Admiralty investigated the matter further. It concentrated on the first and original (1830) expedition of the Beagle to the area, explaining that it was

> "unnecessary to examine all the references to the Beagle Channel contained in the Narrative of the second expedition of 1831–1836; for such allusions are only inserted to make the narrative of events continuous, and no longer assist in giving a correct geographical definition of the waterway.
>
> The best proof of this assertion is contained in the fact that the descriptions of the Beagle Channel *in the Sailing Directions drawn up on the results of the first, and of the second, voyages, are identical*" [stress added].

The Memorandum took the view that the Beagle Channel, at its eastern end, was constituted by its northern arm, flowing past Picton

(43) This reproduces the *draft* of a communication dated May 1896 from the British Foreign Office to the Argentine Minister in London: but a facsimile of the original letter dated 4 May from the Admiralty to the Foreign Office, in exactly the same terms, is amongst the documents in the possession of the Court.

(44) Colonel Sir Thomas Holdich, traveller and distinguished geographer and military engineer, had, together with Lord Macnaghten and General Sir John Ardagh, been one of the Arbitrators in the Argentine-Chilean arbitral proceedings of 1898–1902, concerning part of the Andean boundary.

and Nueva Islands to a closing line drawn between Cape San Pio on the south shore of the Isla Grande and Punta Waller on Neuva Island (about 8 miles or 12·8 km.); and it accompanied this finding by a map the original of which can be consulted in the Public Record Office in London, showing the Channel, as thus defined, coloured blue. Two paragraphs in particular, occurring in the conclusions arrived at have been noted by the Court. The first reads:

> "If the passage between Picton and Navarino Islands [*i.e.* the southern arm] be regarded as part of the Beagle Channel, that waterway no longer possesses the feature of straightness, so frequently alluded to by the first explorers."

This feature of the main stretch of the Channel between Isla Gordon in the west and Picton Island in the east can be seen on any map of the region. The second passage reads:

> "The opinion of impartial geographers cannot be neglected, and the writers of the best known geographical works of the 19th and 20th centuries appear unanimous in regarding the eastern opening of the Beagle Channel in the manner described in the general conclusions of this memorandum."

The paragraph continues with an admission of certain errors in the relevant Admiralty publications, but in terms that can only strengthen the basic conclusion:

> "It must be admitted, however, frankly, that, at the present moment, the Admiralty Charts and Sailing Directions have, in some respects, departed from *the definition originally given to the Beagle Channel by King and Fitzroy* "(45) [stress added].
>
> "It has been stated, however [earlier in the Memorandum], that these departures from the texts of the original authors *are not geographically admissible* . . ." [stress imparted].

And this was so even though it was acknowledged that the errors concerned were such as to "lend some colour to the arguments now advanced by the Argentine Government". Accordingly, the Admiralty stated that it would normally proceed to correct these errors (for errors it evidently considered them to be) "if no diplomatic questions were involved", but left that to the Foreign Office. As will be seen from the latter's letter to the Admiralty dated 14 January 1919 (*vide* No. 10 in Annex II), it was stated that the Foreign Secretary "would deprecate any change in the charts and sailing directions at the present moment".

(*b*) Although the doubts discussed in the latter part of the above-cited passages, and certain other queries considered in other parts of the Memorandum, in no way affected its basic conclusion (which was incidentally not newly arrived at—see paragraph 97 below), the Court, though believing the Memorandum to express an objective view, and to be of great value as information, prefers to regard it as inconclusive.

(45) There is some conflict between this statement and the Admiralty statement of May 1896—see paragraph 88 *supra*—but little useful purpose would be served by trying to resolve it. Its existence does however reinforce the view expressed at the end of sub-paragraph (*b*) *infra*.

It is for this reason that, as already indicated, the Court has reproduced as No. 5 in Annex II, the letter dated 30 September 1918, emanating from the Royal Geographical Society, London, signed by Sir Thomas Holdich, as President, but undoubtedly also representing his personal views at the time(46). As can be seen, the Admiralty disagreed with some of these views (see also No. 7 in Annex II), and it was in response to a request from the Foreign Office to comment on them that the Memorandum of the Department of the Hydrographer was prepared. In order, however, to illustrate the difficulties of the whole subject, it may be mentioned that twelve years earlier Sir Thomas had expressed himself in somewhat different terms. In his well-known work " The Countries of the Kings Award ", published in 1904, he had shown, in a map(47) contained in or appended to it, a dividing line running north both of Picton and also of Nueva Islands. Asked two years later, at Chilean instance, in a private conversation, to confirm this, during an interview with the Chilean Minister in London (reported to the latter's Government in a despatch dated 9 January 1906(48)), he showed (according to that report) the greatest reluctance to commit himself, but nonetheless said at the end of the interview, in a passage that has about it the ring of truth:

> " As you insist on knowing my opinion, I will tell you, but privately and provisionally, that in my view, and without forgetting that it is a controversial matter, the mouth of the Beagle Channel is the one indicated by the Chilean maps "—[*i.e.* the northern arm, —as to these maps see the footnote below(49)].

Yet the different view he expressed in 1918 about Nueva Island was expressed quite as firmly. These hesitations and changes of mind coming from this highly regarded geographer and expert, conversant at first hand with Argentine–Chilean boundary questions, and familiar with the Beagle Channel region, indicate how unwise it would be to come to any definite conclusion as to the course of the Channel on any purely geographical basis, and confirm the conclusion already reached by the Court in that respect—see paragraph 86 above. They also confirm the lack of profit there would be in trying to choose between the varying accounts, given on various occasions by different explorers—or even by the same ones at different periods and in other circumstances.

(*c*) The Court has of course carefully considered the critical comments made by Argentina on the 1918 Admiralty Memorandum, and on some of the views of Sir Thomas Holdich. These comments are conveniently summarized in paragraphs 14–16 on pp. 287–91 of the Argentine written Reply and, as already mentioned, are reproduced as Annex II A hereto. They do not seem to the Court to affect in any essential particular the conclusions it has reached about the views

(46) He then regarded Picton and Lennox Islands as Chilean, but Nueva as Argentine.

(47) This map figures in the documentation of the case as Chilean Plate No. 92.

(48) Text reproduced in Chilean Annex No. 527.

(49) There is reason to believe that there are no maps of Chilean origin that do not show the PNL group as Chilean, whereas a considerable number of Argentine maps show it, equally, as Chilean, not Argentine. The cartography of the case will be considered later.

expressed in the documents, or on the occasions, described in sub-paragraphs (*a*) and (*b*) above: on the other hand, they do further illustrate the difficulty of reaching any finality on the geographical and historical aspects of the course of the Beagle Channel.

90. *The data available to the negotiators*—As regards the negotiators of the Treaty themselves, it is impossible at this distance of time to know exactly what data they may have made use of. This can only be a matter of conjecture. However, if it could be shown that they did in fact base themselves on certain data that pointed only one way, *even though it was erroneous*, it might be possible to say that this was nevertheless the basis on which they negotiated the Treaty, and hence was what the Treaty must be deemed to mean. But this is not the case. An example is afforded by the only map which, so it seemed to be assumed, the negotiators must have taken account of *for Beagle Channel purposes*, namely British Admiralty Chart No. 1373, founded on those of the early explorers (Chilean Plates 1–4). The 1879—(*i.e.* Treaty-period)—edition of it is annexed hereto as Map C. This chart and its forebears, going back to the ancestor chart of Fitzroy referred to in footnote 50 below, and appearing frequently, in various editions and formats, in the cartography furnished by both sides, was much relied upon by Argentina as tending to show, by a process of negative inference, that the Channel, after the western point of Picton Island, proceeded by the southern arm. This inference was drawn from the fact that whereas the two *western* arms at Isla Gordon were duly designated as the north-west and south-west arms, the eastern arm north of Picton was designated " Moat Bay "—(it does contain a Moat Bay([50]))—while the southern arm, in the section passing between Picton and Navarino, was given no appellation at all. The inference was therefore said to be that this unnamed section must have been regarded as being the true course of the Beagle Channel, and the other (called Moat Bay) not. The Court fully appreciates the point, but does not think it possible to draw any firm conclusion on such an ephemeral basis. The words " Beagle Channel " do appear on the chart, but are confined to the central section, west not only of Picton but even of Gable Island([51]),—and it surely could never be claimed that because the lettering of these words does not reach beyond Gable, therefore the section Gable-Picton is not Beagle Channel. Again, to deduce that the negotiators must

---

([50]) In the British Admiralty Memorandum of 28 December 1918 (*supra*, paragraph 89(*a*)), the question of " Moat Bay " is commented on as follows, first on the basis of an earlier chart and then on that of chart 1373:

> " The only document, which can be stated with certainty to express the ideas of, Fitzroy and of Stokes on the point at issue is the fair chart of the locality, drawn in 1831, at the conclusion of the first expedition [see Chilean Plate 1], and the attached tracing of the eastern mouth of the Beagle Channel has been taken from that source.
>
> An examination of the manner in which the name Moat Bay has been placed with respect to the neighbouring shore line and to the central line of the channel, leads to the conclusion that it was intended to designate as Moat Bay, the bend which occurs in the coast line between Cape San Pio and the Woodcock islands.
>
> This opinion is strengthened by an examination of the first edition of Admiralty Chart No. 1373, where the name, although brought more towards the centre of the channel, is still drawn on a curve which is nearly parallel to the shape of the bay.
>
> A less elaborate, but equally certain method of arriving at the same conclusion, is afforded by the reflection that Fitz-Roy can never have intended to give the name of Moat Bay to an open channel; and that the only feature in the locality corresponding to the accepted notion of a bay, is the one described."

([51]) See paragraph 81 and n. 39 above.

have regarded the section passing between Picton and Navarino as being the Channel merely because the chart did *not* say so, and the words " Moat Bay " are inscribed in the northern arm, appears to the Court to be far-fetched and too conjectural to be acceptable. The same type of criticism may be made of the deductions to be drawn from another of the early explorers' maps, Map 8 of the Argentine Memorial, a copy of the eastern half of which was circulated in the course of the hearings, —a map evidently much relied upon by Argentina. This shows the Channel from its western arms eastwards, as far as Picton, together with the eastern arm between Picton–Lennox and Navarino, but cuts off the entire northern arm except for a bare indication of it just north of Picton. Again, this map confines the words " Beagle Channel " to the central section west of Gable Island; —but from the fact that, at the eastern end, the Navarino arm was shown, while the northern arm was cut off by the edge of the map, the Court was asked to infer that the latter was not regarded as Beagle Channel, whereas the former was. It is not, however, from such tenuous indications that any firm conclusions can be drawn.

91. It has been seen that because the text of the Treaty furnished no direct definition of the course of the Beagle Channel at its eastern end, it was necessary to seek assistance from outside that text. This has been done, but without any really certain result, although it may be thought that the weight of the evidence (and see Annex II) tends to favour the northern arm. The Court therefore returns to the Treaty itself. If it contains no direct definition that would *per se* settle the matter, it may nevertheless provide material from which sufficiently firm conclusions can be reached as to whether the PNL group falls within the Chilean attribution or not.

(x) *Factors pointing to the northern arm as being the " Treaty " arm*

92. *First*, if a process of simple elimination is employed, it will be found to place the group within the Chilean attribution and, in so doing, will also settle what the course of the Beagle Channel must be deemed to be for the purposes of the Treaty. Since it has to be presumed, *prima facie* at least, that the Treaty must be interpreted in such a way as to bring about a complete allocation of all the territories and islands in dispute between the Parties at the time of its conclusion, —and if at the same time it appears that, as has been seen, the PNL group cannot, or cannot with sufficient certainty, be regarded as being part of Argentina's attribution (*supra*, paragraph 79), then the islands of the group must be placed within the Chilean allocation, provided of course that some clause of that allocation is capable of covering them. They cannot by any stretch of imagination be brought within the clause specifying all islands " to the west of Tierra del Fuego ", but they can fall within the terms of the clause " to the south of the Beagle Channel " if the northern arm past Picton to Cape San Pio and Nueva Island is taken to have been intended for the purposes of the Treaty; —and a total failure of the Treaty in respect of the PNL group being the only alternative on the basis of these premisses, and being one that was to be excluded, such an intention can legitimately be presumed.

93. *Next*, there are the very terms of the Chilean attribution. The expression " to the south of " can only imply a direction in relation to which the terms " south ", and " north ", are significant, —in other words, an

east–west, west–east direction which, broadly, is that of the northern arm of the Beagle Channel along the southern shore of the Isla Grande, past Cape San Pio to the sea. But all significance and applicability of the term " south of " is lost in relation to a waterway the general direction of which is already from north to south, so that any islands in the vicinity would normally be indicated as being east or west of it, not north, or south. Up to Picton Island, the Beagle Channel runs indubitably west–east, so that any islands not situated in the Channel itself must be north or south of it. But the same criterion of a north or south localization (as postulated by the wording of the Chilean attribution) can only be preserved for the rest of the Channel, past Picton, if it is deemed to continue to go in an easterly direction by the northern arm, not a southerly one by the other arm. The Court thinks that the negotiators of the Treaty, in specifying a " to the south of " criterion, cannot possibly have contemplated a Channel which, over an important stretch of its course, would depart from the direction in respect of which that criterion was relevant and efficacious, suddenly to assume one that ended by pointing almost the opposite way, —for at the end of Lennox Island, the southern arm adumbrates a turn to the south-west, away altogether from the general course of the Channel, and virtually starts to go back westwards, except of course that, *qua* Channel, it stops there.

94. *Finally* and principally, the Court has considered why it was that the negotiators of the Treaty, having carefully defined all the other boundaries concerned—the north–south boundary down the Andes (Article I), the east–west Dungeness–Andes line (Article II), the north–south Cape Espiritu Santo/Beagle Channel line (first part of Article III)—failed to define any boundary when they came to the west–east Beagle Channel line, and treated the Channel, in effect, as if it were a river line that needed only naming, but not describing as to its direction and flow. The Court thinks that this can be accounted for in one way only, just as there can only be one rational explanation of the fact (see paragraph 87 above) that in the whole record of the negotiations the course of the Channel seems never once to have been discussed. This must have been because the course of the Channel appeared to the negotiators to be so obvious as not to need definition or even discussion. But there was only one basis on which this could have been the case, —and here the Court refers to what it has stated in paragraph 50 above concerning the consequences of the drawing of the perpendicular line in the Isla Grande from Cape Espiritu Santo to Point X near Lapataia on the Beagle Channel, *without any further definition of the part of the Isla Grande thereby attributed to Argentina* except to say that the Isla, " divided in this manner ", and Chilean on the western side, would be " Argentine on the eastern ". As described in the paragraph just referred to, this automatically had the effect of making the south shore of the Isla Grande, from Cape Buen Suceso near Staten Island, back westwards to Point X on the Beagle Channel (with the appurtenant waters), the southern limit of Argentina's allocation under the Treaty, except of course as regards any islands south of that limit that might be attributed to her under the Islands clause of Article III.

95. Another way of arriving at the same conclusion is to consider what was the base line with reference to which the perpendicular from Cape Espiritu Santo was drawn. It cannot have been the Beagle Channel as such, for it was the *whole* Isla Grande that was being divided, and its southern

shore runs along, but extends beyond the Channel, at both its eastern and its western ends. It was this entire southern shore (which comprises, but is not co-terminous with, the north shore of the Beagle Channel) that was the base line, the Channel being mentioned because it was the most prominent feature of the locality, and the terminal to which the Isla Grande perpendicular descended at its southern end. The inevitable effect of this, however, was that the boundary line of the south shore of the Isla Grande not only encompassed the Beagle Channel from Point X eastwards, but coincided absolutely with the north shore of the Channel, *and with the north shore of the northern arm of the Channel*, up to the latter's terminating point at Cape San Pio or possibly Punta Jesse. Or to take the approach from the Staten Island direction, the south shore of the Isla proceeded westwards until the vicinity of these Capes, after which it started to coincide with and automatically became, not only the north shore of the Beagle Channel as far as Point X, but to do so *via*, as the connecting link, the northern arm of the Channel.

96. Given this situation, the Court thinks it almost mandatory, or at least a matter of compelling probability, to conclude that in the circumstances, the negotiators of the Treaty could only have seen the Beagle Channel as continuing past Picton by its northern arm, and to consider it as scarcely conceivable that, without comment, they can have intended a Channel that would turn away from the south shore of the Isla Grande at Picton Island, and proceed in quite a different direction, pointing ultimately towards Cape Horn. That such a direction might assist the Argentine view about the " fringe " islands lying between the PNL group and Cape Horn is not relevant in the immediate context.

97. The foregoing conclusion is re-inforced in certain incidental ways connected with sailings:—

(*i*) The evidence supplied by Counsel for both Parties during the oral proceedings, indicates that in the period from 1848 to 1901, *i.e.* in the periods prior to and after the framing of the Treaty, the passage north of Nueva (the northern arm) was the customary track of vessels in voyages going to and from Staten Island, or the Malvinas (Falkland Islands) or Buenos Aires, and various destinations in the Channel, principally Ushuaia, Woollya and Harberton. Furthermore, the preponderant flow of traffic was to and from localities on the eastern seaboard of the Atlantic, rather than from or towards the south—(for further details see Annex III hereto). The almost invariable use of this northern outlet to the ocean was, of course, not surprising, since the inference is that it must have presented itself to mariners as the most accessible and direct route. The customary use of this entrance or exit would have resulted in its being regarded as the main arm of the Channel by those concerned with it, as were the negotiators of the 1881 Treaty; —and since a point somewhat insisted upon by the Argentine side was the alleged danger to navigation entailed—at least in the days of sail—by the stronger adverse winds and currents said to be a feature of this northern arm, the Court has noted the following remarks in an earlier British

Admiralty memorandum of 26 August 1915[52] (Chilean Annex No. 104) that preceded, but expressed the same basic view as that of 28 December 1918 already considered (*supra*, paragraph 89 (*a*)). These remarks were to the effect that the southern arm had been "much less surveyed and charted" than the northern one, and appeared to be "*distinctly more dangerous and less convenient*" than the one "flowing to the North"—stress added.

(*ii*) The Italian navigator Giacomo Bove, in the first of two reports rendered to the Argentine Government in 1882 concerning his sea-voyages in the Magellanic and Beagle regions, and writing from Slogget Bay on the south coast of Isla Grande near Punta Jesse, and north of Nueva Island—(therefore close to the eastern extremity of the northern arm of the Beagle Channel—see Maps)—duly described this Bay (Sloggett) as situated "at the end of the Beagle Channel and a little to the east of Nueva Island"—(Chilean Annex No. 353, at p. 98).

(*iii*) The Argentine Governor of Tierra del Fuego, in his official report on the sea-voyages he made in 1855, as mentioned in paragraph 5 (*a*) of Annex III hereto—one of which took him along the northern arm of the Channel—stated (Chilean Annex No. 49, at p. 155) that he "spent the night at Banner Cove, *a Chilean port*" (stress added),—Banner Cove being on Picton Island in the northern arm of the Channel.

(*iv*) In the same report the Governor, in recommending the future territorial sub-division of the governorate of Argentine Tierra del Fuego, did so in terms which to the Court appear by clear inference to identify the course of the Beagle Channel with the Channel's northern, not southern arm, and with the south shore of the Isla Grande—see paragraphs 94 and 95 *supra*—(Chilean Annexes, *loc. cit.* at p. 158).

98. *Consideration of possible objections*—Various objections have been made to the above conclusion about the course of the Channel:—

(*a*) *The first* of these can be disposed of very quickly: the "costa seca" or "estéril" objection, —a dry and sterile shore without waters would not be a possible boundary. But of course there would be waters, —the waters that, according to the generally received rules of international maritime law, are regarded as automatically appurtenant to territory—a fact recognized by the Argentine negotiator, Señor

(52) This memorandum was not prepared in the Hydrographic Department of the Admiralty but in that of the Director of Naval Intelligence. It figures as Chilean Annex 104, and well repays study in its entirety. It tended to favour Chile, though without reaching any really hard and fast conclusion; and the Hydrographer, Admiral Parry (over whose signature the later, 1918, memorandum appeared) commented (Chilean Annex 104 at p. 276):

> "It appears possible that further investigation might . . . furnish other evidence in this matter, but at such a time as the present [it was war-time] it is obviously impossible that complete justice can be done in such an important and interesting question."

See further, No. 1 in Annex II.

Irigoyen, himself[53]. The Court has already dealt with this matter in another context in paragraph 6 above—(and see also, below, the section on the islands within the Beagle Channel itself). There may, of course, in given cases, be controversy as to how these rules are to be applied. Nevertheless, in principle, they provide the means of determining the matter.

(*b*) *Next*, it was objected that the conclusion reached above (in paragraph 94) involved a gratuitous and unwarranted substitution for the boundary contemplated by the Treaty (said to be the Beagle Channel) of a different boundary, the Isla Grande shore. But this objection is completely fallacious. The Islands clause of the Treaty did not indicate the Beagle Channel, as such, as a boundary, but merely as a reference line for the attribution of the islands lying to the south of it. Indeed, the negotiators seem to have deliberately avoided drawing any boundary line in, or along the Channel, even for the purpose of determining the title to the islands within it. The Channel was mentioned for quite other reasons, —namely to specify where the north-south perpendicular from Cape Espiritu Santo was to stop, —and secondly, as a means of identifying certain of the islands attributed to Chile. The notion of the Channel as a boundary must have come about largely because of the contingency that what the Court thinks is the real boundary, namely the Isla Grande shore and its appurtenant waters, happens to coincide over about half of its length in the section Buen Suceso to Point X, with such a prominent geographical feature as is constituted by the Channel. But it is with the northern shore and northern arm that it so coincides. The course of the Channel for the purposes of the Treaty being thus evident, no doubt the Channel itself—not originally seen as a "boundary"—became regarded as such, —but that is another matter: it cannot change the fact that, in contrast to what the negotiators did under the other territorial provisions of the Treaty, which necessitated the definition or drawing of boundaries that were artificial or not self-evident, these same negotiators, in this region, drew no lines and specified no boundaries because, as the Court sees it, these were not required. The boundaries of Argentina's Isla Grande attribution, —namely the perpendicular, the Atlantic coast-line, and the line of the south shore to Point X, were self-evident. The rest was done by specific attributions. The Beagle Channel, seen by the negotiators—for the reasons already explained—as proceeding by way of the nothern arm to Cape San Pio, left the PNL group to the south of it, and therefore within Chile's attribution.

(*c*) *Finally*, it may be asked why, if the conclusion just reached is correct, the Chilean attribution did not simply take the form of specifying "all the islands to the south of the Isla Grande (or of Tierra del

[53] Speaking, actually, of the Straits of Magellan (but the principle is the same), he said in his speech which is the subject of paragraphs 113ff. below, at p. 122 (see explanation of this reference in n. 60 *infra*):

"In the case of jurisdiction, the waters cannot be separated from the coasts..... Least of all in the case of a Strait...... jurisdiction cannot be exercised over the coasts by someone with no jurisdiction over the waters which wash them."

Fuego) "[54] instead of " to the south of the Beagle Channel". The The answer clearly is that this was not done because, unless qualified in some detail, it would have resulted in the attribution to Chile not merely of the islands south of the Channel but of the whole Channel itself, east as well as west of Point X, and everything in it. This was what had been done in the case of the Straits of Magellan, but only on the basis that Chile would have the shores and hinterland on both sides of the Straits. In the case of the Beagle Channel, Chile was only intended to have the south shore, with appurtenant waters, in the section between Point X and Cape San Pio or Punta Jesse, Argentina having the north shore, with appurtenant waters. The Court will consider separately, later, the question of the islands lying within the Channel—a question not in terms dealt with by the Treaty.

(xi) *Conclusion on the Chilean attribution south of the Beagle Channel*

99. Therefore, none of the above-mentioned objections appearing to be valid, the Court must hold the islands of Picton, Nueva and Lennox to be situated " to the south of the Beagle Channel ", as that expression is to be understood for the purpose of the Treaty. This view is strongly supported by later confirmatory material, to which the Court will come in due course.

(xii) *The western islands*

" . . . and those [islands] there may be to the west of Tierra del Fuego "

100. The western part of Chile's attribution is not relevant to the question of the PNL group, or of the other islands within the " Hammer ", since on no possible basis could they be regarded as lying " to the west of Tierra del Fuego ". But, as was indicated earlier, in paragraph 63, it is necessary to consider the wording of this attribution because of the potential repercussions that it might have on the analogous expression " to the east of Tierra del Fuego " in Argentina's attribution under the Islands clause. The point involved has been sufficiently stated in the paragraph just referred to, —but briefly, the Argentine contention is to the effect that if the words " to the west of Tierra del Fuego " are interpreted in the same way as Chile contends that Argentina's attribution of islands " to the east of Tierra del Fuego " ought to be interpreted (and unless they are interpreted in the sense that Argentina contends should be given to her own attribution), it will be found that a number of western islands, presumed to be Chilean, are not allocated at all under the Treaty because, although they may be west of the archipelago, they are not west of the Isla Grande, —or else because, being part of the archipelago, they cannot lie " to the west " of it, although they may be on its western fringe[55]. Certain other islands[56], which otherwise might escape these objections by reason of being in any event " to the

---

[54] Such a version of the Islands clause actually appeared in 1889 in a work in French, and was depicted on an accompanying map. This work was sponsored by the Argentine authorities for the purpose of the Paris World Exhibition of that year—see further, paragraph 157(*b*) below. However, the suggestion intended to be conveyed was the opposite one, namely that the PNL group fell within the Argentine attribution under the Treaty, because south of Tierra del Fuego and " on the Atlantic ".

[55] In particular the islands of Clarence, Santa Inés, Ricetrebor, Jacques and Desolación.

[56] In particular those of Stewart, O'Brien, Londonderry and Gordon.

south of the Beagle Channel", are said not to be so because they are only south of the north-west, not of the south-west, arm of the Channel at its western end.

101. With regard to the latter group of western islands, the Court thinks that the Argentine contention is in any case misconceived because the two western arms of the Channel have always had equal status as being "Beagle Channel", and it suffices (for the test of being south of it) that an island is south of either arm. With regard to the other islands (see note 55), said to be unallocated on the basis of this Argentine contention, it seems that the possibility has been overlooked—(a possibility which the Court thinks probably represents the truth)—that these islands were already so admittedly Chilean, and regarded as such by both sides, that they were not intended to be covered by the Treaty settlement at all, because not considered to be part of the "controversia de límites" to which its Preamble refers. The point is graphically portrayed through the medium of a map—see *infra*, paragraph 122—that will also be referred to later for its value as confirming the Court's view concerning the course of the Beagle Channel in the vicinity of the PNL group. It will be convenient to call this map the "Irigoyen" map (Chilean Plate 21) because it was given or sent to the British Minister in Buenos Aires by Señor Irigoyen, the Argentine Foreign Minister and chief Argentine architect of the 1881 Treaty, shortly after its conclusion, in order to illustrate the nature of the settlement. The map does not (in general) do this by indicating boundary lines, but by differential colouring of the territories respectively attributed to Argentina or to Chile. At the same time it shows in white (uncoloured) those territories (that is to say the Argentine territories north of the Rio Negro, and the Chilean territories along the trans-Andean Pacific coast and in the Magellanic and Islands region) that did not come into the Treaty settlement at all, because they were not then the subject of any disputed claim. Amongst those thus shown in white are, precisely, those that the Argentine contention now under discussion would place in the category of being unallocated. Amongst the "Aclaraciones" (clarifications) printed on this map, there appears the following:

> "El Archipelago al Occidente de la Tierra del Fuego (que aparece sin colores) ha sido siempre del dominio incuestionable de Chile."
>
> "The Archipelago west of Tierra del Fuego (that appears uncoloured) has always been under the unquestionable sovereignty of Chile."

In confirmation of this, the Court noted statements made on behalf of Argentina in the course of the oral hearings to the effect that, with reference to the proposal for arbitration put forward from the Argentine side as an alternative to the 1881 Treaty, should the latter fail (see paragraph 66 (*2*) (*c*) above), it was the intention to recognize *a priori*, and as not coming within the scope of the arbitration, all Chilean claims west of meridian 70°. This however covered precisely the islands which it was subsequently alleged would remain unallocated under the Treaty unless the Argentine interpretation of what was attributed to it under the Islands clause was accepted[57].

[57] There are also several passages in Señor Irigoyen's speech referred to in n. 53 above that explicitly admit the absence of any Argentine claim to Chilean territory west of the Andes or at the western end of the Magellanic region—see for instance the last quotation in paragraph 114(*v*) below, and see paragraph 116.

102. The Court can only conclude therefore that no sufficient reason has been shown in this respect why it should not adhere to the views it has already expressed as to the effect of the Argentine attribution.

(6) The small islands within the Channel

103. Within the Beagle Channel, and in the vicinity of the PNL group, there are a number of small islands, islets, rocks, banks, etc., which it will be convenient to refer to globally as " the small islands in the Channel ". As they are all within the area of the " Hammer " (*supra*, paragraph 1), it is part of the task of the Court to declare what their ownership is. This task is assigned to the Court by both the respective Requests of the Parties (*supra*, paragraph 2),—directly in that of Chile, and by implication in that of Argentina which asks for a determination of " the boundary line between the respective maritime jurisdictions " of the Parties. Equally, Article XII of the *Compromiso* bids the Court to include in its decision " the drawing of the boundary line on a chart ". This is formally a distinct exercise from the attribution of the small islands concerned but, as explained earlier in another context (see paragraphs 6 and 53) it seems to the Court to make little practical difference whether the line results from the attributions, or the attributions from the line, provided the principles involved are clear.

104. No difficulty arises over the islands immediately adjacent to the PNL group, the ownership of which follows that of the latter, in accordance with the conclusion already arrived at in paragraph 99 above. There is also no difficulty about the small islands lying in the southern arm of the Beagle Channel, between Navarino Island and the islands of Picton and Lennox since, in conformity with the same conclusion, this arm is wholly Chilean. The problem is therefore confined to the section of the Channel running from Point X near Lapataia to Picton Island, and thence along the northern arm, between the Isla Grande and Picton and Nueva as far as the eastern limit of the " Hammer "—a limit represented by a line running due south from a point just west of Punta Jesse on the Isla Grande, and passing Nueva Island about a quarter of a mile to seaward of its easternmost extremity—(this line is in fact that of meridian 66°25′). It is in respect of this section of the Beagle Channel, from Point X to the " Hammer " limit between the Isla Grande and Nueva, that the Court has drawn the red boundary line on the chart that accompanies the present decision entitled " Boundary-Line Chart ".

105. The effect of this line, which represents the Court's decision as to the boundary between the respective territorial and maritime jurisdictions of the Parties, is to attribute to Argentina all the islands and other formations within the area of the " Hammer " lying to the north or (at its eastern end) north-east of the line, and to Chile all those to the south or south-west. But before stating the principles on the basis of which the line has been drawn, the Court must explain how the attributions that result from it in respect of the small islands in the Channel fit into the general structure of the Treaty of 1881.

106. The small islands do not fall within any of the specific attributions made under the Islands clause of Article III of the Treaty: they are neither to the east nor to the west of either Tierra del Fuego or the archipelago, and being in the Beagle Channel itself cannot lie to the south of it. Having

regard to this, Chile put forward a scheme of allocation based on a principle of appurtenance derived from the Treaty, to which the Court will come in a moment. But first it will be convenient to consider an alternative view advanced by Chile, which was to the effect that, failing everything else, all of the small islands in the Channel must be deemed to have been attributed to her by virtue of the global effect of Article II, which (as she contends) allocates her all territory south of the Dungeness–Andes line subject only to the effect of Article III (see paragraph 32 *supra*). Hence, since these islands are not attributed at all by Article III, they are automatically Chilean. Argentina rejects this view on the ground that, as already described (paragraph 33 *supra*), Article II does not have the effect contended for by Chile, and only allocates her the territories lying between the Dungeness–Andes line and the Straits of Magellan, but nothing south of the Straits.

107. Irrespective of which of these views about the effect of Article II is correct—a question on which it has not thus far been necessary to reach any definite conclusion (*supra*, paragraph 49, but see now paragraph 110 below)—the Court regards the Chilean view as unacceptable in the context of the small islands situated within the Beagle Channel itself, —because applied in that context it would have the effect of allocating to Chile not only these islands, but the Channel as such, and all its waters. This would be incompatible with the specific attribution to Argentina, under the first part of Article III of the Treaty, of the whole north shore of the Channel from Cape San Pio to Point X, as part of the south shore of the eastern half of the Isla Grande that went to Argentina according to that provision; —for the Court considers it as amounting to an overriding general principle of law that, in the absence of express provision to the contrary, an attribution of territory must *ipso facto* carry with it the waters appurtenant to the territory attributed; and therefore, on the Channel, those extending up to some sort of median line—see paragraph 98 (*a*) above. This principle could not be regarded as negatived by a simple general attribution of all territory south of a given line such as, according to Chile's contention, resulted in principle for her from Article II of the Treaty; —and in any case that attribution was itself, by reason of the " without prejudice " clause it contains (see *supra*, paragraphs 15 and 32), made subject to Argentina's allocation under Article III of the eastern half of the Isla Grande, an allocation which the Court holds must include the appurtenant waters. But a division of the waters of the Channel along a boundary line must necessarily entail—subject to certain adjustments to be explained later—a corresponding division of the small islands lying in it, depending on which side of the line they are situated.

108. Since it was only as an alternative that Chile put forward the argument just considered, it need not be further discussed. Her principal view regarding the islands in the Channel was that although the Treaty of 1881 did not in terms attribute them, it provided a principle of attribution on the basis of which they could, by implication or analogy, be allocated. This the Treaty did by instituting a north-south test of attribution in relation to the Beagle Channel, the north shore from Point X to Cape San Pio or Punta Jesse being Argentine, the south shore (Islas Hoste, Navarino, etc.) Chilean. An obvious principle of appurtenance required that accessory and minor formations not specifically allocated, should be deemed so to have

been by implication, together with the larger pieces of territory to which they were immediately appurtenant. Combined with this, however, was a criterion of the main waterway, which has nothing to do with appurtenance as such, but may provide a basis of selection in the case of islands in mid-stream. Chile accordingly furnished the Court with a list of the islands which, in her view should, on these premisses, be regarded as Chilean: the rest would be Argentinean. Argentina, for her part, furnished a map tracing a line in mid-Channel as far as the vicinity of Picton Island. This line was, in principle, a median line, but deviated somewhat from the true median in certain places.

109. As was conceded during the oral hearing (and see also paragraph 53, *supra*), little practical difference would result from these two methods as regards the islands that would become attributed, or would be left to each side respectively, in the section of the Channel between Point X and the vicinity of Picton Island. Thereafter, the results are bound to differ, since according to Argentina, the whole northern arm, and the islands in it, should be hers, and also the eastern half of the southern arm,—whereas, according to Chile, only half the length of the northern arm (along the Isla Grande coast), split horizontally, would be Argentine, while the whole southern arm would be Chilean. Apart from the effects of this difference of view (now resolved in the light of the Court's findings in favour of the northern arm as being the " Treaty-arm "), the only other difference of substance was in respect of the Islas Bécasses (Woodcock Islands) which are situated in mid (northern) Channel, between the Isla Grande shore and the extreme western point of Picton (Punta Ganado or Point Gilbert). Despite the fact that this little group, if not by much, is still definitely somewhat nearer the Isla Grande shore than that of Picton Island, it was yet claimed by Chile, on the ground that the main waterway normally used by shipping ran between the group and the Isla Grande shore. The Court shares the Chilean view about the applicability in general of the principle of appurtenance, but for that very reason thinks that the Bécasses group should be allocated to Argentina, the " main waterway " criterion not being compelling enough—at least in this locality—to justify any derogation.

110. In drawing its own line on the attached Boundary-Line Chart, as described in paragraphs 104 and 105 above, the Court has been guided by the considerations indicated in Annex IV hereto (which shows how the line has been traced),—in particular by mixed factors of appurtenance, coastal configuration, equidistance, and also of convenience, navigability, and the desirability of enabling each Party so far as possible to navigate in its own waters. None of this has resulted in much deviation from the strict median line except, for obvious reasons, near Gable Island where the habitually used navigable track has been followed.

(7) The unresolved question of the Chilean allocation under Article II of the 1881 Treaty

111. It will be recollected (see paragraph 49) that the Court left unresolved the question whether the Chilean allocation under Article II of the Treaty extended in principle to all territories south of the Dungeness–Andes line (subject only to the effect of the " without prejudice " clause), or was

confined to the area between that line and the northern and western shores of the Straits of Magellan,—see generally paragraph 32 *et seq.*, above. That question had no direct relevance to the interpretation either of the Argentine or the Chilean attribution under the Islands clause of Article III, but could become material in any one of three ways;—(*a*) if it had proved to be the case that on the basis of the Islands clause standing alone, the PNL group would remain unallocated to either Party; (*b*) if, having regard to the way the Court has interpreted the expressions " to the east of " and " to the west of ", in the Islands clause, certain western islands would have proved not to have been directly allocated, and this would have had repercussions on the question of the interpretation to be given to the Argentine attribution under that clause—(for the explanation of this, see paragraphs 63 and 100 above); and (*c*) if the Treaty had afforded no adequate guidance as to the principles on which the small islands within the Beagle Channel should be allocated (see paragraph 106). In any of these eventualities it would have been Chile's contention that under the global, residuary, or " catch-all " effect of her allocation under Article II, everything south of the Dungeness–Andes line must fall to her (other than what was attributed to Argentina or denied to Chile by Article III). In that case it would have been necessary for the Court to reach a positive conclusion on the question of the extent of the Chilean allocation under Article II. Recourse to that Article is however unnecessary, since it is clear that independently of it, the PNL group, and the small islands within the Channel, can be attributed under the Islands clause of Article III, and that the question of the western islands can be disposed of in the manner specified in paragraph 101 above. Hence the Court thinks that, for the purposes of the present dispute, there is no need for it to decide this question, the various aspects of which have been fully discussed in their appropriate context.

IV

CONFIRMATORY OR CORROBORATIVE INCIDENTS AND MATERIAL

112. The conclusions reached above find confirmation or corroboration, directly or indirectly, in a number of ways, some of which have more appropriately received mention earlier—see for instance paragraphs 73, 76, 89, 97, and footnote 42 *supra*. There are various others, and without attempting any logical classification of these, the Court will deal according to convenience with the various matters involved, confining itself to those that appear to be specially significant or noteworthy, and stressing that its substantive conclusions are not based upon them.

1. The immediate post-Treaty period

(*a*) *Argentine acts*

(i) *Señor Irigoyen's speech of August/September 1881*

113. Between five and six weeks after the signature of the 1881 Treaty, Señor Irigoyen, the Argentine Foreign Minister and principal negotiator on

the Argentine side, made a speech in the National Chamber of Deputies, continuing over three days from 31 August–2 September, partly in presentation and explanation of the Treaty, partly in defence of certain of its aspects. This speech has been greatly relied upon by Argentina in support of the view that she had obtained, or retained, under the Treaty, all the Atlantic islands down to Cape Horn,—or at least that such was the belief of this distinguished statesman who, as one of the chief architects of the Treaty, could be assumed to be in a position to know. A careful study of the speech does not, however, bear out the interpretation Argentina has placed upon it.

114. *The Atlantic coasts and Cape Horn*—The speech is in fact mainly—indeed to quite a striking extent—devoted to the question of the Straits of Magellan and the Magellanic region,—to a lesser, but still considerable extent, to that of Patagonia north of the Dungeness–Andes line,—and only moderately to Tierra del Fuego, and then chiefly in the sense of the Isla Grande: but there is hardly a word about the islands as such, beyond what may indirectly be implied from one or two references to the Atlantic coasts and Cape Horn such as that which has already been quoted in paragraph 66 (*3*) above, to which the Court cannot attach any decisive value for the reasons there given. Other considerations endorse this view:

(*i*) There is reason to think that the appellation " Cape Horn " was often used figuratively as a convenient means of reference,—and rhetorically in such expressions as " hasta el Cabo de Hornos " (" as far as Cape Horn "),—in order to convey the idea of contingent claims, or assertions of title, extending in a general southerly direction, to which, however, no precision was given, and which therefore cannot be regarded as juridically meaningful: pointers rather than designations. This comes out particularly strongly in such passages as that quoted in sub-paragraph (*iii*) below.

(*ii*) It is however most apparent in the context of Staten Island, where the reference to Cape Horn was, so it has been suggested, used as " a shorthand form " for identifying the extent of the Argentine main Atlantic coastal claim, down the eastern shore of the Isla Grande of Tierra del Fuego, to and including Staten Island as a sort of limit. The tendency to regard Staten Island as a terminal can be seen more especially in the passage quoted in sub-paragraph (*iv*) below. This tendency, and the way in which such references to Cape Horn lack any precise application, is apparent in, for instance, the Argentine Law No. 269 of 6 October 1868, granting to one Luis Piedra Buena, as a reward for his pioneering activities, the ownership of the Isla de los Estados (Staten Island) " situada sobre el Cabo de Hornos " (situated on Cape Horn),[58] which can scarcely be said of Staten Island (see next sub-paragraph) though it is in the same general region.

(*iii*) The same figurative use of the Cape Horn appellation was made by Señor Irigoyen himself in a Note to the Chilean Minister in Buenos Aires, dated 30 May 1877 (*i.e.* in the very period of the negotiations

([58]) Annex 36 to the Argentine Reply.

for the 1881 Treaty), in which he similarly said that he wished " to recall the 1868 concession of the Isla de los Estados, situated 'sobre el Cabo de Hornos', that is to say in the southernmost part of this Continent, to Captain Luis Pedra Buena "(59). It may not be entirely without significance that the Argentine translation of this passage gives it as " situated *towards* Cape Horn "—(stress added), but according to Chile the Spanish original says " sobre "—on. Moreover, even if Spanish usage enables " sobre " to be rendered as " towards ", this would still constitute a figurative use of the notion of Cape Horn, 120 miles (192 km.) distant (south-west) from Staten Island, and hardly in the same direction except that it is in the far south of the continent. Further confirmation of this representational use of the term " Cape Horn " is to be found in a passage in Señor Irigoyen's speech(60), in which he went so far as to place that term within quotation-marks:

> ". . . I did not wish to conceal the possibility that national jurisdiction might be interrupted over any part of the extensive coast stretching as far as 'Cape Horn'".

This passage is of course significant in another way also, but in any case there is no " coast " as a continuous line stretching as far as Cape Horn, which is on an island in the Wollaston group—a group separated by varying stretches of sea from its neighbours.

(*iv*) A clue to the real character of Argentine thinking at this time in regard to the extension southward of the " Atlantic " claim, is to be found in a Note of 30 June 1875 from the then Argentine Foreign Minister to the Chilean Minister in Buenos Aires, in which the following passage occurs (it is quoted in full to bring out the significance of the relevant part occurring at the end)(61):

> " The discussion on boundaries in 1872 was opened by a solemn undertaking by the Government of Chile not to hinder Argentine jurisdiction over the Atlantic coasts. It is to be noted that Chile undertook this obligation after the acts of possession of these coasts were carried out pursuant to the laws enacted by the Argentine congress between 1868 and 1871, by virtue of which jurisdiction was extended *to the extreme end of the Continent, that is, to the island of Estados* "—[stress added].

(*v*) The absence of any references to the islands as such in Señor Irigoyen's speech, except for a bare recital—not even of the Islands clause of the Treaty—but of the *Base Tercera* of 1876 (*supra*, paragraph 25), and without comment or discussion—is rendered all the more striking by the fact that there are several places where a specific allusion to the southern islands was to be expected if these were

(59) Annex 10 to the Argentine Counter-Memorial, p. 57.

(60) Speech, p. 103—the reference is to the typed copy of the English translation made available by Argentina in the course of the oral hearing, and the only complete one in the documentation of the case.

(61) Chilean Annex 17, at p. 32.

really claimed, or were regarded as being within Argentina's attribution under the Treaty. For instance, at one point,(62) the Minister tells the Chamber—referring to the line of the 52nd parallel (part of the Dungeness–Andes line)—that

> "we still hold to the South of this line part of the Territories of Tierra del Fuego [meaning here the Isla Grande],(63) Isla de los Estados and the area between the said line, the Strait [of Magellan] and the foothills of Monte Aymond [north of the Strait]."

There is no mention here of any of the islands, apart from Staten, as being still held by Argentina. Again,(64)

> "Patagonia, which will continue (65) to be ours, and the eastern part of Tierra del Fuego [*i.e.* of the Isla Grande], which will remain(66) ours, are located on free seas and neutralized channels."

So were the islands, and in this context a mention of them, if not necessarily to be expected, would have been appropriate. There was none, nor was there any at the end of Señor Irigoyen's speech when, as part of his peroration, he said(67):

> "And on far-away Staten Island where, on a courageous and bold day, a valiant sailor from the Republic set foot, the country's flag will fly forever free."

Assuming the flag was also to fly over the other southern islands up to Cape Horn (still further away), and if this was considered to be the effect of the Treaty, here was an obvious opportunity for saying so. But most striking of all, are the places where Señor Irigoyen refers to the ambiguous meaning of the appellation "Tierra del Fuego" which, almost everywhere in his speech, he is clearly using (in the context) as denoting the Isla Grande. In the one passage in which he really does refer to the islands, though without any indication that some of them are considered to have been allocated to Argentina under the Treaty, he says this(68):

> "Tierra del Fuego is a geographical name which can be understood in diverse ways. Some geographers apply it to the group of islands to the south of the Strait of Magellan—[this would be the Isla Grande and the rest of the archipelago]. Others use this name to refer only to the principal island which is east of peninsula Brunswick—[*i.e.* the Isla Grande]. The remaining islands have received diverse names.
>
> I will take it in the broader sense, *even if it is its less correct one*—[stress added]—that is, I will understand by Tierra del Fuego the group of islands south of the Strait [of Magellan, *i.e.* the whole archipelago], from the Atlantic to the Pacific."

---

(62) Speech, pp. 91–92.

(63) The context clearly indicates this—see final quotation in this sub-paragraph.

(64) Speech, p. 120.

(65) (66) These expressions are not really compatible with the fact that the Treaty made *attributions* of the territories named—and see the first citation in paragraph 116 below.

(67) Speech, p. 164.

(68) *ibid.*, p. 90.

Here then, if anywhere, the speaker might have been expected to go on to indicate how the Treaty dealt with these various groups of islands. He did not do so. He continued with several paragraphs about the difficulty of determining where the Cordillera of the Andes died away in the Magellanic region, and therefore by implication, where Chile "west of the Andes" ended and coalesced with the western islands, —and he then went on to speak about the division of the Isla Grande effected by the first half of Article III of the 1881 Treaty(69):

> "We have divided, then, in equal parts, the extensive island East of Peninsula Brunswick which is commonly known as Tierra del Fuego—[*i.e.* the Isla Grande].
>
> We left out Peninsula Brunswick as belonging indisputably to Chile. . . . To resolve the matter in the Continental part, we have taken the map of the Republic, and . . . we have admitted that the territory in question is that to the South of [parallel] 52°. . . ."

And it was here, after a few words about the character of the 52nd parallel line (part of the stretch Dungeness–Andes), that he ended with the passage quoted at the start of the present sub-paragraph, to the effect that Argentina still held, south of this line, "part of the territories of Tierra del Fuego [*i.e.* the eastern half of the Isla Grande, as he had just mentioned], Isla de los Estados, and the area between the said line, the Strait [of Magellan] and the foothills of Monte Aymond". Thus, a certain amount was said about the western islands, —not a word about those to the east or far south.

(*vi*) It almost looks therefore as if Señor Irigoyen, if not deliberately avoiding the question of the islands, was not much interested in it; but if so, it is not necessary to suppose that a statesman of his known ability and experience had simply overlooked the matter or was unaware of it. There is evidence in several places in his speech that he regarded the far south in general as a region scarcely worth having, —see for instance the following remark(70):

> "And what is Tierra del Fuego, especially for us?
>
> It is a sombre and unknown region, frozen at certain times of the year, which has resisted all investigations and all hopes. The maritime powers have travelled along its coasts and have left them: none of them has set foot on those inclement rocks.
>
> And were they not [*i.e.* "If they were not"] devoid of suitable conditions for population and prosperity, they would not see themselves today deserted and desolated, and visited only by an Evangelist Mission which reaches its beaches to dispense the benefits of its propaganda to the few savages that wish to hear it."

And, paradoxically, Señor Irigoyen quotes a high Chilean source as speaking to the Press in Chile about the results of the Treaty in similar terms(71):

---

(69) *ibid.*, p. 91.
(70) *ibid.*, p. 86.

182915 G

"The zones left to Chile on the continent and in Tierra del Fuego are so miserable that it is impossible that any kind of industry could be developed on a large scale there."

115. It seems to the Court therefore, that no firm conclusions can be drawn from the references to the Atlantic coasts and Cape Horn in Señor Irigoyen's speech, and none at all as to the situation, under the 1881 Treaty, of the eastern and southern islands which, as such, he seems never to have discussed, apart (significantly) from Staten Island. There is much else of great interest in the speech, but no one can read the full text without being struck by the extent to which it is taken up—not with the question of the islands, never really entered into—but of Patagonia north of the 52nd parallel and, above all, the Magellanic region. The speech was basically a defence of the renunciation of all Argentine claims to that region, and to the control of the Straits.

116. *Tierra del Fuego*—On the other hand, it can definitely be concluded that when Señor Irigoyen mentioned Tierra del Fuego in his speech, as he frequently did, he meant solely the Isla Grande, not the archipelago, unless he expressly indicated the contrary. This he did but once (in the penultimate passage cited in sub-paragraph (*v*) of paragraph 114 above)—and then only coupled with an admission that this "broader sense . . . is its less correct one". The limitation to the Isla Grande is clearly shown in several of the passages cited in that sub-paragraph, and there are others, for instance(72),

". . . we ensure . . . the dominion over half the island called Tierra del Fuego, *over which our rights are questionable*" [stress added];

and finally, referring to earlier negotiations with Chile conducted by a former Minister, Señor Frias, he said(73):

"It is vital to bear in mind that by Señor Frias' proposal, the Peninsula Brunswick, together with all the islands to the west of it, was definitively recognized as Chilean. So that, when he was speaking of Tierra del Fuego, he could only be referring to the principal island, to *the large Island* [Isla Grande] if I may use the word, *which, in the maps of this area of the world, is generally called Tierra del Fuego*"—[stress added].

These various passages, in particular the last one, afford very strong support for the Chilean view that the expression "to the east of Tierra del Fuego" in the Islands clause of Article III of the Treaty, meant east of the Isla Grande as such, a designation that could not have included the PNL group of islands. Also, the reference to "all the islands to the west of" Peninsula Brunswick, as being "definitively recognised as Chilean" confirms the conclusion arrived at in paragraphs 101–102 above, that certain western islands(74) cited by Argentina in support of the contention described in paragraphs 63 and 100, fell outside the scope of the 1881 Treaty entirely, being recognized as already Chilean.

---

(71) *ibid.*, p. 21.

(72) *ibid.*, p. 143. It may be noted that the half referred to, over which Argentine rights were stated to be "questionable", was the Atlantic side half.

(73) *ibid.*, p. 67.

(74) *supra*, nn. 55 and 56.

(ii) *The "Apuntes" (Notes, Comments) of October 1881*

117. The 1881 Treaty was ratified on 22 October of that year. Already on 27 July Señor Irigoyen had sent a circular communication to all Argentine diplomatic posts abroad enclosing—not the text of the Treaty itself which, pending its ratification, had not been published—but a statement of its main points. On 24 October, subsequent to ratification, he sent a certified copy of the final text to those same posts but, in the case of a small selection, added a personal letter, accompanied by commentaries (" Apuntes ", " *mises au point* "), on the principal aspects of it, intended to serve those concerned as guidance for publicity purposes (" para que los tome como base en los comentarios que publique sobre el Tratado ")([75]). The accounts that appeared in the Press of the countries concerned closely followed these commentaries, the relevant part of which in the present context ran:

> " By this mutually honourable agreement the Argentine Republic remains owner of the vast region of Patagonia, of all the coasts on the Atlantic as far as Cape Horn; and the Strait [of Magellan] remains subjected to an international servitude for the benefit of world commerce."

Argentina has insisted on the effect of these words as a demonstration of the validity of her claim that the 1881 Treaty was regarded as conferring on her all the Atlantic islands on the eastern side of Cape Horn. The Court is unable to see it in that light. There is no specific mention of the islands as such. The phrase " all the coasts of the Atlantic down to Cape Horn " echoes previous rhetorical statements to the same effect, the figurative character of which has just been commented upon above, and is also open to the doubts about the exact meaning of the terms " coasts " and " Atlantic " noticed earlier in paragraph 65 *et seq*. Señor Irigoyen may have had no more than Staten Island in mind—the island that he had already characterized as being situated " sobre el Cabo de Hornos "—see paragraph 114 *(ii)* and *(iii)* above. It is not possible to say with any certainty; but be that as it may—and the Court has no wish to deduce from casual indications a conclusion that might be as little reliable as its opposite—such inferences as might otherwise be drawn from the " Apuntes " in favour of Argentina seem to the Court to be completely negatived by the further events now to be described, connected with three specific maps—the so-called " Mapa García "; the " Irigoyen " map, as it may conveniently be called; and the 1882 " Latzina " map.

(iii) *Señor Garcia and British Admiralty Chart No. 786*

118. Shortly before sending out the " Apuntes ", as above described, Señor Irigoyen had authorized one of the recipients of these, Señor García, the Argentine Minister in London, to seek an interview at the Foreign Office, mainly to discuss the question of the neutralization of the Straits of Magellan. The interview (with the Under-Secretary of State, Lord Tenterden) took place

([75]) The letters sound a note of caution—(" Todo esto con reserva ")—which was understandable, for in neither Argentina nor Chile were certain aspects of the Treaty popular, particularly as regards the Straits of Magellan. In Chile the permanent neutralization of the Straits effected by Article V of the Treaty, was a good deal criticized.

on 27 October 1881. Señor García was able to inform Lord Tenterden of the recent ratification of the Treaty. In reporting this to his Government (despatch of 30 October) he said (in the Argentine version of the English translation of this despatch—the Chilean version, where different, is given in square brackets)(76):

> " As Lord Tenterden told me that he was anxious [very much wished] to know the terms of that agreement [stipulation], I showed him the Treaty [expounded the Treaty to him] and, after translating [for him] the Article in question,(77) added that [telling him that] my Government had requested me to leave [charged me with leaving] a copy at Her Majesty's Ministry [for the Ministry of Her Majesty]."

Thus there can be no doubt that Señor García was instructed to leave something purporting to be a copy of the Treaty, and did so. But there has been considerable disputation between the Parties as to what exactly this copy represented. Suffice it to say that it was a version that had appeared in an Argentine newspaper, the " Tribuna Nacional ", on 24 July, the day after the signature of the Treaty. In this version, Article I (there called the " *Base Primera* ") is identical in substance with the Treaty Article I, but there are differences of wording. Article II and the first—(Isla Grande)—half of Article III (" *Base Segunda* " and part of the " *Base Tercera* ") are identical with the Treaty in all respects. In the Islands clause of this (" Tribuna Nacional ") version of Article III (the rest of the " *Base Tercera* ") there is a difference in the wording of the Argentine attribution(78), the effect of which was to make it substantially similar to the " Valderrama proposal " of 3 June 1881 that was not adopted—see paragraph 67 above,—and the Court has already (paragraph 68) indicated the reasons there are for thinking that it would in any case have made little essential difference to the scope of this attribution, even if it had been adopted,—while the Chilean attribution of " todas las islas al Sud del Canal Beagle hasta el Cabo de Hornos " is exactly the same in the " Tribuna " version as in the Treaty, with the exception of the spelling of the word " Sud " instead of " Sur ". These details are noted here because of the Argentine contention that what was given to the British Foreign Office was an incorrect or superseded version of the Treaty (Señor García could not on 27 October have received the text as ratified on the 22nd(79)). The reason for this contention, already referred to in paragraph 71 *supra*, will be made clear in a moment,—but in any case the Foreign Office was not misled, for the official annotation on the back of what Señor García handed over reads " This is not the actual Treaty but the bases of what it is believed has been signed."(80)

---

(76) See Annex 45 to the Argentine Counter-Memorial, and Chilean Annex 46a.

(77) This would be Article V of the Treaty, neutralizing the Straits of Magellan.

(78) In the Treaty expression " los islotes príximamente inmediatos a ésta y las demás islas que haya . . .", etc., the " Tribuna " version adds the word " isla " after " ésta ", replaces the " y " by a comma, and changes " las demás islas " to " demás " simply, thus reading ". . . los islotes príximamente inmediatos a ésta isla, demás que haya . . .", etc. It has already been indicated (paragraph 68) why, given the retention of " demás " and " al oriente de ", etc., it made no real difference to speak of " islotes " rather than " islas ".

(79) This might account for the otherwise inexplicable official communication by an Argentine representative of a version of the Islands clause now claimed by Argentina herself to be incorrect and unfavourable to her, and also not adopted in the Treaty text.

(80) Annex 49 to the Argentine Counter-Memorial.

119. Simultaneously with the text that he communicated on this occasion, Señor García made Lord Tenterden a presentation of a copy in French of a work entitled "La Conquête de la Pampa" by an Argentine geographer, Lt. Colonel Olazcoaga, together with—(Argentine version)—"the plan of the southern regions which contain the new frontier". The Chilean version of this is "the plan of the southern regions which includes the new boundary"—thus clearly relating the word "includes" to "the plan", whereas the plural sense of the Argentine "contain" relates that word, not to the plan, but to "the southern regions". The original Spanish text appears to be "el plano de las regiones australes que encierra (not "encierra*n*") la nueva frontera". Therefore the correct English rendering is that given by Chile ("include*s*" or "contain*s*"), from which the natural inference would be that the plan was one that showed the Treaty settlement. This plan has, in fact, never been found, and Argentina has contended that it was not a plan of the settlement at all, but a map in the Olazcoaga book showing the frontier with the Indians in the Pampa. Yet Señor García's account reads as if the plan he handed over was not in the book itself or part of it, but separate. The map incorporated in the book (which appears as No. 11 in the Counter-Memorial volume of Argentine Plates) concerns a totally different region, on the Rio Negro, not the Treaty areas at all; and Señor García could scarcely, in the context of giving Lord Tenterden information about the Treaty, have handed him the "map-of-the-book" as being what he called "the plan of the southern regions which includes the *new* boundary"—(stress added).

120. Be these things as they may, the real point is different. Whatever was received from Señor García was passed on to the British Admiralty, with a request that a map should be prepared showing the new boundaries on the basis of the information as received. This was done, and numbered as Admiralty Chart 786, sometimes referred to as the "1881 Admiralty Map"(81), figuring in the documentation of the case as Chilean Plate No. 20. As sent to the Foreign Office by the Admiralty, it is endorsed with an official annotation reading "F.O. 6/372 (extracts). Map to illustrate Boundary Treaty between Chile and Argentine Republic—*as commd.* [*communicated*] *by Señor García Oct. 27 1881* [stress added] and procured from the Admiralty by the Librarian"(82). It shows the line as running along the south shore of the Isla Grande; and the words "Beagle Channel", placed at the exit, clearly indicate the northern arm, not the southern arm by Navarino and Lennox Islands. Argentina has contended that since, as she maintains, this map was based on incorrect information concerning the contents of the Treaty (*supra*, paragraph 118), its value as evidence is "absolutely nil". But the information given to the Admiralty was not in any case incorrect in respect of Chile's attribution of the islands south of the Beagle Channel, and

(81) The Court has not overlooked the earlier Admiralty Chart 789, published on 11 July 1881, *before* the signature of the Treaty, though apparently given a later serial number (Argentine Counter-Memorial Plate 10 and Chilean Plate 173). However the Court believes that the explanation of this map given in paragraph 133 (pp. 180–181) of the Chilean written Reply is the correct one.

(82) To be noted is the definite statement that Señor García did communicate a map illustrating the Treaty settlement. The Librarian and Keeper of the Papers (*i.e.* Chief Archivist) at the Foreign Office, at this time, was Sir Edward Hertslet, a well-known authority on boundary-treaties, and the author of several books on the subject.

for reasons already stated (*ibid.*) was unlikely to mislead concerning Argentina's attribution.

121. Moreover, it so happened that on 26 October 1881, the British Minister in Santiago (Chile) had received from the Chilean Foreign Ministry a copy of the Treaty as ratified, and an illustrative map, appearing in the case as Chilean Plate No. 16—identical with a number then made available to foreign Legations in Santiago and by them sent to their Governments (Chilean Plates Nos. 13–15 and 18)([83]). It quite clearly showed the PNL group, both by line and colouring, as Chilean. This map was passed on by the Foreign Office in London to the Admiralty, under cover of a letter dated 15 December 1881, as having been "received from Her Majesty's Minister at Santiago showing the boundaries agreed to under the Treaty recently concluded between the Argentine and Chilean Republics". The Admiralty also received the same map (shown as Chilean Plate No. 17) direct from the Hydrographic Department at Santiago—(see paragraph 131 below). It seems to the Court inconceivable that the British Admiralty, thus obtaining information about the same Treaty from both the Parties to it, and finding (if that had been the case) some significant discrepancy, would not at once have started an enquiry, especially as it either just had drawn up, or was in the process of drawing up, a map, chart 786, based on the information obtained from one of these sources. Clearly the Admiralty interpreted the expression "to the south of the Beagle Channel", which appeared in what was received from both Parties, in such a way as to leave the PNL group to Chile. Nothing received from the Argentine side contradicted this interpretation, while that coming from the Chilean side confirmed it. The Court also finds it difficult to believe that the Argentine Government could have remained in complete ignorance of the dissemination to foreign Legations in Santiago of a map so entirely at variance (in respect of the course of the Beagle Channel) with the view that Argentina is now alleged to have then held concerning the attribution to her of the PNL group. True, Argentina was not at the time in diplomatic relations with Chile, but she maintained a Consul-General in Santiago—(Chilean written Reply, pp. 337–8). Yet no record exists of any Argentine protest made, or dissent expressed,—although in the course of the present proceedings the probative value of the Chilean map was challenged,—a matter on which the Court will comment later. Even more significant, however, was the next incident, to which the Court now comes.

(iv) *The "Irigoyen" map*

122. This map, appearing in the documentation of the case as Chilean Plates Nos. 21 and 175, has already been mentioned in an earlier connection (paragraph 101). On 20 December 1881, Mr. George Petre, British Minister in Buenos Aires, who had already, at the end of October, sent the Foreign Office in London an (as he put it) "official copy of the Boundaries Treaty

([83]) In his despatch of 27 October transmitting the text of the Treaty and the map, the British Minister, Mr. J. Pakenham, said that he also enclosed "three copies of a map defining the limits as now established, and which, as they were given to me yesterday by the Under-Secretary of State at the Moneda [Chilean MFA], may I presume be looked on as authentic for all practical purposes"—(see Chilean Annex 46 at p. 148).

. . . of July 23 ", wrote again enclosing two copies of " the map showing the line of frontier established by the Treaty " which, he added, " Dr. Irigoyen has been good enough to send me privately ". This map, Mr. Petre explained, showed the results of the Treaty attributions in colour, and

> " the part which is coloured a deeper shade of crimson, comprising the Straits of Magellan, half of Tierra del Fuego [*i.e.* of the Isla Grande], *and all the southern islands* [stress added] represents what has been actually ceded to Chile by the recent Treaty."

The part coloured the " deeper shade of crimson " included the PNL group; and Mr. Petre concluded, significantly, that the Argentine Republic, as the Foreign Office would see, was " left in full possession of the Atlantic seaboard ". This, coupled with the mention of " all the southern islands " as being attributed to Chile, shows that Mr. Petre did not, on the basis of this map, understand the Atlantic seaboard as extending to or comprising the southern islands, amongst which the PNL group is numbered.

123. The Chilean contention was that the importance of this incident lay in the fact of the *communication* of the map to a foreign diplomat who would be certain to send it to his Government(84), —and by a Minister who was not just any Minister, but the Foreign Minister of Argentina who had himself negotiated and signed the Treaty. This could not but constitute the strongest possible evidence of " the intentions of the Argentine Government when concluding the Treaty and their understanding of it immediately afterwards "(85). Argentina contested this on a variety of grounds, mostly addressed to the map itself: it was not an official or authoritative map but one published in a popular periodical, the " Illustración Argentina "; its colouring was suspect; it contained errors(86); its preparation had been begun before the text of the Treaty was published, and it was based on an earlier superseded version and had appeared (on 10 November) before any changes could be made,—finally, it was not communicated officially, but privately by Señor Irigoyen on a personal basis.

124. With the possible exception of the last, it seems to the Court that these objections are irrelevant because they do not touch the main point on which Chile relies, namely not the map itself (though Chile of course regards it as correct) but the fact of its communication to the British Minister by Señor Irigoyen himself, which appears inconceivable unless he regarded it as accurately depicting the settlement. That this communication may not have amounted to an act of the Argentine Government as such, does not seem to the Court to matter, since it would necessarily be taken by Mr. Petre (and Señor Irigoyen could not have supposed otherwise) as meaning that the boundaries and attributions shown on the map as resulting from the Treaty, represented Señor Irigoyen's own view of those results. What counted was

(84) The terms of Mr. Petre's despatch to the Foreign Office, enclosing the map, imply that he must have regarded the latter as representing Señor Irigoyen's own view as to the nature of the Treaty settlement. The annotation made on the map itself in the Foreign Office, amongst others by Sir E. Hertslet (see n. 82 *supra*), show that there too it was regarded as illustrative of the settlement.

(85) See Chilean Memorial, paragraph 26, and Reply, paragraph 141.

(86) This is admitted to have been true, but only in minor respects not affecting the issue.

official conduct in relation to the map, —and a communication of this kind, made by a Foreign Minister in office, to a foreign Head of Mission *en poste*, cannot be evaluated as if it were a purely private act not in any way binding on the Government. But in any event, that is not the way in which the Court finds it necessary to look at the matter. It sees the episode simply as one that has a very high probative or supporting value in favour of the conclusions earlier arrived at (paragraphs 94–98) that the negotiators of the Treaty—of whom Señor Irigoyen was one—regarded the Beagle Channel as flowing along the northern arm past Cape San Pio and Nueva Island. The map sent by Señor Irigoyen to the British Minister, showing the Treaty attributions by colour, brings out very vividly how the south shore of the Isla Grande with, of course, its appurtenant waters, by its coincidence with the north shore of the Channel, including the north shore of the northern arm, places the PNL group south of the Channel and within the Chilean allocation.

125. The Court concludes that it is impossible to reconcile Señor Irigoyen's communication of a map so drawn and coloured, with the view that he could have had the PNL group in mind when he made the observations that he did in his speech to the Chamber of Deputies, and in the " Apuntes ", concerning the Atlantic coasts and Cape Horn. Whether this was because he did not regard the coasts of these islands as being Atlantic coasts within his notion of that expression, or for some other reason, it is impossible to say, —but the fact remains.

(v) *The 1882 " Latzina" map*

126. If anything more were needed to confirm the view that the map sent to Mr. Petre in December 1881 did indeed represent Señor Irigoyen's own opinion concerning the effect of the Treaty in regard to the islands, it would be amply afforded by the publication under his *aegis*, about a year later, of what has been known in the case as the 1882 " Latzina " map (Chilean Plate No. 25). This map is regarded by Chile as the first official Argentine map to be produced under government auspices—though its official character was subsequently denied by the Argentine Government, and this is discussed later (see paragraphs 153–156 *infra*). The point is however that the map was brought out under the auspices of the President of Argentina, and of Señor Irigoyen (who had by then become Minister of the Interior), for inclusion in, or to go with, a publicity work entitled " The Argentine Republic as a field for European Emigration ", and subtitled " A statistical and geographical review of the country, and its resources, with all its various features ". Supervision was entrusted to Dr. Francisco Latzina, Director of the National Statistical Office.

127. This work, headed " Publicación Official ", was issued in five languages (Spanish, French, English, German and Italian). It included a map prepared by the lithographic firm of Stiller and Laas. The Argentine Congress officially approved the project and authorized the publication of a large number of copies for distribution throughout Europe. Like the

Irigoyen map (*supra,* paragraph 122) this Latzina map leaves no doubt as to the attribution to Chile of the PNL group of islands. In 1883, Señor Irigoyen, in making his Report to the Argentine National Congress, had occasion to assess the value of the publicity project, when requesting additional funds to continue the distribution. In the course of his Report he declared: " The map which Dr. F. Latzina was entrusted with, was printed last year, and distributed in Europe and America with excellent results "—(Chilean written Reply, paragraph 123 on p. 334). It cannot be accepted that the chief negotiator for Argentina of the 1881 Treaty would thus have given his personal backing to the publication of a map which showed the islands as Chilean unless, as previously, he believed this to be a correct representation of the Treaty settlement.

128. The Latzina map of 1882–3 provides an excellent example of the relevance of a map not so much for its own sake—(it could, theoretically, have been inaccurate)—but for the circumstances of its production and dissemination, making it of high probative value on account of the evidence afforded by this episode, namely of official Argentine recognition, at the time, of the Chilean character of the PNL group. The force of this, as illustrative of Argentine official opinion in the immediate post-Treaty period, is therefore in no way lessened by the fact that the 1882 Latzina map fell out of favour with the authorities a decade or so later,([87]) or that Dr. Latzina himself, having again, in 1888, published a map (Chilean Plate No. 48) showing a Chilean attribution for the PNL group, proceeded the year after, in 1889, to publish or at least write an introduction to a work containing a map (Argentine Counter-Memorial Plate No. 25) showing the group as Argentine—(this is discussed in paragraph 157 below).

(*b*) *Chilean acts in the immediate post-Treaty period*

129. The point about Argentine conduct in the post-Treaty months, as above described, is simply that it was not consistent with the interpretation of the Islands clause of the Treaty which Argentina is now maintaining, and which she contends was the one entertained by the Argentine authorities of the time. Alternatively, as in the case of Señor Irigoyen's speech, Argentina's conduct was too uncertain and inconclusive to afford that interpretation any real support. The corresponding Chilean acts seem to the Court to justify a quite different conclusion. This is not because Chile could by her own acts confer upon herself rights or territorial attributions not provided for by the Treaty, but simply because these acts were consistent with, and bear out, the interpretation of the Islands clause which Chile now, *as then,* puts forward as being the correct one.

(i) *Señor Valderrama's speech of September 1881*

130. The Chilean Foreign Minister and chief negotiator of the Treaty for Chile during its latter stages, Señor Valderrama, also made a speech to his Chamber of Deputies in the weeks following upon its signature (as Señor Irigoyen in Buenos Aires had done). The relevant passage about the islands occurring in this speech has already been quoted in paragraph 66 (*3*)

([87]) After a change in official Argentina policy about map production—as to which see *infra*, paragraph 156.

above. Unlike that of Señor Irigoyen, it contained a clear statement concerning the effect of the Treaty in this connexion (Chilean Annex No. 41 at p. 113):

> "The Treaty ensures for Chile dominion of . . . all the islands to the south of the Beagle Channel and to the west of Tierra del Fuego. . . ."
>
> . . . .;

and "in other words" there belonged to Chile

> "all the territories extending to the south [of the Straits of Magellan] with the exception of Tierra del Fuego bathed by the Atlantic and the Island of los Estados. . . ."

(ii) *The Chilean Hydrographic Notice No. 35/233 and "Chile's 1881 Authoritative Map"*

131. The Chilean Hydrographic Notice issued on 10 November 1881 was entirely consistent with the above quoted statement. After referring to the line from Cape Espiritu Santo to the Beagle Channel, it stated that the boundary went

> "thence along this channel until it entered the Atlantic. Thus the South-Eastern point of Tierra del Fuego and the island of Los Estados remain in the possession of the Argentine Republic."

The whole drift of this passage suggests a course along the northern arm of the Channel. When this Notice was sent by the Chilean Hydrographic Department to the Hydrographic Department of the British Admiralty, a map was attached to it which placed the Chilean view beyond all doubt (Chilean Plate No. 17). This was in fact the same map as that which will be discussed in paragraphs 132–134 below. It showed the PNL group as Chilean both by colouring and by line. The line is of interest, being stated to be that of the "proposal of July 1876". This was one of the original Irigoyen "Bases" of that year, set out in paragraph 25 above, and reflected in the eventual 1881 Treaty without any change of substance so far as concerned the "Islands clause".

132. The map just referred to, which subsequently became known as "Chile's 1881 Authoritative Map" (Chilean Plate No. 16), or as the "Prieto map" (after its cartographer), had been published under Government instructions by the Chilean Hydrographic Department, in August 1881, and appeared in the Chilean papers "Mercurio" and "Ferrocarril". Because at that time the Treaty, although signed, had not yet been approved by the Chilean Congress nor, hence, ratified, the legend on the map did not refer to the Treaty as such, but showed the Treaty attributions in colour against the indication "proposal of June 1881" ("proposición de Junio de 1881"), which was in fact the same as what eventually appeared in the Treaty text signed on 23 July. The line showing the Beagle Channel boundary was labelled as being that of the "proposal [*i.e.* "Basis"] of July 1876" which, as already mentioned, was in fact equally the one reflected in the

Treaty; —and to place the matter beyond doubt the following note was printed on the map:

> " Esta división coincide con la de 1876 . . . en todo su transcurso al traves . . . del Canal Beagle."

> " This division coincides with that of 1876 . . . over the whole of its course through . . .the Beagle Channel."

That this map also showed—by means of an entirely different pecking—the line of a proposal of 1879 that was not adopted, does not seem to the Court to affect in the slightest degree the *bona-fides* of the indications given on the map in regard to the other lines and divisions which, in the opinion of Chile, *had* been adopted.

133. This same map was also that mentioned in paragraph 121 above as having been made available to foreign diplomatic and consular posts in Santiago, and by them sent to their respective Governments at varying dates, in all cases *soon after the ratification and publication of the Treaty* (Chilean Plate Nos. 13, 15 and 18). These included (shown as Chilean Plates Nos. 16 and 17) the maps received by the Foreign Office and Admiralty in London in November–December 1881 (see paragraph 131). An identical map was received by the Royal Geographical Society in London, in January 1882 (Chilean Plate No. 19), and one had also been received in Paris from the French Minister in Santiago (the Baron d'Avril), enclosed in his despatch of 24 October 1881; while in the Bulletin of the Société de Géographie (7th Series, 3rd Vol.; Paris 1882, First Quarter), the report of the Secretary-General, M. Charles Maunoir, on the 1881 Treaty contained the following statements:

> " La solution de cette année s'accorde à peu de chose près avec les propositions présentées en 1876. . . . D'après le traité le Chili . . . a toutes les îles de l'ouest et du sud. La République Argentine, *avec la seule île des Etats* [stress added] et le tiers de la Terre de Feu, aura la large zone continentale qui renferme [la Patagonie] ".

134. Argentina has challenged the probative value of the Chilean Authoriative, or Prieto, Map, on grounds similar to the principal ones urged against British Admiralty Chart No. 786 (*supra*, paragraph 123), namely, in particular, that having emerged before the *publication* of the Treaty, it was based on an older and incorrect version of it, —specifically, on the Valderrama proposals of 1881 (see *ante*, paragraph 67) which had not been accepted, and which did not appear in the final, definitive, text of the Treaty. But having regard to what is stated in paragraphs 123 and 132 above, the Court must regard this contention as not well-founded. The map stated quite explicitly that it exhibited the boundary-line resulting from both the June 1881 and July 1876 proposals, which coincided " over the whole of its course through the Beagle Channel "—(and on that basis showed the PNL group as Chilean). It seems scarcely possible that a map bearing indications of this kind should have been prepared under the *aegis* of the official Chilean Hydrographic Department, and subsequently published and disseminated, unless it was a *bona-fide* representation of the Chilean view of the effect of the Treaty, the terms of which, though not yet

published, were of course fully known to the Chilean authorities. It is not credible otherwise that the latter should have sponsored this map.

135. But, as observed earlier—the time for the Argentine authorities to have challenged the authenticity of the map was during the period of its original emergence or reasonably soon after, instead of many years later. It is before minds have had time to change or to visualize possibilities not originally thought of, that the real trend of contemporary acts and attitudes can most clearly be seen. Unquestionably, the map almost immediately became well-known in Buenos Aires. According to one account published in the Argentine newspaper "La Nación" in February, 1895 (Chilean Annex, No. 364):

> "*a few days* [stress added] after this document (the Treaty of 1881) was signed, a map of the Magellanic region arrived in Buenos Aires, issued by the Chilean Hydrographic Office whose seal it bears, circulated by "El Mercurio" of Valparaiso . . . " [This map] "was considered official on account of its origin, and . . . has served as a pattern for the dozens of maps that even now [*i.e.* fourteen years later] are sold in the book stores of Buenos Aires *and are in use in the schools of the Republic*" [stress added].

It is not relevant for present purposes that the writer of this article, Dr. Francisco Moreno, disagreed with what the map showed as being the boundary along the north–south line of the Andes—always a controversial matter, as the two subsequent arbitrations of 1898–1902 and 1965–66 were to show. He was a recognized Argentinean expert, a member of the standing Argentine–Chilean Boundary Commission (set up in consequence of Article IV of the 1881 Treaty), whom Señor Irigoyen had consulted many years before, and whom he quoted in his speech earlier referred to(88). He in no way disagreed with the Chilean 1881 map as regards the way in which it showed the result of the attributions made under the Islands clause of the Treaty. On the contrary, he considered the PNL group to be Chilean. The proof of this is contained in his notable memorandum of 23 July 1918 (Chilean Annex No. 113), further referred to in paragraph 158 below. At the present juncture, the object of the above citation from "La Nación" is simply as evidence that the Chilean version of the effect of the Islands clause of the Treaty, and the map illustrating it, were well-known in Argentina immediately after the conclusion of the Treaty; and neither then, nor for a long period thereafter, did these elicit any express dissent.

2. The cartography of the case considered as corroborative material

136. The present case has been noteworthy for the number, quality and interest of the maps, charts, plans and sketches produced by both sides. Apart from many furnished loose, in leaf form, or enclosed in folders, the Parties have, between them, tabled seven large folio volumes of plates of great beauty, numbering over 350 in all. Many of them show more than one map, so that the total for maps exceeds 400. Having regard to this;

(88) See his August-September 1881 speech (paragraph 113 and n. 60 above), at pp. 137–138. See also n. 9 above.

to the care and trouble taken by the Parties in the preparation and presentation of this cartography; to the prominent part it has played in the case; and to its usefulness for understanding the physical and geographical aspects of the dispute; —the Court proposes to consider the question of its legal effect, both generally and as regards certain particular examples of it, even though the Court's decision has been reached on grounds independent of cartography as such—principally those indicated in paragraphs 55–111 above. An additional reason for so proceeding is that the Court has already had occasion to refer to and comment on certain particular maps or charts([89]), not so much for their value as actual cartography, but because of the part they played in events closely connected with the conclusion of the 1881 Treaty. The Court will now consider the cartography from the point of view of the principles which, in the present case, are applicable to its evaluation; its general weight; and also, in respect of certain individual maps, for the light they throw on different aspects of the dispute.

(*a*) *Relevance of cartography as such*

137. Historically, map evidence was originally, and until fairly recently, admitted by international tribunals only with a good deal of hesitation: the evidence of a map could certainly never *per se* override an attribution made, or a boundary-line defined, by Treaty,—and even where such an attribution or definition was ambiguous or uncertain, map evidence of what it might be was accepted with caution. Latterly, certain decisions of the International Court of Justice have manifested a greater disposition to treat map evidence on its merits([90]). In the present case it is not a matter of setting up one or more maps in opposition to certain Treaty attributions or boundary definitions, but of the elucidation of the latter, —in which task map evidence may be of assistance. The problem involved in the present dispute arises from the difficulties created by the structure and language of the 1881 Treaty already discussed, not from its incompatibility with some map, or *vice versa*, —and the solution has to be found through the ordinary processes of interpretation, to which cartography may contribute. Thus maps or charts in existence previous to the conclusion of the Treaty in 1881 might be relevant if, in the circumstances, they could (for instance) throw light on the intentions of the Parties, or give graphic expression to a situation of fact generally known at the time or within the actual, or to be presumed, knowledge of the negotiators. Equally, maps published after the conclusion of the Treaty can throw light on what the intentions of the Parties in respect of it were, and, in general, on how it should be interpreted. But the particular value of such maps lies rather in the evidence they may afford as to the view which the one or the other Party took at the time, or subsequently, concerning the settlement resulting from the Treaty, and the degree to which the view now being asserted by that Party as the correct one is consistent with that which it appears formerly to have entertained. Furthermore, as has been seen in the case of the "Irigoyen" and 1882 "Latzina" maps (*supra*, paragraphs 122–125 and 126–128), the importance

([89]) *i.e.* principally, Admiralty Charts 554 and 1373; and 786 and 789; the "Irigoyen" and 1882 "Latzina" maps; and the 1881 Chilean "Authoritative" map—see *supra*, paragraphs 58(*3*), 90, 119–122, 126, and 131–133.

([90]) See the cases of the *Minquiers and Ecrehos* (I.C.J. Reports 1953, p. 1); *Sovereignty over Certain Frontier Land* (Reports 1959, p. 209); and *Temple of Préah Vihéar* (Reports 1962, p. 6).

of a map might not lie in the map itself, which theoretically might even be inaccurate, but in the attitude towards it manifested—or action in respect of it taken—by the Party concerned or its official representatives. Its effect may sometimes be indirect, yet specific, as for instance in the case of the map (Chilean Plate No. 34) published in 1885 by the Argentine Geographical Institute " under the auspices of the Honourable National Government ", one aspect of which has been mentioned earlier, in paragraph 65 (*e*), —and see further paragraphs 148 and 157 (*d*) below.

(*b*) *The Argentine attitude regarding the cartography of the case*

138. Since, as a matter of bulk and weight, the cartography of the case favours Chile, at least in respect of the number of maps that, either by line, colour or toponymy (indication by place-name), show the PNL group as Chilean, it is the character of the Argentine objections to this cartography that the Court has principally to consider; —for, as was only to be expected in these conditions, Argentina, although herself adducing many maps, has questioned the probative value of cartography, not only as regards particular specimens of it, but generally, as a category, except in a narrowly restricted class of cases. Accordingly, Argentina has contended that, in the first place, a clear distinction must be drawn between, on the one hand, privately printed and published maps, having no official endorsement, and, on the other hand, official or quasi-official maps which, whether actually produced and published by an agency of the Government, have appeared under its *aegis* or with its official *imprimatur*, —or else have subsequently been officially adopted. The Court itself, while willing to consider the matter on the basis of this distinction, feels that in the circumstances of the present case it is only of relative importance whether a map is, technically, " official " or not. At a time when many governments did not possess intramural printing or publishing facilities of their own, and had to rely on outside resources, much that appeared bearing such indications as " under government auspices ", " with government approval ", " at government request " must rank as having at least some quasi-official status. *Per contra,* even an indubitably official map, produced and published by the government as such, is not thereby rendered infallible or objectively correct. But it will in principle be good evidence of the view the government took, or wished to be regarded as taking, at the date of publication; and it may, for that reason, assist, or, as the case may be, not assist, the contentions that such government advances in a subsequent litigation, or at a later date. The Court will, however, now consider the matter on the basis of the distinctions propounded on behalf of Argentina.

139. *The Argentine view on non-official cartography*—With regard to this category of maps, charts and plans, Argentina maintains, first, that it is neither attributable to, nor imputable against the Government. This is in principle correct, subject to such exceptions as may be entailed by privately produced and printed maps that nevertheless have a quasi-official aspect as just described. Next, Argentina contends that non-official cartography lacks all real probative value unless a more or less complete concordance of view is thereby manifested, —and points to some twenty maps of private origin, eight of them Argentine, and twelve produced in third countries (but none Chilean, *vide* paragraph 144 (2) below), which

show the PNL group as Argentinean([91]). Hence, whatever the number that show the contrary, there is no "concordance": "Many good and important maps", it was said, "favour the Argentine position, and the only generalization that could be made—if one must be made—is that most possible interpretations of the Treaty could find a map to support them."([92]) This is in itself true, although, for reasons to be stated later, the Court believes that the question of whether there is concordance or not is closely bound up with, and needs to be considered in relation to, the period within which the maps concerned were published. In any event the Court thinks that the attitude adopted by Argentina is too restrictive. As a matter of normal use in such a context, the notion of concordance must mean a general, and not necessarily an absolute, unqualified, concordance. But in the opinion of the Court, concordance as such is an unrealistic test for a dispute in which there is much to be said on both sides. What counts is not concordance (hardly to be expected) but preponderance, provided it is sufficiently marked and that its components are sufficiently significant having regard to the point sought to be established. When a tribunal is faced by a conflict of evidence, it cannot simply rule it all out on that account, unless the weight of it on each side, qualitatively or quantitatively, really does balance and cancel out that on the other. Where there is a definite preponderance on the one side—particularly if it is a very marked preponderance([93])—and while of course every map must be assessed on its own merits—the cumulative impact of a large number of maps, relevant for the particular case, that tell the same story—especially where some of them emanate from the opposite Party, or from third countries([94]), —cannot but be considerable, either as indications of general or at least widespread repute or belief, or else as confirmatory of conclusions reached, as in the present case, independently of the maps.

140. *The Argentine view on official and semi-official cartography*—Here the Argentine contention is that official maps or charts have probative force only if they come within the category of what might broadly be called "agreed cartography", —and this they would do only in two classes of cases, —viz. for present purposes (i) if the map concerned could be regarded as being part of the 1881 Treaty settlement as such, being either attached to the Treaty, or, though not so attached, referred to in it, or else shown to have been utilized or worked upon by the negotiators *in common*; (ii) if, though not part of the Treaty settlement itself, under any of these heads, the map had been subsequently drawn up by the Parties or agreed upon by them, as correctly representing the settlement, or if they agreed upon an independent map as doing so. With regard to class (i), it is evident that no map in the present case comes within it, unles it were British Admiralty

([91]) Oral Proceedings, VR/16, p. 11. The more important of these maps are the subject of special comment in paragraphs 149–161 below.

([92]) *ibid.*, p. 22. But as will be seen later, some of the "possible" interpretations of the Treaty settlement represented on certain of these maps are such as could not conceivably be derived from any reading of the Treaty.

([93]) Apparent preponderance may of course be reduced when some maps are merely copied from others, or based on a common ancestor.

([94]) But allowing for the fact that such maps are often taken from nationally produced ones.

Chart No. 1373 and the earlier maps on which it was based (*supra*, paragraph 90)([95]); but it has already been shown (*ibid.*) that this chart is " neutral " on the question of the eastern course of the Beagle Channel, or at best inconclusive. With regard to class (ii), Argentina maintains that there are no maps that have ever been agreed upon between the Parties as correctly illustrating the Treaty settlement, even if a tacit process by conduct were admitted to be sufficient to constitute agreement—e.g. through the parallel, though independent, utilization of the same maps, or of maps showing the same thing([96]).

141. Again, the Court believes that these views are too restrictive. There was certainly no map that was actually part of the Treaty settlement([97]): if there were, it would of course be conclusive, and there could be no dispute unless some technical error in it came to light later. Much the same would apply in the case of any map subsequently agreed upon between the Parties, —and none exists in the present case. But it is precisely in the absence of such reliable indications that boundary disputes come before international tribunals; and it cannot be the case that non-agreed maps, produced, acted upon or adopted unilaterally by a Party, even if they have no conclusive weight or effect of themselves, must, merely on account of their unilateral provenance, be regarded as devoid of all value. They can have such value, in varying degree, in any of the ways described in paragraphs 137–139 above.

(c) *Applicable principles of evaluation*

142. Notwithstanding the foregoing observations of a general character, the fact remains that when it comes to the actual use and evaluation of cartography, as part of the process of deciding a dispute, generalizations are in practice only of secondary value. In relation to each chart or map, whether official, quasi-official or non-official, certain concrete questions have to be asked. In such a context as the present one, the chief of these would be:

(*1*) *Provenance and indications*—(*a*) *Maps emanating*([98]) *from the Parties themselves*—Clearly, a map emanating from Party X showing certain territory as belonging to Party Y is of far greater evidential value in support of Y's claim to that territory than a map emanating from Y itself, showing the same thing. Yet that is not the whole story,—for (subject to the chronological aspect considered in sub-paragraph (*3*) below) a consistent or very general emission from Y of maps favouring its claim will at least show a settled belief in the validity of that claim; while the opposite, or a low level of such emission, though in no way conclusive *per se*, will tend to show, if not necessarily disbelief or disinterest, at any rate doubt or absence of concern or serious conviction.

([95]) And also perhaps Admiralty Chart No. 554 (see paragraph 58(*3*) *supra*); but this had no direct relevance to the region of the eastern Beagle Channel.

([96]) Chile, as will be seen later, contends that in the period of maximum significance, namely in the 1881 Treaty decade, Argentine and Chilean maps were in substantial accord.

([97]) There were however certain maps closely linked with the Treaty's emergence—see paragraph 162 below.

([98]) The word " emanating " is used here because the principle involved is the same whether the maps are official or not, though it may apply more forcefully in the case of the former.

(2) *The same—(b) Maps produced in third countries*—While maps coming from sources other than those of the Parties are not on that account to be regarded as necessarily more correct or more objective, they have, *prima facie*, an independent status which can give them great value unless they are mere reproductions of—or based on originals derived from—maps produced by one of the Parties,—or else are being published in the country concerned by, or on behalf, or at the request of a Party, or are obviously politically motivated. But where their independent status is not open to doubt on one or other of these grounds, they are significant relative to a given territorial settlement where they reveal the existence of a general understanding in a certain sense, as to what that settlement is, or, where they conflict, the lack of any such general understanding.

(3) *The temporal or chronological factor*—The principles indicated in sub-paragraph (*1*) above, however valid in themselves, nevertheless require to be applied in close relation to the temporal or chronological setting in which the map concerned appears. This element can be relevant with respect to both the above classes of cases, but is particularly so—indeed constitutes an essential ingredient—in the evaluation of the first,—namely maps emanating from the Parties. The significance of a map illustrating a territorial settlement or disputed boundary may vary greatly according to the date when, or the period within which, it is issued or published. Where there is controversy, the implications of any given map can be correctly assessed only if account is taken of the date of its publication,—and also of the circumstances of the time. Thus, maps appearing contemporaneously with the territorial settlement or within a relatively short period after it will, other things being equal, have greater probative value than those produced later when the mists of time have obscured the landscape and the original participants have left it. Clearly, since the object of a study of the cartography of a dispute, where a territorial settlement by treaty is involved, is to assist in understanding what the settlement was, the closer in date the map is to the period of the treaty's conclusion, the higher its probative value will be. Similarly, as a broad proposition, maps produced before any controversy over the settlement has arisen will tend to be more reliable than those coming afterwards.

143. It is in the light of the considerations set out above that the Court will now attempt a limited evaluation of the cartography of the case generally, and an assessment of the role of certain of the more important individual maps, in so far as this has not already been done in earlier sections.

(d) Some general facts

144. Without intending to attach undue importance to them, the Court has noted the points tabulated below. For these purposes it has to be understood (i) that an Argentinean (or Chilean) map means a map of Argentine (or Chilean) origin or provenance—*i.e.* authorship or production—irrespective of which Party has submitted it; (ii) that, in consequence, the notion of maps " submitted " by Argentina (or Chile) is not confined to Argentinean or, as the case may be, Chilean, maps, but covers any map submitted by the Party concerned, whether Argentinean or Chilean; and

182915 H

also covers (iii) " third country maps ", which term is used to denote those originating in other countries—and these again may be amongst those submitted by either side. The points of fact that seem relevant are as follows:

(1) Without attempting any exact computation, it can be said that out of those maps (submitted by either Party) that depict an attribution of the PNL group by line, colouring or toponymy (*i.e.* by nomenclature, for instance placing the words " Beagle Channel " along or partly along, or juxtaposed to, an arm of the Channel), the number showing an attribution to Chile is markedly the greater.

(2) It appears that there are no Chilean maps that show the PNL group as Argentinean. Hence the maps submitted by Chile that do show this are all Argentinean or third country maps. This therefore also applies to any maps submitted by Argentina that show the group as Argentinean: they are not Chilean maps.

(3) On the other hand there are many Argentinean, as also third country maps that show the group as Chilean. Those Argentinean maps that show an Argentine attribution are mostly of doubtful value for the reasons stated in paragraphs 149–160 below.

(4) No map at all, whether Argentinean or Chilean, traces a dividing line along the Cape Horn meridian—(for the significance of this see paragraph 62 (*c*) *supra*).

(5) Whereas Chilean cartography, whenever attributive of the PNL group, consistently shows a division along the northern arm of the Beagle Channel, between the Isla Grande of Tierra del Fuego and Picton and Nueva Islands, the Argentine cartography that rejects this division is far from adopting a consistent alternative, or one that always conforms to the present Argentine claim to a boundary running along the whole southern arm between Navarino and Picton and Lennox Islands. Many Argentine maps variously show lines corresponding to all those that are possible after Picton Island is passed, when exiting from west to east, as described in footnote 2 to paragraph 3 above. They reflect the lack of uniformity with which the Argentine claim has been envisaged at different times, entailing a resulting inclusion in, or exclusion from, that claim, of either or both of Nueva and Lennox Islands. As regards Picton, there are lines cutting right across it, not laterally but vertically—a configuration that could not possibly stem from any normal interpretation of the Islands clause of the 1881 Treaty. The same applies to other maps with lines cutting across Navarino or even its western neighbour, Hoste Island. (Details are given in later paragraphs.) In fact, so Chile alleges, there is only *one* Argentinean map *dating from the Treaty decade*[99] that shows a line of division conforming to the present Argentine claim to all three islands of the group.

[99] This was the map (Plate No. 23 to the Argentine Counter-Memorial) produced in 1889 for insertion in the Argentine Official Catalogue for the Paris World Exhibition of that year. Its reliability is open to question for reasons of the same order as those given in paragraph 149 below, and onwards. It should be compared with the map (Chilean Plate 28) that formed part of the Argentine Catalogue a few years earlier at the Bremen Geographical Society Exhibition of 1884, which showed the PNL group as Chilean, —and see also the last few lines of n. 118 *infra*.

(6) Most "third-country maps" support the Chilean claim. The comparatively small number that do not are of dubious value for the reasons stated in paragraph 161 below.

145. From the foregoing data the Court has derived the impression that as far as weight of cartography goes (and leaving particular maps for later consideration), the balance is very much in Chile's favour, and tends to confirm the conclusions already arrived at concerning the interpretation of the Treaty words "to the south of the Beagle Channel". This view finds further support from a consideration of the "time-frame" aspect, to which the Court now comes.

(*e*) *Temporal considerations—the "Time-frame"*

(i) *In general*

146. Although the relevance of this element can to some extent be more easily appreciated in connexion with certain particular maps to be discussed later, it will be convenient to say something in general about it first. The nature of the operative principle has already been stated in paragraph 142 (*3*) above. Since Chilean cartography has, from the start—that is from the year of the conclusion of the 1881 Treaty—consistently depicted the PNL group as Chilean, it is with reference to Argentinean cartography that the question mainly arises.

147. However, before proceeding further, it should be mentioned in parenthesis that the Court sees little point in enlarging upon its earlier discussion of that part of the pre-1881 cartography that consists of the maps drawn up by, or based upon those of the early explorers(100). The reasons for this have already been indicated in the section dealing with the Chilean attribution under the Islands clause of the Treaty (especially in paragraphs 88 and 90 *supra*.) The utility of the cartography of a case lies in the evidence it affords as to what those who produced, authorized, sponsored, published or disseminated it, regarded as constituting a correct representation of the territorial settlement concerned. Cartography appearing before 1881 cannot do this, although some of it might contain pointers—(see paragraph 162 below). The minds of the early explorers in particular, in drawing up their charts (and the same applies to later charts based on these) cannot have been directed to a treaty settlement which they could not anticipate,—still less to the negotiating and political factors that might enter into the drafting of it. They necessarily based themselves on purely geographical considerations, and the Court has already (*supra*, paragraphs 84–86) stated why it does not think such considerations to be in themselves determinant for resolving the problem of the "Treaty" issue of the Beagle Channel. That geographical elements, *inter alia*, were present to the minds of the negotiators, the Court does not doubt (*supra*, paragraphs 50 and 51, 93–94 and 98 (*b*)). But it is not possible to know with any certainty what maps or charts they made use of; while those that may be presumed to have been available to them gave no conclusive indication as to which of the Channel's arms was to be seen

(100) Quite different is the case of certain maps (see paragraph 162 *infra*) of the period 1876–1881, that were closely connected with the emergence of the 1881 Treaty.

as the major one. In consequence, just as it was in the Treaty itself that the Court had to find a solution, it is only from just before or near the date of the Treaty that cartography becomes definitely relevant for elucidating or confirming its correct interpretation.

(ii) *The 1881–1887/8 period*

148. There can be no doubt that in the immediate post-Treaty period, that is to say from 1881 to at least 1887/88, Argentine cartography in general[101] showed the PNL group as Chilean; and this was true of the cartography that, for the reasons given in paragraph 138 above, has to be regarded as having an official character, or at least aspect, such as the 1882 Latzina map already considered (paragraphs 126–128), and also the 1886 map of the Argentine Geographical Institute, reproduced in Chilean Plate No. 34 (*supra*, paragraph 65 (*e*)), both showing the PNL group as Chilean. Another and rather striking example is afforded by the map published in 1888 by the Argentine Bureau of Information in London (Chilean Plate No. 38) which actually corrected a similar publication of 1887 (shown on the same Plate) that had depicted a completely fanciful line of division that could have no possible warrant under the 1881 Treaty[102]. Another Argentine map of the period to which, though not actually official, the Court thinks a special degree of credence can be attached on account of the high standing of its authors, is the "Moreno-Olazcoaga" map of 1886, reproduced in Chilean Plate No. 35, which shows the boundary line unequivocally as passing along the northern arm of the Beagle Channel. Dr. Moreno was a boundary expert whose qualifications have already been mentioned—(*supra*, paragraph 135, and see further paragraph 158 below)[103]. Lt. Colonel Olazcoaga was the author of the book that had been given by Señor García, Argentine Minister in London, to Lord Tenterden, Under-Secretary at the Foreign Office, in October 1881 (*supra*, paragraph 119); and he was, or became, the Chief of the Military Printing Office of the Argentine Army.

149. *The "Paz Soldan" maps*—These fall into two periods:

(*a*) *1885*—Argentina contends that there was at least one important exception to the alleged quasi-uniformity of Argentine cartography during this period. This exception is said to be constituted by what

(101) One private map of the period, published in 1888, the "Estrada" map (Chilean Plate No. 39), which attributes by means of colouring, and is regarded by Chile as showing the PNL group as Chilean (see the Chilean volume of "Some Remarks, concerning the cartographical Evidence", at p. 37) has its colouring so equivocally shaded that it could be taken to depict the group as Argentine. But in any case the benefit of the doubt must go to Chile since a second Estrada map published in the same year quite clearly shows the group as Chilean. Another Estrada map of 1887 must be discounted for reasons similar to those given in nn. 102 and 105 below, while one of 1889 shows the group as Chilean;—both these are on Chilean Plate 44.

(102) This, in two respects: (i) since under the first part of Article III of the Treaty, the perpendicular in the Isla Grande of Tierra del Fuego, from Cape Espiritu Santo to the Beagle Channel, was deliberately stopped there, a map showing a line of division which, by prolonging the perpendicular, *crossed* the Channel, and proceeded southward through the Murray Sound and past the Wollaston group, could not possibly represent the division contemplated by the Treaty; (ii) this map, thereby, and equally by colouring, showed, not only the PNL group, but also Navarino Island and the Hermite group, as Argentine. But these localities were "to the south of the Beagle Channel" according to any possible interpretation of that phrase in the Chilean attribution under the Islands clause of the Treaty.

(103) The later maps (1901–2) issued under Dr. Moreno's name, showing only Lennox Island as Chilean, but Picton and Nueva as Argentine, and repudiated by him in this respect, are commented on in paragraph 158 below.

is known as the " Paz Soldan " map of 1885 edited by Carlos Beyer (Argentine Plate No. 17 to the Counter-Memorial, and Chilean Plate No. 176). It was not actually an official publication, though to be regarded in a special light on account of the reputation of its author(104). But this map, equally, showed a fanciful line unrelated to the Treaty basis of division,—see footnote 105 below. Consequently, it has to be discounted as not amounting to any real break in the general uniformity of relevant Argentine maps of the 1881–1887/8 period, and provides no real exception to that.

(*b*) *1887–1890* (*the " Lajouane " versions*)—After Señor Paz Soldan's death in 1886, four more maps based, or purporting to be based, on his cartography, were published in 1887 (two), 1888 and 1890, not (as in 1885) under the editorship of Carlos Beyer, but of Felix Lajouane. Both those of 1887 (Chilean Plates 36 and 37), unlike the maps of 1885, show the PNL group as Chilean. But those of 1888 and 1890 (Argentine Counter-Memorial Plates 21 and 26), show them as Argentine, with a line of division down the southern arm of the Beagle Channel between Navarino and Picton/Lennox, and going on to Cape Horn in such a way as to leave part of the Wollaston group east of it. Two volte-faces of this kind within one five-year period—for which no explanation seems to have been offered—must throw doubt on the credibility of the whole series of Paz Soldan based maps. It also raises the question of the reason for it. To that, the considerations mentioned in sub-section (v) below may be material.

150. Thus, if concordance is the test, there was, in what the Court regards as the critical period of six to eight years following upon the conclusion of the Treaty of 1881, before any queries or controversies had arisen, a virtually complete concordance of Argentine-Chilean cartography in respect of all maps that do not have to be discounted as portraying a line of division that could not on any possible interpretation of the relevant Treaty provisions, be that contemplated by them.

(iii) *The post 1881–1887/8 period*

151. Chile has contended(106) that the quasi-uniformity of Argentinean cartography in the immediate post-Treaty period, and its concordance with Chilean official cartography in the sense that the PNL group was Chilean, continued on the basis, not of a complete, but of a " substantial " concordance of official Argentine maps up to 1908, apart from certain " doubtful exceptions ". By 1908, the existence of a latent controversy about the group had become evident, and in 1908 the official Argentine map that figures as Argentine Counter-Memorial Plate No. 57 was published (107). This did not

(104) Señor M. F. Paz Soldan was a highly reputed Peruvian geographer, publishing in Buenos Aires at this time.

(105) Exactly the same observations as are made in n. 102 above apply in this case also, but even more strongly, since the Isla Grande perpendicular was prolonged across the Channel to cut through Hoste Island, both in its northern part and through Peninsula Hardy; after which it went on to Diego Ramirez Island and then to Antarctica, leaving to Argentina everything east of it,—that is to say not merely east of the Cape Horn meridian but east of a meridian west of that at (approximately) 68° 60′.

(106) See for instance the Chilean written Reply, p. 356, paragraph 175.

(107) Published by the Argentine Office of International Boundaries as one of the Annexes to the book " La Frontera Argentino-Chilena, Demarcación General ".

actually depict the three islands—or only the beginning of Picton—but it traced a line in the Beagle Channel which, before it was cut off by the map edge, adumbrated the turn towards the south between Navarino and Picton Islands. This was followed up in 1909 by a map published by the Meteorological Office of Buenos Aires showing the PNL group, by colouring, as being Argentine(108). Maps to the same effect were published by the Argentine Ministry of Agriculture in 1910 and 1911(109). There can therefore be no doubt about the Argentine official position, cartographically speaking, from this period on, —but it was inconsistent with that manifested in the post-Treaty period, which the Court holds to have the superior probative value.

152. The instances characterized by Chile as " doubtful exceptions " to the general rule of substantial Argentine cartographical conformity in depicting the PNL group as Chilean (see paragraph 151), were (*a*) the " London Argentine Bureau of Information map " of 1887 (Chilean Plate No. 38), already commented on in paragraph 148 above as showing a merely fanciful line of division unrelated to the provisions of the 1881 Treaty, and in any case corrected by the same Bureau on its map of the next year (also on Chilean Plate 38); (*b*) the so-called " Zeballos map " that was included as part of the Argentine case against Brazil in the *Territorio de Misiones* Arbitration, 1893–4, of which there were two versions, both shown on Chilean Plate 64, and both, either by line or colouring, exhibiting a basis of division that, for the reasons given in footnotes 102 and 105 above, could not be derived from any possible interpretation of the 1881 Treaty; and finally (*c*) " Map XIV, 1901 ", attached to the Argentine evidence in the (Andes) Boundary Arbitration of 1898–1902 (Chilean Plate No. 84, and Argentine Counter-Memorial Plates 42 and 44), —showing, not indeed (like the other two) a line wholly underivable from the Treaty, but one that claimed Picton and Nueva Islands, while leaving Lennox Island to Chile. Of these three " exceptions " to the general situation of Argentine quasi-uniformity, the first two must therefore be discounted, and the third, while not to be discounted, appears to be an isolated instance, and in any event occurred twenty years after the conclusion of the Treaty.

(iv) *The same—The " Pelliza" map*

153. Argentina has, however, claimed that another map, known in the case as the " Pelliza map ", published in 1888 (Argentine Counter-Memorial Plate No. 19), was

> " the first depiction officially *recognized* [stress added] by the Argentine Government of the Argentine-Chile boundary line; the first that may be considered as *an official graphic representation of the 'Boundary Treaty'* " —[stress in the original](110).

The ground of this claim is that the map in question was published by Señor M. Pelliza, Argentine Under-Secretary for Foreign Affairs at the time, as part of a book by him entitled " Manual del Imigrante en la República Argentina ", which was adopted as an official publication. However, before commenting on the claim thus made, the Court will refer to the physical characteristics of this map.

(108) Argentine Counter-Memorial Plate No. 58.
(109) *ibid.*, Nos. 61 and 62.
(110) Argentine Counter-Memorial, paragraph 23, p. 231.

154. The map shows a line that starts to run along the north shore of the northern arm of the Beagle Channel, along the Isla Grande coast opposite Picton Island, but then, when over against what is roughly the mid-point of Picton, facing, say, Isla Gardiner, turns abruptly at right angles, crosses the Channel, crosses Picton Island which it cuts in two, and, on the other side of it joins the southern arm of the Channel off Lennox Island and passes on between the latter and Navarino,—thus attributing to Argentina, Lennox and Nueva Islands and the south-eastern end of Picton, and to Chile the other, north-western, end of Picton. This result, even if not absolutely underivable from any possible interpretation of the Treaty, is so eccentric that it can hardly be taken seriously; it would entail that the Treaty concept of the Beagle Channel should be that of a waterway which, after proceeding some distance along the northern arm, breaks off, and resumes overland with the lower end of the southern arm. This is explained by Argentina as a printing error, but other versions of the map show the same configuration, and in some of them (Chilean Plate No. 179, and Argentine " Additional Charts and Maps ", Nos. 4–7) there are variations,—the line appears to follow, not the south shore of the Isla Grande but the north shore of Navarino Island,—then to cross over to the northern arm of the Channel—or else to Picton itself—but in any case to divide Picton and afterwards proceed by the southern arm past Lennox Island. The Court is obliged to conclude therefore that the Pelliza map is of too uncertain a character to have the requisite probative value,—and the same must apply to another map specifically cited by Argentina that clearly belongs to the same complex as the Pelliza map, namely the " Lajouane " map of 1890 (Argentine Counter-Memorial Plate No. 27), which shows similar features,—in this case, making the Isla Grande perpendicular cross the Beagle Channel and then proceed along the north shore of Hoste and Navarino Islands, cutting Picton Island in two.

155. On the other hand, the Court does not think it necessary to pronounce on the Chilean claim that the Pelliza map was not of Señor Pelliza's own making at all, but was a copy of the later series of Lajouane maps already noticed (paragraph 149 (*b*)). The real point is that, whatever the origins of the map, it is claimed to have been officially *adopted* and moreover recognized by Argentina as correctly representing the boundary-line. If so however, it was in complete contradiction with the 1882 Latzina map published six years earlier, also in the context of immigration (*supra*, paragraphs 126–128). Argentina now maintains that the Latzina map had no official character and that it was the Pelliza map which was the first to accord with Argentine Government opinion: but the Court has already given its reasons for regarding the first (1882) Latzina map as reflecting the views both of the President of Argentina, and of Señor Irigoyen, the chief Argentine negotiator of the 1881 Treaty, and as doing so not only at the time of the conclusion of the Treaty but also the year after, when, as Minister of the Interior, Señor Irigoyen officially sponsored the map and caused its widespread dissemination abroad as part of a government campaign to promote European immigration into Argentina. The Pelliza map of 1888 could therefore only have represented, not an original view, but a change of view, for which there could be no convincing explanation since nothing else had changed in the meantime, and nothing was known in 1888

concerning the Treaty that was not equally, if not better, known in 1881–1882. This however brings the Court to a phenomenon that, since it affects several maps or series of maps, must receive notice.

(v) *The Argentine change of policy in 1889, and the Decrees of 1891 and 1893*

156. By a Decree of 21 December 1891, the Argentine Government created an International Boundaries Office at the Ministry of Foreign Affairs. The Decree referred to the " deficiencies and inaccuracies which characterize the great majority of the geographical charts . . . at least on boundary areas ", and added that State subsidies should only be interpreted as incentives for intellectual work(111). The Decree of 1891 was followed in 1893 by another, providing that works on national geography already published should not be considered as officially approved unless accompanied by a " special statement " from the Department of Foreign Affairs(112). This Decree made, and also elucidated, the same point as the earlier one, reciting that, in the case of many publications, these had been

> " promoted by means of official acts, either taking them for the purpose of teaching or propaganda, or aiding them through subsidies granted by public decrees of the Nation, which could give them, at least outwardly, an extensive importance which, in fact, they cannot have as a result of these acts."(113)

But these preoccupations had already existed for some time previously, having (as the Decree of 1891 recited) given rise to the

> " note of 2 November 1889, in which this Ministry [of Foreign Affairs] conveyed to the Ministry of Justice, Worship and Education, the decision of the President of the Republic to deny any official character of [*i.e.* to] those charts and maps . . . "(114)

In consequence of these Decrees, and of the policy underlying them, it was obvious that it would thereafter be impossible to publish as having any kind of official character or approval (and sometimes not easy to publish at all), maps not endorsed with the *imprimatur* of the Argentine Foreign Ministry, which would presumably not be given unless the map corresponded to the official view. This may be the explanation of what would otherwise be the inexplicable process by which authors of certain Argentine maps, already published and showing the PNL group as Chilean, brought out, or became associated with, later editions that, without indicating any reason for the change, showed the group as Argentinean. Some examples of this will now be given(115).

---

(111) Annex 57 to the Argentine Counter-Memorial, p. 197. It may be that this admonition was intended to convey disapproval over the State support given to the Latzina map of 1882, which both President Roca and Señor Irigoyen approved, and which seems to the Court tellingly significant in determining what was *then* officially regarded as the Treaty boundary line.

(112) Annex 58 to the same, p. 202.

(113) *ibid.*, p. 201.

(114) *loc. cit.* in n. 112.

(115) In a sense the Pelliza map, which Argentina now wishes to substitute for the Latzina map as an expression of the then official Argentine view (though, as the Court thinks, without convincing effect), is itself an example of this; —but it was of course the act of the Argentine Government, not of a private party.

157. *The later " Latzina " maps*—The following points call for notice:

(*a*) In 1888, Dr. F. Latzina who, when Director of the Argentine National Statistics Board, had published the " Latzina map " of 1882, as part of the work referred to in paragraph 126 *supra* (showing the PNL group as Chilean), published another map as part of a new work entitled " Geográfia de la República Argentina ", which equally showed the group as Chilean (Chilean Plate No. 48,—map on the left). This work obtained the " Rivadavia Award " of the Argentine Geographic Institute; and a large number of copies of it where ordered by the Argentine authorities for distribution in Europe and elsewhere. This makes it even more difficult than it already was to account for the official Argentine adoption, apparently in the very same year, of the Pelliza map of 1888, as described above in paragraphs 153–155, and diminishes yet further the credibility of the latter map. Even more unaccountable was the re-issue, only two years later in 1890, of Dr. Latzina's " Geográfia " in a French edition, said to be an " enlarged and corrected " one, but this time with a map (Chilean Plate No. 48,—the map on the right) that was not the Latzina map of the previous (1888) edition and, to all intents and purposes, was the Pelliza map of that year with the same eccentric line cutting Picton Island in two (*supra*, paragraph 154), and showing Nueva and Lennox Islands as Argentine. No explanation of this change was given. Adding to this confusion, in between the dates of these two Latzina editions of 1888 and 1890, there was published a " Carte de la République Argentine " (Plate 25 to the Argentine Counter-Memorial) as part of a work entitled " L'Agriculture et l'Elevage dans la République Argentine ", officially sponsored for the purposes of the Argentine participation in the Paris World Exhibition of 1889. This " Carte " shows yet a third variation of the Pelliza line (for the others, see paragraph 154 *supra*) with a line along mid Beagle Channel as far as Picton Island which, this time, it seems just to fail to cut, and then down by the southern arm. According to Chile, Dr. Latzina was not the author of the publication of which this map was part; but he did write an introduction to it, in which he thanked a certain Dr. José Chavanne for " his generous help in the drawing of the maps ", from which it would seem to follow that the latter favoured the Pelliza alignment. Yet in 1890 (*i.e.* the very next year) Dr. Chavnne published his own map entitled " Mapa Físico de la República Argentina " which, as can be seen from its reproduction on Chilean Plate No. 50, indicated the PNL group as Chilean. For such changes and variations, within so short a period, in maps all purporting to illustrate the effect of the same Treaty, which had not itself changed at all, there cannot have been any objective reason, and the conclusion seems warranted that these were due to some sort of extraneous cause, stemming perhaps from the change in official Argentine policy that began in 1889, as described in paragraph 156 above.

(*b*) In the particular case of the 1889 " Carte " (see above) there was another possible explanation of what the map showed, which the

Court has noted. In the work of which this map was a part[116], the version there given of the Argentine attribution in the Islands clause of the 1881 Treaty, was seriously incorrect. It was as follows:

"... appartiendront à la République Argentine: l'île de los Estados, les îlots qui l'entourent et les autres *îles de l'Atlantique au Sud de la Terre de Feu* et des côtes orientales de la Patagonie ..." [stress added].

"... to the Argentine Republic shall belong Staten Island, the islets that surround it, and the other *Atlantic islands to the south of Tierra del Fuego* and of the eastern coasts of Patagonia" [stress added].

The notion of islands "south" of the "eastern" coasts of Patagonia is scarcely realistic, while the category referred to of Atlantic islands south of Tierra del Fuego (which must here denote the Isla Grande), is not specified anywhere in the Islands clause of the Treaty. It does however correspond closely to the interpretation of the expression "to the east of Tierra del Fuego" that Argentina has been contending for in the present proceedings,—namely that this should be regarded as comprising all the islands fringing the eastern side of the archipelago down to Cape Horn (see opening of paragraph 60 *supra*),—with the implications described in paragraphs 60 (*2*) and 62 (*c*). Be that as it may, the error of description contained in the work under discussion ("L'Agriculture et l'Elevage", etc.) would both fully account for the way the "Carte" attached to it was drawn, and also entirely deprive it (and, by association, other maps of "Pelliza" genus or derivation) of all probative value.

(*c*) The Chilean written Reply states (p. 365) that in the same work of which the "Carte" was a part, there were three other maps that all showed the PNL group as *Chilean*, one of them actually carrying the appellation "Canal Beagle" in such a way as to indicate the northern arm, between Picton/Nueva and the south shore of the Isla Grande. The latter observation is correct,—but these maps (as reproduced in Chilean Plate No. 181) are on an exceedingly small scale, and if viewed through a powerful magnifying glass appear, by colouring, to attribute the PNL group to Argentina, not Chile, in the same way as the "Carte" does by line. In the result, one of these maps—the one indicating the northern arm as being the "Canal Beagle"—shows the PNL group both as being south of the Channel, and yet as being Argentinean. The fact that Argentina invokes the work in which this map appears, lends colour to the surmise (see previous sub-paragraph) that for Argentina, the consideration that must prevail in determining whether a given island comes within her attribution under the 1881 Treaty is that of presence "on the Atlantic" (see paragraph 60 (*3*)),—a view which the Court has been unable to accept, and which has caused Argentina to put forward the strained interpretation of the expression "to the east of Tierra del Fuego" which the Court has characterized as such in paragraph 65 (*a*) above.

---

[116] *i.e.* as indicated in sub-paragraph (*a*) above, "L'Agriculture et l'Elevage dans la République" sponsored by the Argentine authorities for the purposes of the Paris World Exhibition of 1899.

(*d*) In connexion with the point just discussed, the Court has compared the two maps reproduced as Chilean Plates Nos. 34 and 63—of which the first has already twice been commented upon above, in paragraphs 65 (*e*) and 148. Both were of quasi-official character, being made and published (" construido y publicado ") by the Instituto Geográfica Argentino " under the auspices of the Honourable National Government ". Both are entitled " Gobernación [Governorate] de la Tierra del Fuego y de las islas Malvinas "; but whereas the first, published in 1886, shows the PNL group as Chilean, the second, published in 1893, shows only Lennox Island as Chilean, and Picton and Nueva as Argentinean([117]). It is however another difference that is of interest in the immediate present connection, namely that the ocean south of Tierra del Fuego and of the archipelago which, in the 1886 map was, as already noticed (paragraph 65 (*e*)), called the " Oceano Antartico ", became split into two in the 1893 map, the part west of Cape Horn and the Wollaston group being called " Oceano Pacifico ", whereas that east of the Cape, between the Wollastons and Staten Island, is called " Oceano Argentino "([118]). At the same time the Wollaston group on this map is shown as Chilean, unlike that of the previous year (1892) described in footnote 117 hereto. Consequently—and see also footnote 118—it becomes difficult to avoid the impression of a confusion and inconsistency in Argentine cartography at this time, so great as to deprive it of real evidential force.

158. *The " Moreno " maps*—The map published by Dr. F. P. Moreno in 1886 together with Lt. Colonel Olazcoaga (Chilean Plate No. 35), and showing the PNL group as Chilean, has been described earlier (paragraph 148). Three other maps, published later and attributed to Dr. Moreno, are reproduced on Chilean Plate No. 118, and one of them appears as Argentine Counter-Memorial Plate No. 43. The first of these later maps was published in 1889 under the *aegis* of the Royal Geographical Society, London, as being " from a survey under the direction of Dr. Francisco P. Moreno ". Neither by line nor by colouring does it show any attribution at all for the group. The remaining two—which are in fact one and the same map—appeared in the 1901 and 1903 editions of a work published in Paris, the " Annales de Géographie " by MM. de la Blache, Gallois and de Margerie. This is clearly taken straight from the " Popper " map of ten years earlier and shows the " Popper line "—see footnote 118 below. It is

([117]) Yet in a map (also reproduced on Chilean Plate 63) dated the previous year (1892), published by the same Institute and under the same auspices, and apparently part of the same Atlas, not only are all three islands of the group shown as Argentine, but so equally is the whole Wollaston group.

([118]) This map is clearly copied from the " Popper " map of 1891 (Chilean Plate 55) where the words " Mar Argentino " appear, and which divides the group by the same line (that has come to be known as the " Popper line ") passing between Navarino and Picton, but then between Lennox and Nueva. The " Popper " map was drawn up to illustrate a lecture given by the Roumanian geographer and explorer, Julio Popper, to the Argentine Geographical Institute and published by the latter. It contains a number of unusual features, and was a good deal copied. No reason for the particular line of division shown seems to have been given, and in his despatch to Lord Salisbury at the Foreign Office, dated 10 April 1892 (Chilean Annex No. 60(9)), enclosing a copy of the " Popper map ", the British Minister in Buenos Aires drew specific attention to the difference between it and the map of the Argentine Geographical Institute of a few years earlier (Chilean Plate 34—see paragraphs 65(*e*), 148 and 157(*d*) above) which showed the whole PNL group as Chilean—(see also n. 99 *supra*).

this map, showing Picton and Nueva Islands as Argentine, that appears as Argentine Counter-Memorial Plate No. 43, there entitled "Map by F. P. Moreno published in the 'Annales de Géographie', Paris, 1901". Commenting on these various maps in his Beagle Channel Memorandum of 17 July 1918([119]), Señor Moreno confirms that the one he drew up in 1889 shows no attribution for the PNL group:

> "In the map attached to the text of the lecture which I gave before the Royal Geographical Society in London on the 29th of May 1889, I only indicated the line from north to south"—[*i.e.* the Isla Grande perpendicular from Cape Espiritu Santo to the Beagle].

But as regards the 1901 and 1903 maps "which maps bear my name"—and speaking of the fact that "the boundary line as there marked includes the islands of Picton and Nueva in Argentine territory", he says he "must here declare" that

> "the demarcation was made by the Argentine Legation in London contrary to my opinion. I had to consent to it so as not to increase further the many difficulties I experienced during the whole of my stay there . . ."

Whether these allegations were or were not justified, is not the question, and the Court does not rely upon them: the point is simply that Dr. Moreno repudiated the maps of 1901 and 1903 bearing his name, as not correctly representing his opinion on the subject of the title to the PNL group, which elsewhere in this Memorandum he very definitely stated to be (in his view) Chilean—(pp. 287–288 of the Chilean Annex No. 113).

159. *The "Hoskold" maps*—These maps, one of which is considerably relied upon by Argentina, provide another example of a series that goes through a sort of process of metamorphosis:

(*a*) Señor A. D. Hoskold was a mining engineer of repute in Argentina who became Director of the Argentine National Department of Mines and Geology, and Inspector General of Mines. His first map (see Chilean Plate No. 61) appeared in 1892, in illustration of a paper entitled "Mines in the Argentine Republic" which he read in that year at the Newcastle (England) session of the Institute of Mining and Mechanical Engineers. It shows the PLN group as Chilean,—and since neither the occasion, nor the map itself, had any sort of official character, it can be taken as undoubtedly representing his own individual personal view. Yet two years later—in 1894—he published—this time under the official seal of the International Boundaries Office of the Argentine Ministry of Foreign Affairs (see paragraph 156 above)—another map, entitled "Mapa Topográfico de la República Argentina" which now showed the group as Argentinean. This map also is on Chilean Plate No. 61, and on Plate No. 22 to the Argentine Memorial. The seal of the Boundaries Office can plainly be seen on the cover, and the legend not only records this, but bestows high praise upon the map. There can

([119]) Chilean Annex 113. This was written in response to a request from the British Minister in Buenos Aires, Sir Reginald Tower, at a time when the possibility of the Beagle Channel question being referred to the British Government for arbitration was being invoked.

therefore be no question but that, if not technically an official map, it had full official approval and reflected the official view as existing at that time. Yet, as has already been mentioned, that view had come to differ completely from the one that had been manifested for some seven or eight years in the immediate post-1881 Treaty period, and is consequently open to the same type of criticism as that made in paragraphs 150, 151 and 155 above. The Hoskold map of 1894 carries a further statement to the effect that it has been " drawn on the basis of the most recent data ", but no indication is given, either there or anywhere else, of what recent data it was that had caused islands represented as Chilean in one year, to be represented as Argentinean two years later—(indeed, possibly only one year later—see next sub-paragraph). In the interval, neither the text of the Treaty nor the geography of the area had altered.

(*b*) The original of the 1894 Hoskold map seems to have appeared in 1893, when it won the first prize at the Chicago Fair of that year—(this is stated on the 1894 map cover). This original (1893) edition is reproduced as Argentine Counter-Memorial Plate No. 31. It is supposed to represent the PNL group by colouring as being Argentinean(120), but even with the aid of a powerful magnifying glass the Court has not been able to detect a sufficient differentiation in the colouring to enable it to be seen what the attribution is. If this is correct, then the Hoskold maps exemplify the same process as the Moreno maps, of starting by showing the group as Chilean, proceeding to neutrality (no attribution shown) and ending, after they have come under official influence, as showing it as Argentinean. If, however, the attribution on the 1893 Hoskold map is indeed Argentinean, then, as already mentioned, Señor Hoskold must have changed his mind from one year to another, on the basis of undisclosed data. In any case, the attribution was definitely Argentinean in the 1894 map. The only clue afforded appears to be a statement in one of Señor Hoskold's later writings(121) to the effect that the " first proof " (of this 1893–4 map) " merited the highest award at the Chicago Fair of 1893, and since then has been corrected on two occasions by the Boundary Office of the Ministry for Foreign Affairs, "—but there is no indication as to what these particular corrections related to. On the other hand there is at least some evidence from the later writings (122) to suggest that Señor Hoskold had not changed his former personal view on the basis of which his first map of 1892 attributed the PNL group to Chile.

(*c*) A further peculiarity of the 1893–1895 Hoskold maps is the appearance of the words " límite a fijar " (" boundary to be fixed ") in the sea, off the south point of Lennox Island. Since no boundary line at all is shown (the attribution being by colouring) the meaning of this is obscure, unless it foreshadowed an intention to introduce

(120) This is stated by both Parties.

(121) See the Chilean volume entitled " Some Remarks Concerning the Cartographical Evidence ", p. 49, and n. 40 on p. 85.

(122) See Chilean written Reply, paragraph 159, pp. 350–351.

into later editions a line tending towards Cape Horn. But, in the circumstances, such an intention can hardly be ascribed to Señor Hoskold personally.

160. *The 1903 " Delachaux" map*—This map (Argentine Counter-Memorial Plate No. 47), the last of the eight maps of Argentinean origin to be specifically cited by Argentina (paragraph 139 *supra*), went through something of the same process as the others noted above. Appearing in 1903, it showed the PNL group as Argentine. Yet nine years earlier, in 1894, Señor Delachaux([123]) had published a map showing the group as Chilean. The explanation of this change proffered by Argentina (Counter-Memorial, p. 525) in that the earlier map was produced under the influence of (erroneous) Chilean cartography, but that this was " corrected . . . on the [1903] map . . . which was based, as stated in its legend, on ' official [*i.e.* Argentine official] documentation ' ". If this is so, then it would seem that neither map constituted an independent expression of Señor Delachaux's views, unaffected by external considerations, and that there is no ground upon which the Court could rely upon the one more than the other.

161. *The " third-country " maps* (see paragraphs 142(*b*) and 144(6) above)—In addition to the eight Argentine maps specifically cited by Argentina (paragraph 139), all of which have now been considered, she also cites (*ibid.*) twelve produced in countries neither Argentine nor Chilean. These are shown, as Argentine Counter-Memorial Plates Nos. 13–15, 18, 22, 28–30, 34 and 35, and Plates Nos. 3 and 9 of the Argentine volume of Additional Charts and Maps. The Court has examined these maps, with the following result. All of them, with two seeming exceptions([124]), attribute the PNL group to Argentina. Six (or—if one of the seeming exceptions is counted—seven) show an attribution—either by line or by colouring—that could not be derived from the 1881 Treaty inasmuch as they show Navarino Island (unquestionably south of the Beagle Channel) as Argentine; and seven also show the Hermite group, west of Cape Horn, and no less unquestionably south of the Beagle Channel, as Argentine. Two of these moreover show a line that crosses the Channel at Point X and proceeds on down through the Murray Channel, leaving all to the east of it to Argentina. The remaining four show a line passing between Navarino Island and Picton/Lennox Islands, which however then goes on to cut through the Wollaston group (Cape Horn). Consequently, a question mark has to be placed against virtually all of these maps. Most of them show attributions that are not derivable from the 1881 Treaty at all, and are therefore open to the criticisms made earlier in paragraphs 148–155 and related footnotes, in

([123]) Señor Enrique Delachaux was a distinguished Argentine engineer and geographer, head of the cartographic section of the Argentine Museo de la Plata, and associated with the Argentine–Chilean Boundary Commission (1881 Treaty, Article IV); but the Court has no information as to the dates or periods involved.

([124]) One of these, a Russian map (Plate 3 in the Argentine Additional Charts and Maps), attributes Navarino Island to Argentina but appears to attribute the PNL group to Chile. However, the colouring is so ambiguous that no certainty is possible. The same applies in the case of Plate 14 to the Argentine Counter-Memorial; but assuming that an attribution can be detected on it, this is said on page 504 of that Counter-Memorial to be one that gives the PNL group to Argentina but leaves Navarino uncoloured, " as not being awarded to either Party ". Yet this Island is unquestionably south of the Beagle Channel (part of its south shore in fact) and therefore Chilean under the 1881 Treaty.

respect of various Argentine maps, of which some of them appear to be copies. In such circumstances the fact that a map shows an Argentinean attribution for the PNL group is of small probative value.

(f) *Conclusion on cartography*

162. The conclusion the Court reaches is that Argentine cartography, viewed as a whole, does not support the present Argentine contentions, or is subject to too many doubts, queries and inconsistencies to do so effectively, — while much of it supports the Chilean position. In marked contrast is the cartography of Chile([125]). Even the only Argentine map of the immediate *pre*-1881 Treaty period, that was indubitably an " official " one, favours Chile. This was the " Elizalde " map of 1878 (Chilean Plate No. 9), sent by the then Argentine Foreign Minister, Señor Rufino de Elizalde([126]), to the Chilean Minister in Buenos Aires, and chief negotiator for Chile, Señor Barros Arana, on 30 March 1878. It proposed an entirely different boundary line for the Magellanic region and in the Isla Grande of Tierra del Fuego. But once it had reached the Beagle Channel, at a point approximately where the later Ushuaia was to be, and only a small way east of the eventual Point X of the 1881 Treaty (see map B hereto), it proceeded along the Channel and out into the ocean by the northern arm, leaving the whole PNL group south of it, on the Chilean side.

163. Finally, the Court wishes to stress again that its conclusion to the effect that the PNL group is Chilean according to the 1881 Treaty has been reached on the basis of its interpretation of the Treaty, especially as set forth in paragraphs 55–111 above, and independently of the cartography of the case which has been taken account of only for purposes of confirmation or corroboration. The same applies in respect of the particular maps discussed in, and from, paragraph 119 onwards.

3. Acts of jurisdiction considered as confirmatory or corroborative evidence

164. Chile has contended that her title to the PNL group, resulting, as she maintains (and as the Court has found) from a correct interpretation of the 1881 Treaty, is confirmed by numerous acts of jurisdiction in and relative to the three islands of the group—in manifestation of sovereignty over it—and to the total exclusion of any comparable acts on the part of

([125]) In addition to the remarks on Chilean cartography contemporaneous to 1881 already made (*supra*, paragraphs 131–133), attention may be drawn especially to four maps closely connected with the negotiating period of the 1881 Treaty, —namely the map (Chilean Plates 8 and 169) stated by Chile to have been sent to Santiago by Señor Barros Arana in 1876 in illustration of the " Bases " of that year—see paragraphs 25 and 34 *supra;* the first sketch of Baron d'Avril, French Minister in Santiago, of 1877 (Chilean Plates 12A and 170); the Barros Arana sketch map of 1878 (Chilean Plate 10), and the El Mercurio Map of 1878 representing the terms of the Fierra-Sarratea Treaty of that year (Chilean Plate 11). These maps and sketches uniformly depict the PNL group as Chilean. Argentina has registered objections to their probative value, both in general and in particular, and the Court mentions this without further comment.

([126]) He had replaced Señor Irigoyen, who had been Foreign Minister when the negotiations for the Teaty were at the 1876 stage, and who returned for the later stages, ending in 1881.

Argentina. She has supplied the Court with a voluminous number of documents in support of this contention([127]). Argentina, on the other hand, has argued that in the circumstances of the present case, and as a matter of law, such acts have no probative value.

165. The Court does not consider it necessary to enter into a detailed discussion of the probative value of acts of jurisdiction in general. It will, however, indicate the reasons for holding that the Chilean acts of jurisdiction while in no sense a source of independent right, calling for express protest on the part of Argentina in order to avoid a consolidation of title, and while not creating any situation to which the doctrines of estoppel or preclusion would apply, yet tended to confirm the correctness of the Chilean interpretation of the Islands clause of the Treaty.

166. An analysis of the record reveals the following:

(*a*) Until 1892 there were no significant acts of jurisdiction specifically referable to the PNL group. This is explained by Chile on the ground that owing to the sparseness of the population and the character of the region, no exercise of authority on the islands was called for. Argentina has maintained that her presence in the Beagle Channel area was, during this period and even earlier, more conspicuous than that of Chile owing to the founding of Ushuaia in 1884; the assumption of authority in Staten Island; the functioning of various scientific expeditions in the area; and the flow of water traffic which, while moderate, was predominantly in Argentine vessels. This is in keeping with Argentina's emphasis on the importance of "maritime" jurisdiction as a focus of enquiry. However, she does not claim at any time to have engaged in any acts of jurisdiction or to have maitained any presence in the PNL group as such.

(*b*) Beginning in 1892, owing partly to the discovery of auriferous deposits on Lennox and Nueva Islands, and partly to a more positive attitude on the part of the Chilean authorities in Punta Arenas (Straits of Magellan), there began a series of administrative activities on the part of Chile. Thus in 1892 a decree fostering colonization was published in the Official Gazette of the Republic, and a sub-delegation was established on Lennox Island; in 1894 a system of land leases through public auction was inaugurated as a consequence of a law of 1893, also published in the Official Gazette; in 1896 a concession on Picton was granted to a British settler of distinction, Thomas Bridges; in 1905 a postal service was established. Indeed, in the period extending from 1892 through 1905, numerous official documents dealt with acts of jurisdiction in the three islands and many of them described the islands as lying south of the Beagle Channel.([128]) Particularly revealing is the comprehensive Report of 1892 by Governor Señoret on the founding of Puerto Toro on Navarino

([127]) These documents, numbering 320 and running to 572 pages, are reproduced in chronological order from 1826 to 1971 in the Chilean Memorial, vol. III. Approximately two-thirds are devoted to the period 1881–1915, of which some 110 are prior to 1906.

([128]) Chile has placed particular emphasis on the following documents dealing with this period: Chilean Memorial, vol. III, Documents 24, 25, 28, 64, 67, 86, 88, 102, 114(*a*), 133, 152; Oral Proceedings, VR/5, p. 123.

Island opposite Picton,—a Report sent to the Chilean Minister for Foreign Affairs and equally published in the Official Gazette of the Republic of Chile. Motivated by the need to investigate the activities of the gold miners on Lennox Island, it contained a detailed description of various islands described as being south of the Beagle Channel, including the PNL group, and provided reasons for their colonization as part of the complex of southern islands which, without hesitation, were assumed to be Chilean (Chilean Memorial, vol. III, Document 28, p. 41). During the ensuing years Chile engaged in many other State activities, customarily associated with the existence of sovereignty, such as the provision of public medical services and education, the exercise of civil and criminal jurisdiction—etc.

(*c*) Chile contends, and the evidence appears to support the contention, that most of these activities (which were openly carried out) were well known to the Argentine authorities. Thus in the period between 1892–1898 the Argentine Governor at Ushuaia specifically and on several occasions drew the attention of the authorities in Buenos Aires to various Chilean acts on the islands, but without eliciting any positive reaction. According to Chile, at no time did Argentina register any reservation of rights, or initiate any protest, until 1915, and even this protest was limited to two of the three islands.

(*d*) Chile further fortifies her contentions by citing several Argentine official Decrees dealing with the Administrative Divisions of the Argentine National Territories, issued in the period between 1883 and 1904. None shows the PNL group as being under Argentine administrative control. This is all the more significant inasmuch as the Decrees indicate specific boundaries. The southern boundary of the department of which Ushuaia is designated as the Capital is stated to be "Beagle Channel, boundary with Chile"—(Chilean Counter-Memorial, vol. II, Annex 368, pp. 131–132)—and see *supra*, paragraph 97(iv). Likewise a critically significant quasi-official Argentine map appearing in 1886, dealing specifically with the "Governorate of Tierra del Fuego and the Malvinas", failed to depict any part of the PNL group as falling under Argentine governorship[129].

167. Cast against this background (and it could be filled in with other types of evidence) the Chilean legal position emerges. Stated succinctly it is that:

"In these circumstances the Argentine failure to protest for 34 years after the conclusion of the Treaty constituted an adoption or recognition of the allocation effected by its provisions".[130]

(129) This map (shown on Chilean Plate 34 and Argentine Plate 18) has been cited earlier to illustrate different points—see *supra*, paragraphs 65(*e*), 148, and 157(*d*). Produced in 1885, it was published in 1886 in Buenos Aires in the Atlas of the Instituto Geográfico Argentino, "under the auspices of the Honourable National Government". That a similar map, similarly published under the same auspices some nine years later, and depicting the same Governorate (Chilean Plate 63), showed a "Popper" line (see n. 118 above), was merely an example of the same process as that described in paragraphs 156–160 *supra*. These two maps are commented on further in paragraph 157(*d*); and see also n. 117.

(130) Oral Proceedings, VR/7, p. 23.

And after denying that Chile was relying on the concept of estoppel, it was explained that:

> " The Chilean Government is relying upon the conduct of the Parties as a source of guidance in the interpretation of the Treaty. The subsequent conduct of the two Governments, confirms the Chilean interpretation of the Treaty, if it be the case that the textual approach is not considered to be conclusive."(131)

168. In keeping with her general emphasis on " maritime jurisdiction " Argentina, as previously stated, maintains that her presence in the whole area was more significant than that of Chile, —without however claiming that she exercised authority in any of the three islands. In general, she does not dispute the accuracy of the Chilean claim to have exercised such authority in the manner indicated earlier, although she asserts that many of the alleged concessions were merely paper claims. Her basic objections to the Chilean thesis rested rather more on legal than factual grounds. They are as follows, and the Court's views on them are given below in paragraph 169:—

(i) First and foremost Argentina invokes the express terms of the Vienna Convention, Article 31, paragraph 3(*b*), which specifies that in interpreting a treaty

> " There shall be taken into account, together with the context:
>
> (*b*) Any subsequent practice in the application of the Treaty which establishes the agreement of the Parties regarding its interpretation."

The key word in this article, according to Argentina, is " agreement ", and the Protocol of 1893 (see *supra*, paragraphs 73–78) is cited as a typical illustration of what was intended. She interprets the Convention as requiring a manifestation of the " common will " of the Parties and denies that the " unilateral acts " of Chile can be said to manifest any kind of agreed interpretation or common will. This being so, she asserts that the entire Chilean argument lacks relevance. Chile's answer to this line of reasoning takes the form of a simple denial of the meaning of the Vienna Convention advanced by Argentina. The concept of " agreement " in the clause cited does not require a formal " synallagmatic " transaction. It means consensus, and can be satisfied if " evidenced by the subsequent practice of the Parties which can only involve the acts, the conduct, of the Parties duly evaluated " (Oral Proceedings, VR/19, p. 184). The agreement, so Chile maintains, stems *from conduct*—in this instance from the open, persistent and undisturbed exercise of sovereignty by Chile over the islands, coupled with knowledge by Argentina and the latter's silence. In support of this conclusion, Chile points out that it would be quite inconceivable for a State to seek agreement in the exercise of its asserted sovereign rights. By their very nature such rights are

(131) Oral Proceedings, VR/7, p. 23.

unilateral and intended to be exclusive to the State performing them; —put concretely, a State does not ask another State's agreement to establish a postal service or to exercise civil and criminal jurisdiction.

(ii) Argentina's second argument is tied to the first and consists in a denial that any relevance can be attributed to Argentine silence. This silence can be put down to an attitude of reasonable and prudent restraint during a period of tension and cannot therefore be considered as evincing consent to Chile's acts, or agreement with the interpretation she seeks to place on them. To this Chile replies that Argentine "motives" are legally irrelevant, especially as her reticence and her failure to speak out on an issue as important as that of the exercise of sovereignty under a treaty is admitted to have been due to deliberate policy.

(iii) Finally, Argentina maintains that all non-agreed acts unilaterally performed by one Party are irrelevant when a boundary treaty provides for its own measures of demarcation. Until such measures are taken, there are zones of doubt and uncertainty and the other Party is on notice of this fact. She contends that the process of allocating sovereignty is not finished when the Treaty is signed and ratified. That would only be the first step, and therefore the activity or non-activity of a Party during the time when demarcation is pending is not "very useful evidence, —for the final, legally authoritative, meaning of the Treaty is still to be made known by the authority constituted by both Parties for that very purpose" (Oral Proceedings, VR / 13, p. 172.([132])

169. The Court's views on the above described Argentine arguments, briefly stated, are as follows:

(*a*) *Regarding paragraph 168, heads* (*i*) *and* (*ii*), the Court cannot accept the contention that no subsequent conduct, including acts of jurisdiction, can have probative value as a subsidiary method of interpretation unless representing a formally stated or acknowledged "agreement" between the Parties. The terms of the Vienna Convention do not specify the ways in which "agreement" may be manifested. In the context of the present case the acts of jurisdiction were not intended to establish a source of title independent of the terms of the Treaty; nor could they be considered as being in contradiction of those terms as understood by Chile. The evidence supports the view that they were public and well-known to Argentina, and that they could only derive from the Treaty. Under these circumstances the silence of Argentina permits the inference that the acts tended to confirm an interpretation of the meaning of the Treaty independent of the acts of jurisdiction themselves.

(*b*) *Regarding paragraph 168, head* (*iii*), the Court equally cannot agree with the Argentine contention that merely because the Treaty provides procedures for demarcation on the ground, no subsequent conduct

([132]) The Argentine written Reply, paragraph 40 at pp. 215–216, contains a particularly trenchant summary of Argentina's position.

182915 I 2

of the Parties, including acts of jurisdiction, can have any probative value. The purpose of such procedures is not to delay the allocation of sovereign rights over territories, which it is the very object of a boundary treaty to determine, but simply to make adjustment of such particular lines as may not be sufficiently clear from the necessarily general terms of the Treaty, —that is to say lines which can be adjusted in the light of purely local conditions without affecting the principles on the basis of which they were adopted. True, this may affect the application of the terms of the Treaty within an already allocated area, but this is a far cry from concluding that the Treaty itself is inoperative for as long as delays, tardiness or other circumstances hold up the demarcations, and that in the meantime it creates no capacity for either Party to act within the area it considers allocated to it(133).

170. Two further points are made by Argentina: (*a*) she asserts that through the publication of certain Argentine cartography, Chile was put on notice that Argentina did not agree with the Chilean interpretation of the Treaty (the maps referred to are the "Pelliza" map, those of Paz Soldan and the later "Latzina" and "Hoskold" maps—the Court's comments on these maps will be found in paragraphs 126–128, 149, 153, 157 and 159 above); (*b*) Argentina argues further that as "soon as it was obvious that there was a difference of opinion between the two countries as to the proper interpretation of Article III . . . there took place the negotiations of 1904–05 with a view to its settlement" (Counter-Memorial, p. 411), —and while these negotiations failed, Argentina yet insists that they are significant as disclosing a lack of concurrence on the meaning of the Treaty.

171. The Court cannot accept the implications that Argentina seeks to derive from these two points. The mere publication of a number of maps of (as the Court has already shown) extremely dubious standing and value, could not—even if they nevertheless represented the official Argentine view—preclude or foreclose Chile from engaging in acts that would, correspondingly, demonstrate her own view of what were her rights under the 1881 Treaty, —nor could such publication of itself absolve Argentina from all further necessity for reaction in respect of those acts, if she considered them contrary to the Treaty. In the same way, negotiations for a settlement, that did not result in one, could hardly have any permanent effect. At the most they might temporarily have deprived the acts of the Parties of probative value in support of their respective interpretations of the Treaty, insofar as these acts were performed during the progress of the negotiations. The matter cannot be put higher than that.

172. The important point throughout is not whether Argentina was under a duty to protest against Chilean acts in order to avoid the loss of the islands because of unilateral acts performed outside the terms of the Treaty (which obviously could only be devoid of legal effect): the important

(133) These observations, although the Court has thought it desirable to make them, are really in the nature of *obiter dicta* since (see paragraph 78 *supra*) the 1881 Treaty makes no provision for any demarcation of the boundary in the Beagle Channel region, —a fact which tends to bear out the conclusion reached earlier (paragraphs 94ff.) that the negotiators were in no doubt as to what it was.

point is that her continued failure to react to acts openly performed, ostensibly *by virtue* of the Treaty, tended to give some support to that interpretation of it which alone could justify such acts.

173. An additional argument needs to be considered, based on Article VI of the Treaty—(for text see paragraph 15 above). It has been suggested that this Article strips all confirmatory evidence, whether in the form of cartography or acts of jurisdiction, of any probative value. Article VI of the Treaty, commented on in paragraph 19 *supra*, provides that the two Governments shall perpetually exercise full dominion over the territories which respectively belong to them "*according to the present arrangement*", and that any dispute shall be submitted to the decision of a friendly Power, but that in any case "*the boundary specified in the present Agreement will remain as the immovable one* between the two countries"—(stress added). The argument appears to be that the words italicised, and forming part of the conventional relations between the Parties, are sufficient to act as notice to both that their rights cannot be altered or affected in any way by the unilateral acts of either. The Treaty and the Treaty alone is controlling.

174. The Court cannot accept this line of reasoning. It is clear that the Treaty is controlling, but the critical issue is, what does the Treaty mean? In the event of a dispute, as in the present case, the Parties are not concerned with the immovable character of the frontier but with the problem of what the frontier is. This is precisely the question that has to be decided. The true effect of Article VI is that, pending arbitration in the event of a dispute, the boundary cannot be *changed* by the unilateral action of either Party: nor could a Party be permitted to adduce evidence in support of the existence of a right to do so, —for Article VI negates any such right. But the question in the present case is not one of attempting to change the boundary, but of determining what the boundary is. For that purpose (the matter having been submitted to arbitration, the Parties must be free to adduce any relevant and legally admissible evidence they can, in support of their respective views, —and for the reasons already stated the Court thinks that evidence of acts of jurisdiction performed by either Party in the disputed area is relevant and legally admissible—not to alter the rights granted by the Treaty or to add to these, or create new rights—but in confirmation of the validity of that interpretation of the Treaty which is alleged to have the effect of conferring the rights concerned. Article VI could not operate to prevent this completely normal process without impeding the very courses of arbitration which the Article itself provides for.

175. The Court therefore, after a review of certain of the principal aspects of the matter, holds that, as with the cartography of the case, evidence of the acts of jurisdiction performed by Chile is admissible and tends to confirm and corroborate the conclusions the Court has reached, affirming her title to the PNL group.

* * *

V. DISPOSITIF

176. Accordingly,

THE COURT OF ARBITRATION, —

Taking into account the foregoing considerations, and more particularly for the reasons given in paragraphs 55–111, —

UNANIMOUSLY[a]

1. *Decides*

(i) that Picton, Nueva and Lennox Islands, together with their immediately appurtenant islets and rocks belong to the Republic of Chile[b];

(ii) that the red line drawn on the attached chart, entitled "Boundary-Line Chart"—which forms an integral part of the present Decision (*Compromiso* of 22 July 1971, Article XII(1))—constitutes the boundary between the territorial and maritime jurisdictions of the Republics of Argentina and Chile respectively, within the limits of the area bounded by the straight lines joining the co-ordinate points ABCDEF specified in Article I(4) of the said *Compromiso*, and known as the "Hammer" (DECISION, paragraph 1);

(iii) that within this area the title to all islands, islets, reefs, banks and shoals, if situated on the northern side of the said red line, is vested in the Republic of Argentina; and if situated on the southern, in the Republic of Chile:

2. *Determines*—(*Compromiso*, Article XII(3))—that in so far as any special steps are necessary to be taken for the execution of the present Decision, they shall be taken by the Parties, and the Decision shall be executed, within a period of 9 months from the date on which, after ratification by Her Britannic Majesty's Government, it is communicated by the latter to the Parties, together with the Declaration constituting it the Award specified in Article XIII(1) of the *Compromiso*:

3. *Directs* the Parties

(i) to inform it, through the Registrar of the Court, of the steps, legislative, administrative, technical, or other, which they deem it necessary to be taken by either or both of them, in order to execute the present Decision;

(ii) to inform the Court in due course, and in any event within the period specified in paragraph 2 of this Dispositif, of the steps actually taken by them, respectively, for the execution of the Decision:

(a) See Section F of PART I (REPORT of the Court).

(b) This wording corresponds to that of the Parties' Requests—PART I (REPORT), Section C, Articles 1(1) and (2).

4. *Declares*, having regard to Article XV of the *Compromiso*, that the Court

(i) continues in being for the purposes specified in paragraph 3 of this Dispositif, until it has notified Her Britannic Majesty's Government that, in the opinion of the Court, the Award specified in Article XIII(1) of the *Compromiso* has been materially and fully executed;

(ii) remains at the disposal of the Parties for the purpose of giving them such guidance or instructions as they may require in order duly to implement the Award.

Done in Geneva this 18th day of February 1977 in a single copy for transmission to Her Britannic Majesty's Government in the United Kingdom in accordance with Article XII(1) of the *Compromiso*, accompanied by the original of the Dispositif dated 31 January 1977 bearing the signature of the four then Members of the Court.

(*Signed*)

G. G. FITZMAURICE
President

(*Signed*)

PHILIPPE CAHIER
Registrar

Judge Gros makes the following declaration*:—

1. I have reached the same conclusion as the Court about the interpretation of Article III of the Treaty of 1881, but by another road and with differences of approach that do not seem to me to call for detailed expression since the Court has not relied upon them, but which I would like briefly to indicate.

2. The present territorial dispute between the two Parties must be viewed from within the complex of its development at the time—from 1810–1881—and in particular from that of the very special relations existing between two States that every factor tends to bring together by reason of their common origins, ethical, political and social outlook and habits of thought in the widest sense. What is in question is not an issue of sovereignty *in abstracto* but—after seventy years of effort—of defining a frontier between Argentina and Chile extending over 5,000 kms. On the specific matter of the disputed islands, information concerning the negotiations of 1881 is still inadequate, but those of 1876 are well documented; and in that context there exists a firm proposal, put forward by the Government of the Argentine Republic, described as non-negotiable, and understood as such by the Chilean negotiator (Barros Arana Telegram of 5 July 1876 and Despatch of 10 July

* The original French text, signed by Judge Gros is in the keeping of the Registrar.

1876, Chilean Annexes 21 and 22). This is of great importance, since Basis 3 of 1876 was carried over to become the text of Article III of 1881. The responsibility for this text, in 1876, was the Argentine Government's; and it is this same text, as also the accompanying circumstances, explanatory incidents of the negotiations, and the way in which the latter developed, together with the official commentaries which were to follow in 1876 and 1881, that constitute the sources for the interpretation of the clause that attributes the disputed islands.

It is by taking into account all the aspects of those negotiations in 1876–1881, and the special social context of the international relations between the two States, that the intention of the Parties may be rediscovered in the text of Article III—an intention confirmed by the declarations of the political personalities responsible in the matter of the frontier. It is this whole complex comprising the text, its historical origins, the general political circumstances of the negotiation, and the explanation given by the negotiators and statesmen, which decided me to vote for the Decision of the Court.

3. One of the consequences of this approach to the case is a different appraisal of the use to be made of cartography and the acts of the Parties subsequent to the Treaty.

The Parties having chosen in 1876 and 1881 not to make any map, or even a sketch of the frontier in the islands, the Treaty is therefore a treaty without a map. After the Treaty no map at all became the subject of a joint discussion or study during the progress of the dispute, or which could in my view be used to elucidate the meaning of a provision of the Treaty which has already been interpreted by the Court on the basis of the intention of the Parties as revealed by the text itself. However, since the two Governments had devoted a very large part of the written submissions and the pleadings to the question of cartography as corroborative evidence in case difficulties or defects in the interpretation of the Treaty should make that necessary, the Court proceeded to a study in depth of that aspect of the matter. Personally, while recognizing the interest and utility of that study, I would point out, on the one hand, that it was not necessary from the legal point of view once the meaning of Article III had been decided on the basis of the text and of all the historical circumstances, and, on the other, that the Parties themselves, at the time of the Treaty and in the years which followed, attached to that same non-concordant cartography only a minimal degree of interest (cf. the Chilean Minister for Foreign Affairs in 1892 when the British Minister at Santiago had submitted to him a problem concerning contradictory Argentine maps: documents 60a and 61b; Chilean Annexes, pp. 187a and 188b). The maps submitted to the Court are facts which cannot by themselves prove anything against the Treaty when the meaning of the text is held to be or recognized as clear, and they should simply be considered within the context of the relations of the two Parties *inter se* as I have described them to be. In these special relations concerning frontier problems, the situation is as the Chilean Minister said, namely that " with such a precise description of the possessions of the two countries in the Treaty it [is] immaterial what geographers chose to publish on the subject "—speaking of two maps of which at least one is considered to be an official Argentine map (quotation from a document of 1892 cited above).

Furthermore, the objections of principle put forward by the Argentine Government with reference to the question of maps as evidence of the meaning of the Treaty, appear to me to be based on a correct interpretation of a formal legal undertaking contained in Article VI of the Treaty of 1881. According to that Article (Decision of the Court, paragraph 15) the two Governments shall exercise their full sovereignty over the territories defined by the Treaty; thus no act imputable to one of the States can compromise that frontier, whether or not with intention to modify it, and it is difficult to see what effect such a unilateral act could have on the treaty rights of the other State, if those rights exist by virtue of the Treaty—and if they do not exist, *cadit quaestio.* Moreover, Article VI goes on to bind the Parties to submit to arbitration any dispute whatsoever arising out of the Treaty, stating expressly that " in any case the boundary specified [in the Treaty] will remain as the immovable one between the two countries ". There is thus, consolidating Article 39 of the 1855 Treaty of Perpetual Peace, Friendship, Commerce and Navigation, a permanent two-fold obligation between the two Parties, to negotiate and submit to arbitration all questions of their treaty relations concerning the frontier. The treaty relations, in conjunction with the special historically interwoven pattern resulting, above all, from the intra-American international law rule of *uti possidetis juris* interpreted and affirmed in the Treaty of 1881, render any unilateral act void of legal effect as a claim to, or evidence of a revision of the frontier as laid down in the Treaty. For these reasons the study of the cartography, however interesting it may have been, appears to me devoid of legal relevance. The same applies *a fortiori* to the cartographical studies and technical analyses of the movements or tracks of ships in the area, contained in Annexes II and III to the Court's decision.

4. It is clear that, for the reasons given in paragraphs 2 and 3 above, I cannot follow the Court in its views concerning the conduct of the Parties after the Treaty, which is equally lacking in relevance, if account is taken of the treaty relations and general principles of law binding on the Parties in the period under consideration.

The conduct of the Parties can only be understood by looking to the effect which they themselves attributed to it at the time, and not by a retroactive introduction of principles totally alien to the attitude of the two States in question; and it is easy to see that neither the one nor the other attached importance to the acts of either in the islands region as regards the interpretation of Article III of the Treaty. When difficulty became apparent in 1904, the conduct of the Parties shows that they regarded the question of the frontier in the islands as remaining to be settled by negotiation; and the Chilean Government accepted this as something normal (cf. Chilean Documents 72, 73 and 74), without in any way relying on its acts in the islands. The two Governments thus recognized, by that date at the latest, that the problem was one of the application of the Treaty. It does not seem to me possible to reconstruct *a posteriori* a present day interpretation of the relations between the Parties, in order to draw conclusions from these that are not based on what they really were.

ANNEXES

ANNEX I

The Chilean Notes of 11 December 1967, exclusive of Annexes B—D thereto
(see Decision, paragraph 2)

Chilean Ambassador in London to the British Foreign Secretary

London, 11th December, 1967.

No. 43
VSC/BS

MONSIEUR LE MINISTRE,

I have the honour, on the instructions of my Government, to refer to the General Treaty of Arbitration of 1902 between Chile and the Argentine Republic, under which Your Excellency's Government were good enough, as recently as 1966, to render such important service to the cause of good relations between Chile and the Argentine Republic. As Your Excellency is aware, the Award which Her Majesty's Government then delivered has been fully implemented by both Parties.

I enclose (Annex A) an English translation of a Note that the Minister for Foreign Affairs of Chile is delivering to H.E. The Ambassador of the Argentine Republic in Santiago, in which he refers to another dispute between the two countries. As Your Excellency will observe, the Argentine Republic has been questioning the sovereignty of Chile over certain islands and islets in the region of the Beagle Channel, thus giving rise to the present dispute.

I also enclose English translations of the three Protocols of 1915, 1938 and 1960 (Annexes B, C and D)* referred to in the above-mentioned Note, by which the Governments of Chile and of the Argentine Republic attempted to arrange for a judicial solution of this dispute but without success.

In the Note of the Minister for Foreign Affairs of Chile to the Ambassador of the Argentine Republic, enclosed herewith, mention is also made of further and repeated negotiations during the past three years, which have also proved to be fruitless. Thus the default of agreement between the Parties is made abundantly clear.

As it is imperative to find an early solution to this dispute, and having regard to the above-mentioned default of agreement, the Government of Chile have decided to have recourse to Her Majesty's Government as permanent arbitrator under the 1902 General Treaty of Arbitration, and in this connection to invite them to intervene as Arbiter in the manner provided for in Article 5 of that Treaty.

Accordingly, and under the formal instructions of my Government, I have the honour to request Her Majesty's Government to exercise in relation to the aforesaid dispute the arbitral functions entrusted to them in 1902 and graciously accepted by the British Sovereign in 1903, and to initiate therefore the proceedings provided for in the 1902 Treaty.

---

* Not now annexed.

May I avail myself of the opportunity of stressing the importance which the Government of Chile attaches to this renewed assistance by Her Majesty's Government towards the maintenance of friendly relations between Chile and the Argentine Republic and generally to the furtherance of the cause of peaceful settlement of international disputes.

I have the honour to be, with the highest consideration,

Monsieur le Ministre,

Your Excellency's obedient Servant,

VICTOR SANTA CRUZ
Ambassador of Chile

The Rt. Hon. George Brown, M.P.,
Principal Secretary of State for Foreign Affairs,
Foreign Office,
Whitehall,
S.W.1.

ANNEX A to ANNEX I (see above)

Chilean Foreign Minister to Argentine Ambassador in Santiago

Santiago, 11th December, 1967.

MONSIEUR L'AMBASSADEUR,

As Your Excellency is aware, the Government of the Argentine Republic have been questioning the sovereignty of Chile over certain islands and islets situated in the region of the Beagle Channel.

I may recall that in the past century, after prolonged discussions between our two Governments concerning their territorial limits, they signed on the 23rd July, 1881, the Boundary Treaty which put an end to those discussions.

This Treaty, which determined the immovable frontier between the two countries, refers to the southern part of the Continent in the provisions of its Articles 2 and 3, which read as follows:

"ARTICLE II. In the southern part of the Continent, and to the north of the Straits of Magellan, the boundary between the two countries shall be a line which, starting from Point Dungeness, shall be prolonged by land as far as Monte Dinero; from this point it shall continue to the west, following the greatest altitudes of the range of hillocks existing there, until it touches the hill-top of Mount Aymond. From this point the line shall be prolonged up to the intersection of the 70th meridian with the 52nd parallel of latitude, and thence it shall continue to the west coinciding with this latter parallel, as far as the divortia aquarum of the

Andes. The territories to the north of such a line shall belong to the Argentine Republic, and to Chile those extending to the south of it, without prejudice to what is provided in Article III., respecting Tierra del Fuego and adjacent islands."

"ARTICLE III. In Tierra del Fuego a line shall be drawn, which starting from the point called Cape Espiritu Santo, in parallel 52° 40′, shall be prolonged to the south along the meridian 68° 34′ west of Greenwich until it touches Beagle Channel. Tierra del Fuego, divided in this manner, shall be Chilean on the western side and Argentine on the eastern. As for the islands, to the Argentine Republic shall belong Staten Island, the small islands next to it, and the other islands on the Atlantic to the east of Tierra del Fuego and of the eastern coast of Patagonia; and to Chile shall belong all the islands to the south of Beagle Channel up to Cape Horn, and those to the west of Tierra del Fuego."

The provisions above quoted recognised the sovereignty of Chile over all the territories extending to the south of the boundary line described in Article 2, subject only to the specific exceptions established in Article 3.

The full sovereignty of Chile in this southern extremity of the Continent, which the 1881 Treaty together with its correct interpretation and fulfilment came to confirm, was not disputed by Argentine during the decades after the signature of that instrument.

Only at the start of the present century, and on the basis of varying and sometimes contradictory interpretations of the 1881 Treaty, did some disposition manifest itself in the Argentine to question Chile's title to Picton and Nueva Islands and adjacent islets, over which Chile was—and still is—exercising full sovereignty. Argentine did not then express doubts on Chile's title to Lennox Island.

Notwithstanding that the Government of Chile have always been—as they are now—absolutely convinced of their rights over the islands and islets in question, they agreed to seek together with the Government of the Argentine Republic a formula which would lead to an arbitral solution of the question ultimately raised by the latter concerning Chile's title to those islands and islets.

Following extended negotiations, on the 28th June, 1915, a Protocol was signed in Buenos Aires in accordance with which the Government of His Britannic Majesty was to be asked to determine to which of the High Parties "belonged sovereignty over the islands of Picton, Nueva, Lennox and adjacent islets and islands lying in the Beagle Channel, between Tierra del Fuego to the north and Dumas Peninsula and Navarino Island to the south."

As it may be observed, in this instrument the Argentine Republic sought to place in doubt the Chilean title to Lennox Island.

This Protocol, for reasons which it is not necessary to elaborate, was not completed and did not come into operation, and thus this attempt to reach a solution was frustrated.

A similar result befell the Agreement which, with the same object in view and in the same terms, was signed in Santiago by the Ministers for Foreign Affairs of both countries, on the 4th May, 1938. The distinguished North American jurist, which the Instrument named as arbitrator, was unable to take up his functions for reasons which are well known to Your Excellency's Government.

About fifteen years later, both Governments entered into new discussions on the matter, but these were no less inconclusive.

Negotiations were resumed in 1959 and on the 12th June, 1960, another Protocol was signed in Buenos Aires with a view to resolving the dispute. In accordance with this instrument and in the terms there set out, it was decided to place the dispute before the International Court of Justice. In the text of this document Argentine no longer persists in her pretensions to Lennox Island.

The fate of this Agreement was no better than that of its predecessors; neither the Chilean Congress nor the Congress of the Argentine Republic gave it the necessary approval and thus the solution of the dispute was once more postponed.

This was the position when by a Note dated 30th October, 1964, Your Excellency's Government informed the Government of Chile that " they had decided to submit the case of the Beagle Channel to the International Court of Justice ". When transmitting this " formal decision to have recourse to the principal judicial organ of the United Nations ", the Argentine Foreign Minister expressed in the name of his Government their hope that steps would be taken to place this matter before that Court.

The Government of Chile immediately expressed their concurrence in this Argentine initiative, which gave promise once more of the solution that had been sought unavailingly for so many years. Evidence of this is contained in the Declaration signed by the Ministers for Foreign Affairs of Chile and the Argentine Republic on the 6th November, 1964, in which they expressed their willingness " to initiate conversations with a view to reaching the necessary agreement to submit the case to the Court in question ".

These conversations began, on the initiative of the Government of Chile, early in 1965. Your Excellency's Government are aware of the many negotiations that, as a result of the Joint Declaration, took place in order to reach that agreement.

I should like to point out that in spite of the determined and constant efforts of Chile to facilitate the course of these negotiations and reach the required agreement, the dispute is still unsettled and we have not advanced one step towards the preparation of a formula which would have led to its solution. The common desires which inspired the two Governments when signing the Joint Declaration of 6th November, 1964, have therefore been frustrated, and that Declaration has proved to be no more than another abortive attempt to find the terms for a solution. Thus the default of agreement between the Parties is evident.

The prolongation of this dispute disturbs the cordial relations between both countries and leads to the risk of serious incidents.

In these circumstances, the Government of Chile are glad to be able to recall that the General Treaty of Arbitration, signed by our two Governments on the 28th May, 1902, establishes the very procedures appropriate for the solution of a difference such as that which is now our concern. And this instrument has demonstrated its efficacy, for very recently the Award delivered under the provisions of this General Treaty gave final resolution to another dispute between our two Nations.

The Government of Chile, determined as they are to reach a final solution of this longstanding dispute in the region of the Beagle Channel through legal means, and faithful in their observance of International Agreements, have decided to invoke the aforesaid Chilean-Argentine General Treaty of Arbitration. Having recourse to the right conferred on them by Article 5 of that instrument, they are requesting Her Britannic Majesty's Government to exercise in relation to that dispute the arbitral functions which Chile and Argentine entrusted to them in 1902.

In deciding to exercise the right conferred upon them by Article 5 of the General Treaty of Arbitration, the Government of Chile are seeking a legal solution and also, as Your Excellency will certainly appreciate, the removal of every obstacle that may disturb or delay the ample and general co-operation between Chile and Argentine, so necessary for the full development of both Nations.

I avail myself of this opportunity to renew to Your Excellency the assurances of my highest and most distinguished consideration.

(Signed) GABRIEL VALDES S.

H.E. Señor Don Manuel E. Malbran,
Ambassador Extraordinary and Plenipotentiary of Argentine,
Santiago.

ANNEX II

British inter-departmental exchanges
September 1918–January 1919

(see Decision, paragraph 89)

No. 1

Minute by the Hydrographer of the British Admiralty, September 1918

With reference by my minute of 18th September 1915 on F.O. papers 9th June 1915, (formerly M.04488) in which I observed that a further investigation on the subject of the Beagle Channel Controversy might furnish further evidence, a most exhaustive examination has now been carried out in this Department which it is hoped will throw further light upon this important question, but before submitting the result and conclusions for consideration it is most desirable to ascertain if the question of arbitration has altered in any material point from the aspect which it assumed to their Lordships on 1st October 1915 (see letter of that date to Foreign Office herein).

J. F. PARRY
Hydrographer

No. 2

Letter, The Secretary of the British Admiralty to the British Foreign Office, 9 September 1918

Dear Sperling,

9th September, 1918.

In September 1915 we had some semi-official correspondence about the Beagle Channel Arbitration, and on the information you then gave we said in an official letter of 1st October 1915 (M.04488) that we understood that Argentine and Chile had agreed to defer the definite submission of the matter to H.M. Government until after the war.

Can you say if this is still the position? The reason we want to know is that the Hydrographer has since accumulated some further data on the subject, which he might work up into a considerable statement if there were any chance of the arbitration coming on at an early date. If however that is improbable it would hardly be worth his while to do it when there are plenty of more important things to attend to, especially as still further data may be discovered.

Your sincerely,
W. F. NICHOLSON.

No. 3

Letter, the British Foreign Office to the Secretary of the British Admiralty, 26 September 1918

Foreign Office, S.W.1.

Dear Mr. Nicholson, September, 26, 1918.

In Sperling's absence I am replying to your letter to him of September 9th about the Beagle Channel Arbitration.

The position has not altered since 1915, that is to say His Majesty's Government are not officially pledged to accept the arbitration and it is understood that in any case we shall not be asked to do so by the two Governments until after the war. As a matter of fact the Protocol between Argentine and Chile agreeing to settle the dispute by arbitration appears not yet to have passed the Lower Chamber at Buenos Aires and you will see from the enclosure in a despatch from Sir R. Tower—a copy of which is now being sent to the Admiralty—that there is some reason to think that the matter may never come to arbitration in the end.

In view of the above mentioned despatch we are acting on a suggestion which the Director of Military Operations made some time ago and are asking confidentially for the views of Sir Thomas Holdich who was the Chief Commissioner on the Chile-Argentine Boundary Commission of 1901 and who passed through the Beagle Channel in that year.

In the circumstances it would seem hardly worth while for the Hydrographer to subordinate other important work to the preparation of a statement on the Beagle Channel dispute at the present time.

Your sincerely,

RICHARD SEYMOUR.

No. 4

Letter, the British Under-Secretary of State for the Foreign Office to Sir Thomas Holdich, 26 September 1918

The Under-Secretary of State for Foreign Affairs presents his compliments to Sir Thomas Holdich and begs leave to state that the possibility has arisen of His Majesty's Government being invited at a future date to act as arbitrator in a boundary dispute between Chile and Argentine respecting the Beagle Channel. Mr. Balfour would be grateful if he might be furnished with Sir T. Holdich's views on the matter at issue, as he understands that in the course of the work of the Commission which investigated the Chile-Argentine boundary in 1901, Sir Thomas passed through the Beagle Channel.

The question which the two Governments concerned have proposed to submit to arbitration is defined as follows:—

"To which of the High Contracting Parties appertains the sovereignty over Picton, New and Lennox Islands, the adjacent small islands and the islands which are situated in the Beagle Channel between Tierra del Fuego to the North and Dumas Peninsula and Navarino Islands to the South.

The territorial limits of Chile and the Argentine Republic in Tierra del Fuego are, as Sir T. Holdich is aware, fixed by a line starting from Cape Espiritu Santo at lattitude 52·40, and following longtitude 68·34 West (Greenwich) to Beagle Channel. The Argentine Republic owns Isle de los Estados and the other islands in the Atlantic and East of Tierra del Fuego and the wastes of Patagonia, while to Chile belong all the islands South of Beagle Channel down to Cape Horn and those wast of Tierra del Fuego. The Argentine Republic claims that the three islands of Picton, Lennox and Nueva are situated in the Atlantic and East of a line drawn from the Eastern end of the Beagle Channel to Cape Horn, while Chile maintains that the Beagle Channel continues East between the mainland and the Eastern extremity of Picton Islands, and that therefore these islands lie South of the Beagle Channel and West of a line drawn from its Eastern extremity to Cape Horn.

The question therefore resolves itself virtually into the determination of the Eastern end of Beagle Channel.

Should Sir T. Holdich be able, from his personal knowledge of the region, to express a view of the position of the end of the Channel and on the conflicting claims of the two Republics, Mr. Balfour will much appreciate his assistance in the matter.

Foreign Office, S.W.1.
September 26th 1918

No. 5

Letter, Sir Thomas Holdich to the British Under-Secretary of State for the Foreign Office, 30 September 1918

Royal Geographical Society,
Kensington Gore,
London, S.W.7.

30 September 1918

Sir Thomas Holdich presents his compliments to the Under-Secretary of State for Foreign Affairs and in reply to his No. 153002/2/A referring to the dispute between the Argentine and Chilean Republics concerning the sovereignty over Picton, New and Lennox Islands, begs to submit the following statement.

This dispute was informally discussed when I was navigating the Beagle Channel in the Argentine gun-boat *Patria* during the progress of the Chile-Argentine Boundary Commission in Patagonia; consequently I took note of the position of the islands in question.

The vague geographical definitions which are at the very root of the dispute must necessarily have an arbitrary meaning given to them in order to arrive at any conclusion whatever.

To the eastern "end of the Beagle Channel" the eastern "entrance" to that Channel must be assumed as the equivalent, and the point to determine is, which is the eastern "entrance". The geographical position of

Picton Island divides the eastern approach to the Channel into two actual entrances. That to the west of the island is the one to which Darwin refers in his " Voyage of a Naturalist round the World " as connecting the Goree roads (where the *Beagle* was anchored) with the Channel. That on the north-east side of the island is the one by which the *Patria* entered from Staten Island, and it is undoubtedly in my opinion the main or chief entrance. It was a grey misty afternoon but visibility was good enough to enable me to see the headlines both north (Cape Piu) and south of the entrance, and to note the shallowing of the water over the approach (there is no actual bar). This was certainly regarded as the entrance by the commander of the *Patria* at that time. Whether it was so regarded when the treaty of 1881 between the Chilean and Argentine Governments was made is only to be decided by historical references, which can be readily made if necessary (they will be found in " La Soberania Chilena en las islas al sul del Canal Beagle ", published at Santiago de Chile in 1917), but I am strongly of opinion that it is modern practices in navigation and not historical references which should weigh most deciding a dispute of this nature. On the whole it is clear that the entrance which I noted between Cape Piu and the south-eastern extremity of Picton Island is the one which has been generally accepted and used by navigators.

A line drawn from the eastern " end " of Beagle Channel to Cape Horn must start from some fixed point. Again it must be assumed that the point in question is either at one end of the " entrance " or in the middle of it. It is not a matter of great consequence which point is selected. Taking the middle point, this line would leave the islands of Picton and Lennox to the west and Nueva to the east of it. This would give the first two islands to Chile and the last to the Argentine. Only a line drawn from the centre of the entrance on the south-west of Picton Island to Cape Horn could leave all three islands to the east and consequently to the Argentine. Even then the question would arise whether these islands are south of the Beagle Channel. I think that clearly by " south " is meant " due south " and not south-east, and that consequently Nueva should be adjudged to the Argentine by the terms of the treaty and not to Chile. But the expression " south of the Beagle Channel " does not include islands in that Channel, and here a discrepancy (one of many) arises between the official maps of the two republics and the terms of the treaty. Both maps (the latest Chilean map dates from 1911, but I have no Argentine map later than 1901) agree in carrying the boundary along mid-channel, leaving certain islands off the northern coast of Navarino to Chile. We may consequently assume that no question arises of interpretation of the treaty along this portion of the boundary.

My opinion then is that the islands of Picton and Lennox should be adjudged as Chilean, and Nueva as Argentine under the terms of the treaty. Geographically no doubt all these islands belong to the same group but there are no ethnographical or political problems likely to arise from their possible separation, and the only question is one of naval strategy and security. Undoubtedly Argentine interests prevail in the Beagle Channel. Harberton and Ushuaia are important centres of sheep farming and their timber industry, and the navigation of the Channel is (or was) almost entirely Argentine.

That Chile should retain a preponderating control of the eastern entrance by the occupation of all three islands under modern conditions of naval

182915 K 2

warfare (which admits of submarine bases) appears to be most inadvisable, so that, in spite of the difficulties which may be expected to arise from the division of a geographical group, the award of Nueva to the Argentine appears more likely to lead to a satisfactory issue than any other. I may be permitted to add with reference to certain criticisms that have recently appeared that in my book " The Countries of the King's Award " I purposely made no reference whatever to the dispute.

(Sgd) T. H. HOLDICH

Pres. Royal Geographical Society.

No. 6

LETTER, THE BRITISH UNDER-SECRETARY OF STATE FOR THE FOREIGN OFFICE TO THE SECRETARY OF THE BRITISH ADMIRALTY, 9 OCTOBER 1918

Foreign Office, S.W.1.

October 9th, 1918.

Sir,

With reference to the letter from this department No. 153002 of the 25th ultimo, forwarding a despatch from His Majesty's Minister at Buenos Aires relative to the dispute between the Argentine and Chilean Governments regarding the sovereignty of certain islands in the Beagle Channel, and to the recent correspondence with Mr. W. F. Nicholson on the same subject, I am directed by Mr. Secretary Balfour to transmit to you herewith, to be laid before the Lords Commissioners of the Admiralty, a copy of correspondence with Colonel Sir T. Holdich on this subject.

In view of the opinion expressed by Sir T. Holdich which, as will be seen, differs in some important respects from that put forward in Dr. Moreno's memorandum, Mr. Balfour would be glad if he might, notwithstanding the reply addressed to Mr. Nicholson on the 26th ultimo, be favoured with a considered statement on the merits of the respective claims of the two Governments.

A copy of a despatch which is being addressed to Sir R. Tower on this subject is enclosed herein; a similar letter is being sent to His Majesty's Minister at Santiago.

I am,

Sir,

Your most obedient,

humble Servant,

(Sgd.) (Illegible.)

No. 7

Minute by the Hydrographer of the British Admiralty, 20 December 1918

I attach herewith a memorandum on this subject based on researches which have been carried out in this Department.

It will be seen that the conclusions arrived at in this memorandum differ from the views of the President of the Royal Geographical Society, and attention is drawn to the following remarks:—

(1) The geographical definitions which are alluded to as being vague in paragraph 3 are not considered so in this Department.

(2) It is not considered that any geographical definition found in the "Voyage of a Naturalist round the World" can possibly be as authoritive as those given by the Explorers in their original reports.

(3) The statement that "modern practices in navigation" can be considered in this connection appears quite inadmissible.

(4) It is not considered that this question is in any sense "one of naval strategy and security"; for such considerations, which obviously may vary from time to time, cannot possibly be allowed to affect interpretation of established Treaties.

(5) It is to be observed that although this Department in its Memorandum has drawn attention to the existence of a legal problem arising out of acts of jurisdiction exercised by the Chilean Government over the three islands in question, this aspect has not been dealt with by the President of the Royal Geographical Society; and it is suggested that it is of sufficient importance to be referred for legal opinion.

J. F. PARRY
Hydrographer,
20 December, 1918.

Submitted to send Hydrographer's memo. to F.O. with covering letter at attached. Hydrographer concurs.

W. F. NICHOLSON

No. 8

Letter, the Secretary of the British Admiralty to the Under Secretary of State for the British Foreign Office, enclosing the Hydrographer's Memorandum, 28 December 1918

Admiralty,
28th December 1918

Sir,

In reply to your letter of the 9th October 1918, No. 165125/2/A, I am commanded by My Lords Commissioners of the Admiralty to transmit herewith, to be laid before the Secretary of State for Foreign Affairs, a Memorandum by the Hydrographer of the Navy on the Beagle Channel.

2. This Memorandum treats the subject exclusively from a geographical and hydrographical point of view, and so far as that aspect of the matter is concerned Their Lordships have nothing to add.

3. If it is the view of the Secretary of State for Foreign Affairs that other aspects need to be considered, and that Their Lordships' opinion on such aspects would be of value, I am to suggest that specific questions should be put to this department.

I am,
Sir,
Your obedient Servant,

The Under Secretary of State,
Foreign Office,

W. F. NICHOLSON.

No. 9

MEMORANDUM BY THE HYDROGRAPHER OF THE BRITISH NAVY

With reference to the request of S. of S. for F.A. for a considered statement of the claims of the Argentine and Chilean Governments to sovereignty over Picton, Lennox and New Islands, (M.46549) the following memorandum is submitted.

Before entering into a detailed discussion of the problems raised by the contending claims of the Argentine and Chilean Governments to sovereignty over the islands at the eastern entrance of the Beagle Channel, a brief review of the geographic and diplomatic history of the question will not, perhaps, be superfluous; for it is the opinion of the Hydrographic Department that the controversy turns upon a geographical problem, which, by its importance, entirely dominates all other aspects of the question.

The Beagle Channel runs in a easterly and westerly direction along the 55th parallel of South latitude, through the archipelago of islands lying between the mainland of Tierra del Fuego and Cape Horn, and its existence was unknown until the early part of the 19th century.

After the discovery of the Magellan Straits in 1520, little attempt was made by either Spanish or English navigators to extend their explorations to the south of that waterway; although Garcia de Loayza and Drake were successful in their attempts to navigate into a higher latitude. In 1615, however, a Dutch expedition under Le Maire discovered that a passage between the Atlantic and Pacific Oceans existed to the South of Magellan Straits; the discoverer rounded Cape Horn, and returned to Europe by the Pacific and Indian Oceans.

The results of Le Maire's voyage were confirmed by a Spanish expedition, which set out three years later, under the command of Bartolome Garcia Nodal, Gonzalo Nodal and Diego Ramierz Arellano. Certain erudite persons, inclined to speculation, have asserted that the leaders of this latter expedition may justly be regarded as the first discoverers of the Beagle Channel; but an examination of the arguments by which this statement has been supported is not necessary. The report of the voyage of the Nodales, written in Spanish, is vague and guarded in its wording; and the claims that these explorers were the first discoverers of the Beagle Channel is advanced by no more than an ingenious system of guess-work.

In the 18th century, the expeditions of Cook, of L'Hermite, and of Bougainville, gave to Europeans a more accurate knowledge of the configuration of the archipelago that surrounds Cape Horn, but without actually discovering the waterway traversing it.

In 1825, a British Expedition of two ships set out from Plymouth on a voyage of exploration to the coasts of South America. The "Adventure" was commanded by Captain Philip Parker King, the leader of the expedition; the "Beagle" by Captain Pringle Stokes, who died on the voyage, and was succeeded by Captain Robert FitzRoy in this command.

During the months of March, April and May, 1830, Captain FitzRoy in the "Beagle", acting independently of the "Adventure", discovered and explored the Beagle Channel.

When leader of a subsequent expedition to the coasts of South America, Captain FitzRoy navigated in the Channel which he had previously explored, without adding to, or modifying, his original descriptions of its form and extent.

During the 19th century, missionaries, Argentine and Chilean settlers, and the results of scientific expeditions in the French vessel "Romanche", and the Argentine vessel "Almirante Brown" enlarged our knowledge of the region, and confirmed opinions generally held as to its barren, desolate and inhospitable nature.

In the year 1881 a Boundary Treaty was drawn up between the Chilean and Argentine Governments, wherein the continental and maritime boundaries of the two countries were laid down.

Article 3 of this Treaty defines the boundary in the Beagle Channel; and, as the terms of the article have been the ground of the dispute, it is not inappropriate to quote in extenso:

> "Art. 111. Tierra del Fuego is divided by a line starting from Cape Espiritu Santo at latitude 52°40′ south, and following longitude 68°34′ west (Greenwich) to the Beagle Channel. Divided thus, Tierra del Fuego is Chilean to the west and Argentine to the east. In regard to the other islands, Isla de los Estados belongs to the Argentine Republic with the islets next it, and the other islands in the Atlantic and east of Tierra del Fuego and the coasts of Patagonia; while to Chile belong all the *islands south of Beagle Channel down to Cape Horn*, and those west of Tierra del Fuego".

Chile interpreted this article of the Treaty in the sense that Picton, Lennox and New Islands lay to South of the Beagle Channel, and therefore belonged to her; and acting under this conviction, performed various acts of jurisdiction and possession, the legitimacy of which does not appear to have been disputed for nearly twenty years.

In 1893, a further Boundary Treaty was agreed upon by the Chilean and Argentine Governments; it was termed a "Protocol Aclaratorio", and was intended to give precision to certain provisions of the earlier Treaty, since a correct interpretation of some of the articles of that agreement had been rendered difficult in the light of subsequent geographical exploration in the Andes.

The second Article of this Protocol states clearly the general principle upon which the agreement was based, and runs as follows:

> "Secondly: The undersigned declare, that, in the opinion of their respective Governments, and according to the spirit of the Boundary Treaty, the Argentine Republic shall maintain its dominion and sovereignty over all territory which lies to the East of the main chain of the Andes as far as the shores of the Atlantic; and that the Republic of Chile shall maintain its dominion and sovereignty over all territory to the West of the aforesaid chain, as far as the shores of the Pacific; it is further to be understood, that, by the articles of the said Treaty, the sovereignty of each state over the respective littoral is absolute, so that Chile can have no claim over any point towards the Atlantic, just as the Argentine Republic can have no claim towards the Pacific. If, in the Southern peninsula, in the vicinity of the parallel of fifty-two degrees, the Cordillera shall be proved to lie between inlets of the Pacific there existing, the experts shall make a special study of the terrain, and shall establish a boundary line which shall leave to Chile the shores of the aforesaid inlets, and both governments shall amicably settle all questions arising out of the said examination of experts".

In 1903, the British Government, as arbiter, gave a decision not relevant to the subject of this memorandum, upon the manner in which the boundary between the two Governments should be laid down in the vicinity of Last Hope Inlet.

Having thus reviewed the exploration of the regions now in dispute, and the diplomatic negotiations by which they were partitioned, the arguments advanced by the contending Governments to support their claims of Sovereignty over Picton, New and Lennox Islands, in so far as they are known, may be briefly stated.

It is claimed by the Argentine Government that the form and limits of the Beagle Channel have never been defined so closely as to make it certain that the term "islands to the South of the Beagle Channel" should be regarded as applicable to Picton, Lennox and New Islands; that the eastern mouth of that Channel may be considered to include all the islands in question, which cannot, therefore be assumed to lie to the South of it; or else, that the channel may be regarded as terminating to the West of Picton Island, which, together with Lennox and New Islands must be considered to lie in Moat channel (See attached chart cutting): that the basic principle of the 1893 Protocol, to the effect that the Argentine Government should have exclusive possession of ports upon the Atlantic, and that Chile should exercise exclusive dominion over those situated upon the Pacific, cannot be reconciled with Chilean possession of Picton, New and Lennox Islands, all of which lie on the former ocean and that these circumstances combine to render an arbitrational decision upon the subject imperative.

It is argued by the Chilean Government that an inspection of the works in which the original explorers of the Beagle Channel recorded their discoveries, makes it evident that the form and limits of that channel were defined in such a way as to justify the manner in which the Chilean Government has interpreted the words "islands to the S. of the Beagle Channel"; that the claim of the Argentine Government, to the effect that the islands under discussion lie in Moat Channel, is inadmissible; since the definition of the Beagle Channel, given to that waterway by its first explorers, invalidates the argument: that the acts of jurisdiction, performed by Chile over Picton, New and Lennox Islands, during the years following the 1881 Treaty, confirm the claim of that country to the undisturbed exercise of her sovereign rights over those islands; that the 1893 Protocol referred only to a certain portion of the continental boundary between the two republics, and that neither its basic principle nor particular provisions are applicable to the maritime frontiers of Argentine and Chile.

It is therefore evident that the contentions of the Republics hinge primarily upon two questions:

(1) What is the form and what are the limits, of the Beagle Channel; and

(2) What is the correct interpretation of that portion of the Boundary Treaty of 1881, which has occasioned the present controversy.

The argument of the Argentine Government, upon the degree to which the Protocol is applicable to the litigation, is a secondary one, which can only be answered by International Jurists.

In the opinion of this Department, however, the first question is by far the most important, and its correct solution would appear to settle the controversy in an equitable manner. It is therefore now proposed to examine every passage in the published works of the discoverers of the Beagle Channel, wherein that waterway is described or mentioned to see whether the recorded opinions of the Explorers themselves make it certain what ideas they entertained with regard to its size, shape and extent; to investigate the manner in which they regarded the feature now shewn on the Admiralty charts as Moat Channel, in view of the importance that it has assumed in this controversy; and, finally, to apply the results of this examination to the text of the 1881 Boundary Treaty.

The books, and MSS documents, written by the first explorers should now be enumerated, as it is upon the evidence which they contain that the conclusions of this Memorandum are based.

The works in question are as follows:

(*a*) The report of discoveries made during the first expedition, forwarded by Captain King to the Admiralty under cover of his letter of proceedings dated 15th October 1830, Plymouth Sound. This report has never been published and is at present in the custody of the Public Record Office.

(*b*) A lecture given by Captain King to the Royal Geographical Society in 1831, and printed in the Journal of the proceedings of that Society for the year in question.

(*c*) The Sailing Directions for the coasts of the Eastern and Western Patagonia by Captain Philip Parker King, 1832.

(*d*) The second edition of the Admiralty Sailing Directions for the Eastern and Western coasts of Patagonia written by Captains King and FitzRoy in collaboration, and published in 1852.

(*e*) The 3rd and 4th editions of those Sailing Directions, edited by FitzRoy.

(*f*) The first edition of Admiralty Chart No. 1373, upon which the discoveries of the Beagle and Adventure were shewn.

(*g*) The Narrative of the surveying voyages of H.M. Ships Adventure and Beagle written by King, by FitzRoy and by Darwin in collaboration.

(*h*) All subsequent editions of the Admiralty Sailing Directions.

A few remarks should be added upon the relative trustworthiness and significance of these books and documents. They consist, in the first place, of books and reports written by the first explorers of the Beagle Channel, and, in the second, of books edited at a later date by other persons; these latter, although possibly more complete in certain technical matters than the earlier editions, cannot be considered as being of equal authority to the works of the first explorers in the matter of geographic definitions, for it is an established axiom of geographic science that such nomenclature as the discoverers of any region shall originally have given to its natural features, shall be preserved without alteration; and that all departures from the expressed intentions of the first explorers in such matters, should be condemned, and corrected in so far as later discoveries and explorations permit.

With regard to the Matter before us, viz: the correct geographical definition of the Beagle Channel, —no subsequent exploration has altered such conceptions of its form and shape as were held by those who first discovered it; and it is the object of this Memorandum to give accurate interpretation of their recorded opinions upon the subject.

But, as the works in which Captains King and Fitzroy have described the Beagle Channel are numerous, and were published at widely different dates, it is evident that, in this case, those of later date should carry more weight than the earlier publications, in that in them they may be assumed to have expressed their more considered, and, when necessary, corrected, conclusions.

For this reason the 4th Edition of the Admiralty Sailing Directions for this locality are regarded as the standard text, which must be taken as of more authority than any other in the case of discrepancy. This book was the last edition of Sailing Directions written by Fitzroy, and must therefore be considered to embody his final and considered opinions; all later editions were written by other persons and are, in consequence, of less authority on the point at issue.

Finally, a word should be added about the Narrative of the surveying voyages of H.M. Ships Adventure and Beagle. This work is one of the most popular books in travel in the English language, but its authors were not concerned with giving to the regions explored those exact geographical definitions which appear in the Admiralty Sailing Directions, and such descriptions of natural features as the book contains are primarily introduced for the entertainment of the reader. The Narrative has therefore been regarded as of special importance only where it records the circumstances under which the Beagle Channel was discovered; but such accounts of coasts, bays, inlets and channels are to be found in its pages, have not been considered as of equal weight to those passages in the Sailing Directions wherein the same features are described.

Having stated the principles upon which the original sources of information have been examined, it is now possible to review the circumstances under which the name Beagle Channel was first employed, and to determine what impression was left upon the minds of those who actually discovered it.

The succession of events leading up to the discovery of the Beagle Channel and the manner in which those events were recorded by Fitzroy are as follows:—

March 2nd—March 14th 1830. Mr. Murray, the master, left the ship anchored near Waterman island, and passed up Christmas Sound into the SW'n arm of the Beagle Channel. He returned to the ship on the 14th, and Fitzroy speaks of the discovery in the following manner. (Narrative Vol. 1. p. 417).

"Mr. Murray penetrated nearby to the base of the snow-covered mountains, which extend to the eastward in an unbroken chain, and ascertained that there are passages leading from Christmas Sound to the large bay where the whale-boat was stolen; and that they run near the foot of the mountains. He also saw a channel leading farther to the eastward than eye-sight could reach, whose average width seemed to be about a mile. He left the two children in charge of an old woman whom they met near the westernmost part which his party reached, who appeared to know them well, and to be very much pleased at having them placed in her care".

April 6th—14th 1830. Mr. Murray again left the vessel, which was anchored in Orange Bay, and proceeded to the Northward in the cutter: he entered the Beagle Channel through the Murray narrows, passed up it to the eastward as Gable islands, and then returned to the ship.

Fitzroy describes this further exploration of the newly-discovered channel as follows. (Narrative Vol. 1. p. 429).

"14th. The master returned, and suprised me with the information that he had been through and far beyond Nassau Bay. He had gone, very little to the northward, but a long distance to the east, having passed through a narrow passage, about one-third of a mile wide, which led him into a straight channel, averaging about two miles or more in width, and extending nearly east and west as far as the eye could reach. Westward of the passage by which he entered, was an opening to the north-west, but as his orders specified north and east, he followed the eastern branch of the channel, looking for an opening on either side, without success. Northward of him lay a range of mountains, whose summits were covered with snow, which extended about forty miles, and then sunk into ordinary hills that, near the place which he reached, showed earthy or clayey cliffs towards the water. From the clay cliffs his view was unbroken by any land in an ESE. direction; therefore he must have looked through an opening at the outer sea. His provisions being almost exhausted, he hastened back".

May 4th—May 10th 1830. Mr. Stokes, midshipman, was sent away from the vessel, which was anchored in Lennox Cove at the time, with orders to explore the Eastern entrance to the Beagle Channel. His tracks on the outward and return trips are unknown. The soundings inserted on the fair chart, which was drawn up from these results of these explorations of the region under discussion appear to show that Midshipman Stokes' tracks was approximately as shown on the chart cutting attached. The reason for this conclusion is, that, from the evidence available, it does not appear possible that the soundings in question should have been taken on any occasion but this one. Captain Fitzroy refers to the trip in the following laconic fashion; (Narrative Vol. p. 449).

"Soon after the Master came alongside, Mr. Stokes also returned, having been a long way into the channel first discovered by Mr. Murray, and having examined all the shores about its eastern communication with the sea. He met many groups of Indians, but managed so as not to have any collision or trouble with them".

May 7th—10th 1830. Fitzroy, having left the vessel at Lennox Cove, passed round the South and Southwestern shores of Navarino Island, entered Beagle Channel, and explored it to the westward as far as point Divide. His description of this trip is given [in] the Narrative Vol. 1. p. 439, in the following terms.

"7th. Soon after we set out, many canoes were seen in chase of us, but though they paddled fast in smooth water, our boat moved too quickly for them to succeed in their endeavours to barter with us, or to gratify their curiosity. The Murray Narrow is the only passage into the long channel which runs so clearly east and west. A strong tide sets through it, the flood coming from the channel. On each side is rather low land, rising quickly into hills, behind which are mountains, those on the west side being high, and covered with snow ".

At the conclusion of these boat expeditions FitzRoy considered the Beagle Channel to be completely surveyed and explored from its eastern entrance to Christmas Sound; and the descriptions of the Channel made later on by Captain King were based solely upon the reports of these explorations.

It is therefore unnecessary to examine all the references to the Beagle Channel contained in the Narrative of the second expedition, of 1831–1836; for such allusions are only inserted to make the narrative of events continuous, and no longer assist in giving a correct geographical definition to the waterway.

The best proof of this assertion is contained in the fact that the descriptions of the Beagle Channel in the Sailing Directions drawn up on the results of the first, and of the second, voyages, are identical.

The extracts made from the Narrative shew generally, that the discoverers were impressed by the straightness, and the narrowness of the channel; whilst the Narrative for April 4th, 1830 shews, in addition, that they regarded the *eastern opening of the channel as being partially visible from Gable Island.*

This fact is regarded as of great significance, and attention is particularly drawn to it.

After the return of the two vessels to England, Captain King drew up an accurate report of the discoveries made, and forwarded it to the Admiralty with his letter of proceedings, dated 15th October, 1830, Plymouth Sound. In this document, which is in the custody of the Public Record Office, he speaks of the newly discovered channel in the following terms.

" *Beagle Channel*". Among the most remarkable features of this survey is a channel leading in almost a direct line between Cape San Pio and Christmas Sound, one part of which is within 25 miles of Admiralty Sound ".

This sentence describes the form and limits of the Beagle Channel, and would appear to be decisive even though no other evidence existed; but it is still necessary to examine the texts of those other works in which King and Fitzroy defined the waterway, in order to ascertain that they did not subsequently modify their original opinions.

In the lecture delivered by Captain King before the Royal Geographical Society in 1831, the leader of the first expedition described the Beagle Channel in terms almost identical to those which he employed in his letter to the Admiralty. " The South Shore, or seaward coastline, is principally of greenstone, excepting the shores of the Beagle Channel, which extends from Christmas sound to Cape San Pio, a distance of one hundred and twenty miles, with a course so direct that no points of the opposite shores cross and intercept a free view through, although its average breadth which is also very parallel, is not more than a mile, and in some places only a third of a mile across."

In the "Sailing Directions for the coasts of Eastern and Western Patagonia" by Captain Philip Parker King 1832, the author describes the Beagle Channel in the following terms:

P. 103

"*To the north of Lennox Island is the eastern opening of the Beagle Channel.* It is easy of access, but useless to a ship. Boats may profit by its straight course and smooth water. It runs one hundred and twenty miles, in nearly a direct line between ranges of high mountains, covered always with snow. The highest are between three or four thousand feet above the sea. This channel averages one mile and a half in width and in general has deep water; but there are in it many inlets, and rocks near them".

It must be admitted that the words which state that the eastern entrance of the Beagle Channel as lying to the North of Lennox Island are somewhat ambiguous.

It is stated, on page 1 of the book that "all bearings not otherwise distinguished are corrected for variation are true, so that the words "to the North of Lennox island" might be construed in the sense, that the eastern mouth of the channel lay on a bearing, drawn accurately North (true) from Lennox island; that is to say, it would run between Picton and Navarino Islands.

So rigorous a construction of the phrase hardly commends itself, however; firstly, because the eastern mouth so described could never have been visible, or even partially visible, from Gable Island, as it was stated to be in the Narrative for April 4th 1830; and secondly, because, if the eastern mouth ran in a Southerly direction between Picton and Navarino Island, it could not be reconciled with the straight, *east and west* course, of the waterway, so clearly described in the earlier statements of Fitzroy. It is therefore preferable to infer that the words "to the North of Lennox Island" mean no more than "a general northerly direction"; but, as the substitution of this phrase for that actually in the text would still leave doubt as to the exact position of the eastern mouth, it is necessary to refer to the descriptions given to it by the explorers in later editions of the Sailing Directions which they published.

The volume of Sailing Directions published in 1850 by Captains King and Fitzroy in collaboration dissipates the ambiguity.

At the beginning of this it is stated that "In this work the bearings are all magnetic except where marked as "true" whilst, on page 167, the eastern mouth of the Beagle Channel is again stated to be "to the north of Lennox Island", and the description of the form and limits of the waterway is identical with that of the earlier edition.*

* *Sailing Directions for South America, Part 11 by Captains Philip Parker King and Robert Fitzroy 1852, at page 167:—*

"To the North of Lennox Island is the eastern opening of the Beagle Channel. It is easy of access, but useless to a ship. Boats may profit by its straight course and smooth water. It runs 120 miles, in nearly a direct line between ranges of high mountains, covered always with snow. The highest are between 3,000 and 4,000 feet above the sea. This channel averages 1½ miles in breadth and in general has deep water, but there are in it many inlets, and rocks near them."

This manner of describing the Beagle Channel, its shape, its extent and its eastern entrance may be regarded as an expression of the final opinions of the first explorers, since the 3rd and 4th editions, both published by Fitzroy, contain no alteration in wording. If, therefore, we apply to the description of the Beagle Channel given in the second edition, the principles of argument under which the first was examined, we can only conclude, that, in the final opinion of the discoverers, the eastern mouth of the waterway lay to the north (magnetic) of Lennox Island, the variation at the date in question being about 20° E.

If, at this point, a summary be made of the evidence which has been reviewed, it must be concluded that the Beagle Channel alluded to in the Narrative, and described by Captain King in his letter of proceedings, his lecture, and his sailing directions, is the waterway which has been tinted in blue on the attached chart cutting, whilst its eastern entrance must be regarded as the stretch of water between the coast of Tierra del Fuego to the west of Cape San Pio, and the northern shores of the New and Picton islands. Any other conception of the channel would be at variance either with the straightness of its traject, upon which the first explorers insisted so frequently, or with the eastern and western limits which they defined with such precision.

Attention should now be drawn to a statement already made, that the second edition of the Sailing Directions may be regarded as the final expression of the ideas of King and Fitzroy on the limits and form of the Beagle Channel. The two subsequent editions (3rd and 4th) were, it is true, prepared by FitzRoy, but they merely repeat the geographical definition of the Eastern mouth already made in the second edition. All subsequent editions were prepared by other persons, and cannot therefore be regarded as original, and authoritative documents. For this reason, it is not intended to include in this Memorandum an examination of the definitions given to the Beagle Channel in editions of the Sailing Directions, which have succeeded the one published in 1850, for it is considered that such an investigation would be outside the scope of this enquiry, which is concerned primarily with the opinions and statements of the first discoverers.

Having now examined all the descriptions of the Beagle Channel made by King and FitzRoy, it would be easy to propose a geographical definition, which should describe that waterway, in a manner conformable to the opinions of those who first discoverered it.

Before doing this, however, it has been thought necessary to make an investigation, similar to the preceding one, with regard to Moat Bay, now known as Moat Channel, and to discover if possible how Fitzroy and King would have described the form and limits of that configuration.

This second examination cannot be conducted as rigorously as the one just concluded, because Moat Bay although shown on their original chart is not mentioned in any report or description of the locality made by King or by Fitzroy. Another obstacle to a satisfactory solution of the question consists in the fact, that it would appear that the name of Moat Bay must have been given to that feature during the boat expedition of Midshipman Stokes to the eastern mouth of the channel in May, 1830, and that expedition is only referred to in the briefest manner by Fitzroy.

The only document, which can be stated with certainly to express the ideas of, Fitzroy and of Stokes on the point at issue is the fair chart of the locality, drawn in 1831, at the conclusion of the first expedition, and the attached tracing of the eastern mouth of the Beagle Channel has been taken from that source.

An examination of the manner in which the name Moat Bay has been placed with respect to the neighbouring shore line, and to the central line of the channel, leads to the conclusion that, it was intended to designate as Moat Bay, the bend which occurs in the coast line between Cape San Pio and the Woodcock islands.

This opinion is strengthened by an examination of the first edition of Admiralty Chart No. 1373, where the name, although brought more towards the centre of the channel, is still drawn on a curve which is nearly parallel to the shape of the Bay.

A less elaborate, but equally certain method of arriving at the same conclusion, is afforded by the reflection that FitzRoy can never have intended to give the name Moat Bay to an open channel; and that the only feature in the locality corresponding to the accepted notion of a bay, is the one described.

All the relevant passages from the manuscript reports and the published works of Captains King and FitzRoy have now been quoted and examined, and it is reasonable to conclude on the basis of the available evidence:

I. That the Beagle Channel as conceived by its first explorers is a narrow channel, about 120 miles in length running between Capes Kekhlab, on the Eastern side of Cook bay, and Cape San Pio.

II. That the feature now shewn on the Charts as Moat Channel should really be termed Moat Bay, which should be regarded as lying between Moat Point, on the East, and a round, unnamed point 8 miles to the West of it.

These conclusions make it fairly certain, that, the words in Article 3 of the boundary treaty of 1881 " islands to the South of the Beagle Channel ", include Picton, New, and Lennox islands, which in the opinion of this Department, belong to Chile.

Having thus formulated the conclusions of the preceeding investigation, a few words should be added in explanation of the arguments that might be brought forward to combat the view which has been taken.

The statement in the Admiralty Sailing Directions for 1852, that the Eastern mouth of the Beagle Channel lies to the " North (magnetic) of Lennox islands ", is not wholly satisfactory, and it might be maintained that this definition does not preclude the possibility of including the passage between Picton and Navarino islands within the eastern opening.

This argument is strengthened by the reflection that, in the 5th edition of the Sailing Directions, published in 1860, the editor, Mr. Hull (Master) certainly held that opinion. His description of the Eastern mouth has in fact been the basis of the claims of the Argentine Government, and was worded as follows: "Its eastern entrance lies to the NW. of Lennox and New Islands on either side of Picton island".

Whilst admitting the feasibility of such a standpoint, it must be added that it is seriously weakened by other considerations.

I. Mr. Hull was not an original explorer of the channel, and his alteration of the original description of the Eastern mouth, made by the discoverers of the Channel, cannot be regarded as authoritative.

II. The description given by him was abandoned in the next edition of the Sailing Directions and has not since been revived.

III. If the passage between Picton and Navarino islands be regarded as part of the Beagle Channel, that waterway no longer possesses the feature of straightness, so frequently alluded to by the first explorers.

IV. The inclusion of the above passage in the Beagle Channel gives it two eastern openings, or more properly, an eastern and a south-eastern one; whereas King and FitzRoy distinctly allude to only one, by referring to it in the singular.

V. The opinion of impartial geographers cannot be neglected, and the writers of the best-known geographical works of the 19th and 20th centuries appear unanimous in regarding the eastern opening of the Beagle Channel in the manner described in the general conclusions of this memorandum. It must be admitted, however, frankly, that, at the present moment, the Admiralty Charts and Sailing Directions have, in some respects, departed from the definition originally given to the Beagle Channel by King and FitzRoy.

It has been stated, however, that these departures from the texts of the original authors are not geographically admissible; and, if no diplomatic questions were involved, the mistakes could and would at once be admitted and rectified. But, as the present mis-statements, or ambiguity, of the Admiralty publications lend some colour to the arguments now advanced by the Argentine Government, it would appear as though the British Government had already decided in favour of the Chilean Republic, if the errors in question were now rectified; for such corrections could only be made upon the Admiralty Charts and Sailing Directions, and their appearance would mostly certainly be noticed by such technical experts as are at present advising the Argentine and Chilean Governments.

The Admiralty is therefore faced with the problem of whether it would be better to allow the existing ambiguities in its publications to stand, or to incur the charge of partiality by correcting them. The opinion of the Foreign Office upon this point would be of value.

J. F. PARRY

Hydrographer.

182915 L

No. 10

LETTER, THE UNDER SECRETARY OF STATE FOR THE BRITISH FOREIGN OFFICE TO THE SECRETARY OF THE BRITISH ADMIRALTY, 14 JANUARY 1919

213077/2.A. Foreign Office S.W.1.

Sir:- January 14 1919.

With reference to your letter No. M.46549 of the 28th ultimo, I am directed by Earl Curzon of Kedleston to request you to thank the Hydrographer of the Navy for his memorandum on the Beagle Channel, which has been read with interest.

With reference to the last paragraph of the memorandum, I am to state that His Lordship would deprecate any change in the charts and sailing direction at the present moment.

I am,
Sir,
Your most obedient
humble Servant,
(Signed) R. Graham

ANNEX II A

Paragraphs 14–16 (pp. 287–291) of the Argentine Reply

(See Decision, paragraph 89 (*c*))

The Memoranda of the British Hydrographic Department of 1918 and the opinion of Sir Thomas Holdich

14. Much has already been said in the *Argentine Memorial*(37) and *Counter Memorial*(38) on the value of the opinion expressed by the British Hydrographic Department in its Memorandum of 6th July, 1918; nevertheless, the *Chilean Counter Memorial*(39) insists in giving to this document a decisive relevance. It is therefore necessary to return briefly to this subject to emphasize certain important features of this document.

Mr. Bell is not only promoted by the Chilean Government to the rank of authoritative interpreter of the geographical and historical meaning of the Beagle Channel, but also as a better authority on the Beagle Channel than Fitzroy himself! Mr. Bell was probably never in the area; he relies on King—who certainly was never there—and interprets the " Narrative " 's entry for 4 April 1830(40) freely in order to adjust it to his own pre-conceptions.

Actually, the argument used by Mr. Bell against Master Hull's definition of the eastern entrance of the Beagle Channel in the 1860 edition of the Sailing Directions, can be used against his own Memorandum, since, as he says of Mr. Hull, neither Captain King nor Mr. Bell were the " original explorer of the Channel "(41).

The Memorandum of July, 1918 cannot be considered as a serious alternative interpretation of Fitzroy, not only because of Mr. Bell's very doubtful conclusions, but also because they were quite obviously much influenced by Guerra's book; and were certainly not founded on a careful perusal of all of Fitzroy's original documents.

The Chilean Government considers this Argentine view " gratuitous " and " offensive ", but it is difficult to see what is so offensive about drawing attention to a fact. And it can hardly be " gratuitous " in view of Mr. Bell's own words in the opening of his Memorandum of July 1918(42):

> " *The translation of Dr. Guillermo Guerra's book* upon the Chilean claims over Picton and New Islands, in the eastern mouth of the Beagle Channel, *is submitted.* The work consists of a long and detailed discussion of the geographical and legal aspects of the question; and *no summary of its contents could be anything but inadequate* ". (Emphasis added)

(37) I, pp. 75 ff.

(38) I, pp. 354 ff.

(39) I, pp. 92 ff.

(40) The *Chilean Counter Memorial* I, p. 92, by a printing error quotes " April 4th, *1839* ".

(41) *Chilean Counter Memorial* II, Annex 373.

(42) *Chilean Counter Memorial* II, Annex 373.

After which it is hardly surprising to read at the end of his Memorandum:

"V. The opinions of impartial geographers cannot be neglected and the writers of the best-known geographical works of the 19th. and 20th. centuries appear unanimous in regarding the eastern opening of the Beagle Channel in the manner described in the general conclusions of this memorandum. (*See Guillermo Guerra's book Chapter 3*)" Emphasis added).

15. Mr. Bell's internal Memorandum of July 1918 was copied in full by the British Hydrographer, J. F. Parry, when preparing his Memorandum in December of that same year. Nevertheless, there are some *nuances*:

(*a*) Parry must have been aware of the true bearing noted by Fitzroy in the first edition of the Sailing Directions: "to the north of Lennox Island is the eastern opening of the Beagle Channel" but preferred the later, second edition which wrongly quotes a magnetic bearing, possibly in order not to contradict Bell(43).

(*b*) He further confused the matter by repeatedly referring to Fitzroy and King as the "first explorers of the Beagle" and listing the greater part of the original documentation in a way that the reader might have been led to suppose that King was himself the explorer and surveyor of the Channel.

(*c*) He rejected Darwin's opinion, although Darwin was on board the 'Beagle' with Fitzroy, wrote Volume III of the "Narrative" and, it will be allowed, must have had not inconsiderable powers of observation, and took King instead(44).

(*d*) He stated, in 1918, that "modern practices in navigation" are inadmissible considerations in the case.

(*e*) He added a synopsis of the historical and diplomatic background to the question where it is said, for instance, that the 1893 Additional and Explanatory Protocol "was intended to give precision to certain provisions of the earlier Treaty"(45).

To summarize then, the originally partial view of Mr. Bell was merely taken by Mr. Parry, and enlarged with a historical introduction and a final *caveat* as to the responsibility of the Admiralty for ordering any changes in the British charts and Sailing Directions.

16. It is respectfully submitted to the Court that, if it is indeed desired to canvas the state of opinion within the British Government—when it was at the very edge of being asked to play the role of arbitrator—on the Beagle Channel question, it is proper at least to take in also, besides, the advice emanating from Sir Thomas Holdich.

Sir Thomas Holdich was *first* asked by the Foreign Office to submit his views on the question of the Beagle Channel, well before the Office addressed a letter to the Hydrographer and for the following reasons:

—He was *the Chief Commissioner on the Argentine-Chile Boundary Commission* of 1901–3.

(43) See *Argentine Memorial* I, p. 95.
(44) *Chilean Memorial* II, Annex 121.
(45) *Ibid.*, Annex 122, p. 300.

—*He personally navigated the Beagle Channel* on board the Argentine gunboat " Patria " in 1903.

—He was the President of the Royal Geographical Society and author of " The Countries of the King's Award ".

Sir Thomas Holdich, as well as the Hydrographer and Mr. Bell, knew Professor Guerra's book, although Holdich only mentioned it as a good source for historical references in one paragraph of a letter, strongly to discard the value of historical references to the Beagle Channel question in the next([46]).

It has been seen above (para. 15) that one of the differences between the Hydrographer's opinion and the internal note prepared by Mr. Bell is that the former in the Minute with which he transmits his Memorandum to his Admiralty superiors rejects Holdich's statement that " modern practices in navigation " have to be considered in connection with the Beagle Channel Case([47]). But the point is that the Hydrographer rejected Holdich's idea of the value of " modern practices in navigation ", yet it was solely on these considerations that Holdich rested his thesis of a Channel with *two mouths,* allowing the line Cape San Pio-Picton Island as one of the two. The only significant historical reference that Sir Thomas Holdich incorporates in his text is one that comprises the Argentine thesis:

> " That to the west of the island [Picton] is the one [entrance] to which Darwin refers in his ' Voyage of a Naturalist round the World ' *as connecting the Goree Roads* (where the *Beagle* was anchored) *with the Channel* ". (Emphasis added)([48]).

Holdich then, although disregarding in general the historical references, does recognize the undeniable fact that for Darwin the eastern entrance was situated between Picton and Navarino. He then, *on the basis of the needs of modern navigation,* says that the other sea area to the north of Picton is another entrance.

Moreover, Sir Thomas Holdich foresaw the roots of the strategic and security problems that surely influenced the minds of the negotiators and which lie at the basis of the Beagle Channel question. Indeed, he accurately perceived—after recognizing the needs of modern navigation—the permanence of an historical fact as important and decisive as the historical evidence. He said in his letter:

> " Undoubtedly Argentine interests prevail in the Beagle Channel "([49]).

([46]) See letter of Sir Thomas Holdich to the British Under-Secretary of State for Foreign Affairs, 30.ix.1918, in *Chilean Memorial* II, Annex 119: " Whether it was so regarded when the treaty of 1881 between the Chilean and Argentine Governments was made is only to be decided by historical references, which can be readily made if necessary (they will be found in ' La Soberania Chilena en las islas al sur del Canal Beagle ', published at Santiago de Chile in 1917), but I am strongly of opinion that it is modern practices in navigation and not historical references which should weigh most deciding a dispute of this nature ".

([47]) See *Chilean Memorial* II, Annex 121.

([48]) *Ibid.*, Annex 119.

([49]) *Chilean Memorial* II, Annex 119.

182915 M

ANNEX III

Sea traffic to and from the eastern Beagle Channel region

(Decision, paragraph 97)

1. In the course of the oral hearings (specifically on September 17, 1976), after a few preliminary remarks, the following question was put by a member of the Court to Counsel both for Argentina and Chile (Verbatim Record, VR 12/7 at p. 172 of the English version):

> " To come to the point, the precise question is this: can the Parties supply the Court with information as to the tracks followed by vessels entering the Beagle Channel from the direction of Staten Island or, as the case might be, from the direction of the Wollaston or Hermite Islands; and similarly, as regards the vessels leaving the Channel and going in either of these directions. It would be appreciated, also, if so far as possible, approximate numbers of ships, dates or periods concerned could also be indicated."

2. In the preliminary remarks, it was explained that the enquiry had to do with the customary track of vessels " . . . in the period roughly covered by the negotiating process preceding 1881 and the period shortly thereafter ",—and attention was directed to various voyages in the period 1848–1886 referred to by the Parties in the written pleadings and oral hearings. The specification of a brief period *subsequent* to 1881 was included on the assumption that what was customary at that time was not likely to diverge significantly from what it had been earlier, and that in consequence, it was likely to throw light on contemporary understandings as to the usual course of entry into, or exit from, the Beagle Channel. This seemed justified even though Ushuaia, as the key destination point, was not founded until 1884.

3. Admittedly the question posed a challenge to counsel owing to the passage of time, the difficulty of consulting records (especially logs of journeys) and the limited period for additional research. Nevertheless, the response from both Parties was characteristically thorough and helpful. A wide variety of sources, of a reliable kind, were used to plot on sketch maps the courses of particular vessels. Argentina supplied the Court with eight such sketches of which five covered the period 1848–1881 and three the period 1890–1901. Chile supplied thirty-five, of which seven covered the period 1870–1881; sixteen, the period 1882–1891; and twelve, the period 1892–1903. Argentina supplemented its production of sketch maps with an analysis of the navigational aspects of the problem in which stress was placed on the need to understand the relevance of the destinations and purposes of the voyages, and the special problems imposed by weather hazards in the use of sail prior to 1881, as opposed to the use of steam (independently or in conjunction with sail) thereafter (Verbatim Record, VR/25, pp. 113–142 in the English version). According to Argentina the requirement of safe harbours in the days of sail dictated the track[s] of vessels, and it was only after the advent of steam that major use was made of

" Moat Bay " (*i.e.* the northern arm) in proceeding to and from points within the Channel, notably Ushuaia, Harberton, Woolya and Almanza,—and in this connexion there is no doubt that Argentinean use of the Channel was more conspicuous than that of Chile.

4. Without attempting an analysis of the tracks of every voyage the following facts may be noted:

(*a*) During the " sailing " period a number of voyages were made which employed the northern arm exclusively, both in entering and leaving the region (*e.g.* the six voyages of the " Allen Gardiner " in 1870–1871).

(b) On the other hand, there were a few vessels which, on entering the region, appeared to veer south of Nueva Island and then pursue various courses depending on the mission of the voyage (*e.g.* the " Clymene ", 1848; the " Dido ", 1852). The " Clymene " passed south of Nueva, circled Picton Island, and then took a southern course between Nueva to the east and Picton and Lennox to the west; the " Dido " appeared to track a course south of both Nueva and Lennox Islands, then headed north with Picton on the east before returning to the Atlantic north of Nueva. Another vessel entered the northern arm as far as Picton, then veered south between Nueva and Lennox before returning to Picton (the " Ocean Queen ", 1850). The track of the " Allen Gardiner " (rescue mission, 1855) shows entry by the northern arm, a stop at Nueva, then proceeds to Picton, and afterwards south between Nueva and Lennox before heading north between Lennox and Navarino Island. While the record is not altogether complete, it yet appears that all the vessels whose tracks were made available to the Court, entered the region from the Atlantic seaboard and, with a few exceptions, all left *via* the northern arm.

(*c*) A slight discrepancy exists in the evidence with respect to the route of the " Charrua " (Uruguyan expedition of 1881). According to Argentina it veered south of Nueva before rounding Picton and then heading south. According to Chile it veered south of Picton. Both agree that it left the region *via* the northern arm.

(*d*) It may be assumed that the passage between Navarino and Lennox Islands (the southern arm) was used, especially during the " gold rush " era,—but there is no evidence available from the tracks of vessels as to their routing to and from this waterway.

5. Without ascribing too much importance to something that may well be due in part to fortuitous circumstances, it seems that most of the evidence available to the Court indicates that in the period subsequent to 1881 the northern arm of the Channel was almost exclusively used in entering and (with a few exceptions) also in leaving the region on voyages from and to the Atlantic seaboard, and that it was from and to this seaboard that almost all traffic flowed. A few salient examples will be given:

(*a*) In 1885 Señor Felix Paz, Argentine Governor of Tierra del Fuego dispatched a comprehensive report to the Minister of the Interior of

182915 M 2

Argentina describing his travels and observations. His journey on the "Comodoro Py" took him along the northern arm of the Beagle Channel from Ushuaia past Buen Suceso.

(*b*) Included among the twenty-eight post-1881 sketch maps supplied by Chile, all showing the employment of the northern arm of the Channel in entering or leaving the region are the following:

(i) The routing of the National Transport ships from Buenos Aires. These ships plied the waters without a fixed schedule (Argentine Memorial, Plate 23; Chilean Plate No. 55—1891).

(ii) The routing of the Swedish Expedition of 1895–97 on the "Condor" and "Huemul" (Chilean Plate No. 76—1896).

(iii) The Henry de la Vaux expedition of 1896–97 (Chilean Plate No. 85).

(iv) The expedition of the "Romanche" in 1882, with soundings displaying the use of the northern arm (Chilean Plate No. 33).

(v) The voyages of the "Villarino", the "Ushuaia", the "La Argentina", the "Cleopatria", the "Patria" and many others, including even the voyages of the Argentine training ships for naval cadets, which habitually followed the northern arm of the Channel in entering the region.

6. From all the above, the inference appears justified that, whatever other motives there may have been, the northern arm of the Channel was regarded as the normal route to and from points within the Channel in striking contrast to the passage between Navarino, Picton and Lennox—(and see also paragraph 97 of the Decision).

ANNEX IV

The tracing of the boundary line

(Decision, paragraph 110,—and for additional comments, see paragraphs 103–105, and 108–109)

Sources and modus operandi

1. The documents consulted were the Record of the oral proceedings, VR/25, pp. 183–4, where the Agent for Argentina describes the Channel line; and the letter of 20 September 1976 (No. 131) from the Chilean Agency proposing a division of the islands, islets and rocks between the Parties.

2. The charts consulted were: (*a*), the three put in by the Agent for Argentina at the final session of the hearings—(see VR/25, p. 182), which reproduce the provisional line already indicated on Map 27 to the Argentine Memorial; (*b*) a map consisting of a specially arranged and tinted version of Chilean chart 1307, which proceeded by way of a colouring of the islands to be attributed to the Parties but without showing a line; and finally British Admiralty Charts 1373, 3424 and 3425.

3. However, it is from the second of these groups that the map actually used for tracing the Boundary-Line, namely Chilean chart 1307, on a scale of 1:80 000, has been taken. It has been compared with the Argentine charts of the first group, and various discrepancies have been found in relation to geographic positions, relative positions, and the nature or existence of specific features. In accordance with normal practice the evidence of the Argentine charts has been accepted as to the existence or nature of a feature that lies on the Argentine side of the Channel, and the Chilean chart has been taken as authority for Chilean features. For example, a small islet has been inserted close south of Punta Entrade (meridian 68°30′W. approx.) to accord with the Argentine charts. This islet is also shown on British Admiralty Chart 3425. Similarly, the Chilean depiction of Islotes Solari as an island has been accepted in preference to the Argentine classification of it as a drying reef.

4. The Boundry-Line itself is the resultant of construction lines drawn between opposite, shore to shore, points, sometimes to or from straight baselines. It is in principle a median line, adjusted in certain relatively unimportant respects for reasons of local configuration or of better navigability for the Parties. Over the whole course, account has been taken of sandbanks, siltings etc., which would make a strict median-line unfair, as in the case of certain islets or rocks.

Straight baselines

5. Straight baselines for use in constructing the boundary-line have been drawn as indicated on the Argentine charts between point X and Pampa de Los Indios (meridian 67°06′W, approx.). East of the latter point, straight baselines are shown by firm green lines. Where the Argentine chart ignored Islotes Solari (see above), it has been included here as a basepoint. In general, all those baselines have been omitted that, in the event, have been found to have no effect on the boundary.

6. Between Islas Bridges and Isla Despard, where an equidistant line between basepoints on above-water features would pass too far north in the

narrow channel, a notional baseline (shown by a pecked green line) enclosing the shoal water about three-quarters of a mile south-west of Isla Lucas has been used.

Construction lines

7. "Construction lines" are shown as pecked green lines. They indicate in every case the nearest points on the respective baselines which define the equidistant line. These lines are shown in principle wherever the equidistant line changes direction, and so indicate the features which control any section of the line. Where, however, because of the influence of straight baselines (which are comprised of an infinite number of discrete basepoints), the equidistant line is constantly changing direction around another basepoint, a selection of controlling lines only has been shown.

Tracing of the Boundary-Line

8. The position of the terminal point of the Argentine-Chile land boundary (the Isla Grande perpendicular at meridian 68°36′6W (approx.))—*i.e.* Point X near Lapataia—and of the coastline in its vicinity is markedly at variance between the charts, and therefore that shown on the Chilean chart has been accepted, since otherwise construction of the boundary as an equidistance line in that region would be impossible without re-drawing the coastline. Starting due south at Point X, the line proceeds to a point equidistant from a headland close east of the terminal point and the straight baseline running south-west from Ras Peron. Proceeding eastwards the boundary is a line of equidistance between the straight baselines or the low-water line of coasts and islands, as appropriate and indicated, until it reaches the 100 metre isobath at approximately meridian 68°24′8W. From that point (off the entrance to the Murray Channel) it runs direct (and up to about 400 metres south of a true equidistance line) to a point at approximately meridian 68°10′2W. Thence it continues as an equidistant line to a point north of Bahia Virginia (meridian 67°43′W. approx.). There the line runs straight in an east-north-easterly direction to a position on the leading line that bears 270° from the leading lights on the west coast of Isla Gable, and lies along this leading line until it meets the line indicated by the leading lights situated on Punta Piedrabuena. Thence it runs in a 140° direction along this line, and then in a 100° direction along the leading line formed by the leading lights the front one of which is at Punta Rossales.

9. At a point 1400 metres from the last-mentioned light the boundary turns north-eastwards and runs in a straight line to a point 1100 metres, 294° from the same light, then in a straight line to an equidistant point bearing approximately 332° from the light. Thence it continues as an equidistant line which, east of 67°11′W. (approx.) uses Snipe Island and Islotes Hermanos as Chilean basepoints, and Islas Bécasses as Argentine basepoints, as appropriate. Off the east coast of Picton Island the small Islote Lepper and Isla Reparo have not been used as basepoints for reasons of the kind mentioned in paragraph 4 above, with particular reference to navigability in Argentine waters along the south shore of the Isla Grande.

10. The line ends at meridian 66°25′ West, terminal line of the "Hammer" (see Decision, paragraph 1).

ANNEX V

(See PART I (REPORT) section D, p. xiii)

BEAGLE CHANNEL ARBITRATION

(Argentina vs. Chile)

No. 1

Formal Opening Session, Alabama Room, Geneva, 7th August 1976

Inaugural Statement of Sir Gerald Fitzmaurice, President

Your Excellencies,
Ladies and Gentlemen—

I

We are here today to inaugurate the oral hearing in the Beagle Channel case, and I accordingly now formally declare that hearing open. This case concerns a dispute—the nature of which I shall indicate later—between the Republics—(whom I name in alphabetical order)—of Argentina and Chile. I see before me their Agents and Counsel, and greet them on behalf of my colleagues and myself—members of the Court of Arbitration. This includes also a warm welcome from the Government of the United Kingdom which, I would recall, is—for reasons to be mentioned in due course—formally the Arbitrator in the case, and to whom this Court will eventually transmit its views.

I furthermore welcome the diplomatic or consular and other representatives of the Parties and of the Arbitrator Government, and the representative of the International Labour Organization—and equally, and no less than these, the representatives of the Swiss Confederation and of the Canton and Municipality of Geneva, by whose kindness and co-operation in a number of ways it has been possible for the Court of Arbitration to have its Seat in this city; for the Parties to establish their Agencies here; and, not least, for this formal opening Session to take place in the historic chamber in which we are now sitting, for ever associated with the concept of international arbitration because it was within these four walls that there occurred, a little over a century ago, one of the most famous of all cases of the settlement by arbitral process of a serious dispute between States—a dispute that could otherwise easily have led to war, —the case of the *Alabama Claims* brought by the United States of America against Great Britain.

II

This is obviously not the occasion on which to discuss the *Alabama* case as such, but amongst other things it left two legacies behind it which are not without relevance to our own situation here and now; —*first*, coming when it did, it gave a great impetus to the concept of arbitration as a judicial or quasi-judicial method of settling international disputes, —*secondly*, although the reasons for choosing Geneva as the seat of the tribunal in the *Alabama* case were to some extent fortuitous, there can be little doubt that it furthered the idea of Geneva as an international city—a process that had already started some years previously with the signature of the first of the Geneva Red Cross Conventions in 1864. When I speak of Geneva as an international city, I do not of course mean that it is anything other than a part of the sovereign State of Switzerland. I have in mind simply its unsurpassed record in the promotion of the cause of peace and humanity, of good relations between States, and of the settlement of disputes according to justice and law. As regards the latter, the *Alabama* case of 1872 is far from having been the only occasion on which these premises have been used for such a purpose, —and in that connexion it gives me much pleasure—because of the nationality of two of my colleagues, members of this Court—to recall the quite recent instance of a Franco-United States arbitration that took place in this room some years ago. The tribunal in that case gave its award on 22 December 1963, and for those who are interested a report of it will be found in the *Revue Générale de Droit International Public* for 1965, from p. 189 onwards.

III

As regards the process of international arbitration, which the *Alabama* case helped to promote, I should like to say a few words about that before I come to our own case. Once again this is not the occasion on which to embark upon a history of the subject, and of the various forms that arbitration between States has taken in the past, —entertaining and instructive though that might be; —for today there are, in practice, only two ways in which States can obtain a *judicial* settlement of the legal differences that may arise between them—if it is such a settlement that they desire, —namely to submit the dispute either to a tribunal set up by themselves jointly, or else to a standing international tribunal whose jurisdiction extends to the subject-matter concerned,—in short, and for all practical purposes, either an *ad hoc* specially set up tribunal, such as our own Court of arbitration here, expressly constituted for the particular case, and for that case alone, or else a pre-existing standing tribunal such as the International Court of Justice at the Hague, empowered to deal with any cases referred to it that are within the scope of its jurisdiction.

It is not my intention here to discuss which of these two methods is the more to be preferred. In the international field, both have their place and their utility. What matters is that—for the settlement of legal disputes—States should have recourse to one or other of them as a means of solution. This is what the Parties to the present case—greatly to their credit—have done and, as I shall mention later, not for the first time. Why does it not occur more frequently? Certainly not for any lack of legal disputes between States: these abound. The reasons for the reluctance of States in this area are many and various. I have elsewhere and more than once indicated what, in my view, are the main ones, and I will not repeat them now. What I want to stress is that whatever these reasons may be, the fault does not lie in anything inherent in the international arbitral or judicial process itself. Of course the proceedings are long, because as a rule the disputes involved are long-standing and complicated, and the tribunal and the Parties need time in which to present and hear them, and to come to a properly deliberated conclusion. Of course they cost money, but not unduly so compared with other items of a national budget. Doubtless also, there may be defects of procedure in the practices and methods of international tribunals, but what national or municipal court is perfect in that respect? Finally, the outcome of the case, the decision of the tribunal, cannot, or at least seldom does, please everybody—but this is inseparable from the judicial process everywhere, whether in national or international courts. None of these elements, considered either singly or cumulatively, affords an adequate justification for failing to have recourse to international arbitration or adjudication where that would otherwise be the natural step to take. In such circumstances, appeal to one or more of these elements cannot avail as anything else but a pretext for a reluctance grounded essentially in government policy in respect either of the particular dispute or—alas all too frequently—of the international judicial process as such.

In saying all this, I am not blind to the difficulties of governments in this matter. It is not for nothing that two of my colleagues on this Court and I myself also, were for many years jurisconsults in our respective Ministries of Foreign Affairs. We know what goes on. My concern is simply that responsibility for what really results from the attitudes—possibly the quite understandable attitudes—of governments, should not be laid at the door of the international judicial process, where it does not belong. I believe that if the international community could rid itself of its many illusions in this sphere, it would become easier to see where the true obstacles lie, and easier to embark upon those courses that might, in the fullness of time, provide a solution.

IV

I come at length—and it is time I did so—to the present—*Beagle Channel*—arbitration, which is, so to speak, now safely before this Court. How has it got here? As to this, and other things that I shall have to say about the case, I must ask the indulgence of those of you who are familiar with it, if, the benefit of others, I refer to much that you will already know about.

By Article III of the Treaty of Santiago, signed on 22 May 1902—(a Treaty which is now no longer in force, but which was still in force when this case was originally brought before our Court)—the Parties—the Republics of Argentina and of Chile—nominated His (now of course Her) Britannic Majesty's Government to be the Arbitrator in any dispute between them that might be referred to arbitration under the other provisions of the Treaty. This succeeded to an earlier treaty of 1896 which had conferred a similar function on Queen Victoria's Government. This type of arbitration, namely by reference to a single Head of State, or his or her government, was very common in the 19th century; but, partly under the impulsion of the *Alabama* case, was being increasingly replaced by the modern system of a reference to a *court* of arbitration, or arbitral tribunal, composed of several members of different nationalities. In any event, in all the boundary disputes such as the present one, that have been referred to arbitration under these

Argentine–Chilean Treaties, the Arbitrator—the British Government—has seen fit, with the concurrence of the Parties, to appoint an arbitral tribunal to examine the matter and report to it accordingly. Thus, for the boundary arbitration that took place in London between 1898 and 1902, the tribunal consisted of Lord Macnaghten, one of the English Law Lords, as President, with General Sir John Ardagh and Colonel Sir Thomas Holdich as the other members, both of them distinguished geographers, and Sir Thomas Holdich also a military engineer. This arbitration, because it left certain points unresolved or in doubt, led many years later, in 1965–1966, to another one (the *La Palena* case as it is often called), again held in London, with the tribunal consisting of the late Lord McNair as President, and two expert geographers, Mr. L. P. (now Sir Laurence) Kirwan and Brigadier Papworth, as the other members. In both these cases, it will be observed, the members of the tribunal were all of the same nationality, which was also that of the Arbitrator government, and only one of them was a jurist.

In the present case, there are certain notable differences, much more in line with modern tendencies. We—that is to say my colleagues and I—are all of different nationalities; only one of us, myself, has the nationality of the Arbitrator Government; and we are all jurists. But the fact that, at the date of our appointment, we were all members of the International Court of Justice at the Hague, and that two of us still are, is entirely fortuitous. We were selected for such personal qualifications as we may individually possess, not as members of the International Court, —and it is in our personal capacity alone that we function. I would like to stress that.

V

All these disputes, including the present one, had and have their ultimate origin, or perhaps more correctly cause, in a Treaty of 23 July 1881, between Argentina and Chile (of which we shall hear much in the coming weeks) the object of which was to define the boundaries between the two countries. Like so many treaties however, it involved uncertainties and obscurities that, in default of agreement between the Parties could, in the long run, only be settled by reference to some form of international adjudication. But whereas the earlier arbitrations I have mentioned concerned the boundaries along the chain of the Andes, this one relates to a much more southerly area, not far from the tip of the continent where the territories of the two Parties converge, namely the region of the Beagle Channel, which is a narrow channel running in a general east–west direction and connecting the Atlantic and Pacific Oceans. This Channel has romantic associations for two reasons. *In the first place*, it is named after the British naval survey vessel " Beagle " from which it was seen in 1830 and which is popularly known as " Darwin's ship " because, on a later voyage, it carried the celebrated naturalist Charles Darwin on his voyage round the world in the course of which he gathered the materials for his great work " The Origin of the Species ", and for the theory of evolution by " natural selection ".

Secondly, —and perhaps of greater interest to our Latin-American friends—is the fact that the Beagle Channel constitutes one of the very few examples of what the old Spanish and Portuguese explorers were always looking for—what they called "El Paso"—a channel, strait, river, or waterway of some kind, that would connect the two great Oceans, the Atlantic and the Pacific. There are only three such waterways in the Latin-Americas. The most northerly is the Panama Canal which is man-made and must therefore, presumably, from the standpoint of romance, be discounted, although we can follow the English poet Keats, who, on first reading Homer, felt constrained to place himself in imagination with Cortez at some point on the Isthmus of Panama from which perhaps, on a clear day, both Oceans could be seen, and to utter these immortal lines which have always seemed to me to embody all the wonder of the discovery of the Americas,

"Then felt I like some watcher of the skies
When a new planet swims into his ken;
Or like stout Cortez, when with eagle eyes
He stared at the Pacific—and all his men
Looked at each other with a wild surmise—
Silent, upon a peak in Darien."

The second example, and first discovery of "El Paso", was the Straits of Magellan, the narrow Atlantic entrance to which was found—indeed virtually stumbled upon—in 1520 by the Portuguese explorer Fernando de Magellanes, in the course of the first circumnavigation of the world. Then, approximately 300 years had to elapse before the existence of the third—(at the time the second)—"El Paso" was definitely established, in the shape of the Beagle Channel. It is not surprising that this remarkable, and rather mysterious seaway, much of which could almost have been man-made, should have aroused great interest.

VI

But now we must, for the time being, leave the coasts of romance, and return to the more mundane, if most mellifluous, shores of the Lac Léman, where we shall be remaining until the case is finished. I shall not go into the back history of the dispute from the date when it first arose or began to arise, possibly some ninety years ago—for that history belongs to the substance of the case which we shall be considering during the weeks to come. But it *is* part of my function, on an occasion such as this one, to describe briefly the procedural steps that have led up to the oral hearing on which we are now embarking. Negotiations, which had been going on for a considerable time, led to the signature in English and Spanish, on 22 July 1971, and on behalf of the two Parties and of the Arbitrator, Her Britannic Majesty's Government, of the "Special Agreement" or "*Compromiso*" setting up this Court of Arbitration and defining its terms of reference. Accordingly, I will now ask the Registrar, Professor Philippe Cahier, to read those parts of the *Compromiso* that are of primary relevance and importance for understanding the nature of the case and the situation of this Court, —namely the Preamble and Articles I–III inclusive, IX, and XII–XVII inclusive. He will do this in a French translation. The official texts are of course in English and Spanish, both being equally authoritative:—

. . . .

. . . .

As regards the subsequent steps in the procedure, after the signature of the *Compromiso* in 1971, I propose to go over these very rapidly. From time to time the Court has held informal meetings with the Agents and Counsel of the Parties to settle various procedural points that arose. It has also issued a series of Orders, establishing the seat of the Court here in Geneva, appointing the Registrar, and fixing time-limits for the filing of the various written pleadings of the Parties and the annexed documents in the case. On two matters of considerable importance the position has been left in some sense open. *First*, the Court has not adopted any definite written rules of procedure. With the approbation of the Parties, it simply laid down for itself in Section II of its Order of 10 June 1972, the following general principle, namely that the Court would

> " with such adaptations as the particular circumstances of the present case may require, be guided by the rules and practices customarily applied in modern arbitral proceedings ".

A further clause provided that either Party could at any time bring before the Court any question of practice or procedure, and that the Court would decide it after consulting both Parties and, if so requested, hearing oral argument from them. So far, these arrangements have worked very satisfactorily, and I have no doubt will continue to do so. The *second* matter to some extent left open was that of language. It has from the start been understood that the basic language of the Court, in which its eventual report, for communication to the Arbitrator, the United Kingdom Government, would be drafted, was to be English, —and the various written pleadings filed by the Parties have been in English. It has been left to them to draw up or exchange with each other such translations as they felt they required. A regards the present oral proceedings, the understanding is that the Agents or Counsel of the Parties may address the Court in either English or French, the Registry ensuring a simultaneous interpretation into the other language; —and here perhaps would be the appropriate moment for me to extend on behalf of the Court our best thanks to the President and Registrar of the International Court of Justice at The Hague for the loan of no fewer than three of its interpreters, thus making it certain that we shall have interpretation of the very highest class.

The system adopted for the written pleadings was that of a *simultaneous* deposit with the Court (and exchange between the Parties) of, first, the Memorials by each of them, and then the two Counter-Memorials, and so on —instead of the more usual " successive " system whereby one Party deposits a Memorial, then the other a Counter-Memorial, followed by a Reply from the first Party and then a Rejoinder by the second. The main reason for this was to avoid either Party seeming to be placed in the position of defendant, and to comply with the spirit of that phrase in Article V of the *Compromiso* which provides that the order in which the written pleadings are presented " shall be without prejudice to any question of any burden of proof ".

The various written pleadings were exchanged, as to the Memorials in 1973; as to the Counter-Memorials in 1974; and as to the Replies in 1975. The case would then have been ready for the oral hearing, but in the meantime a question of some moment had arisen, namely the desire of the

Parties that the Court, or at least some of its members, should visit the Beagle Channel region, —what is technically known as a "*descente sur les lieux*"—for which the international arbitral and judicial process affords a considerable number of precedents. At first, the Court was reluctant to accede to this request, partly on account of the delay that would be involved, partly because it felt that it was probably already adequately informed on the basis of the written pleadings, which conformed in every way to the highest standards prevailing in such matters, and above all of the splendid series of maps and cartographical notes supplied by each Party, —for all of which I would like to take this opportunity of congratulating and thanking the Parties in the name of the Court, and of letting them know how greatly it has helped us. However, on account of it, the feeling of the Court was that perhaps a set of photographs of the main features of the Beagle Channel region might suffice, instead of a visit. Nevertheless, in the end, the Court agreed to go, and all of its members participated. We have never regretted it. It would take too long, and exceed any tolerance that I can reasonably expect, and which I have probably already overrun, if I attempted to do anything like justice to an experience that could not have been more interesting and agreeable, both on account of the excellence of the arrangements made, and the overwhelmingly generous hospitality extended to us by the diplomatic, naval and air authorities of each Party; and also on account of the charm of the region and the intrinsic fascination, from the point of view of the case, of seeing everything that we wanted to see and receiving all the information we asked for. Because the occasion involved going about in ships, boats and helicopters, and winter conditions in the region are severe, the visit could only take place in the summer or early autumn months which, in the southern hemisphere, means the period December to April. In fact it could not be arranged before March of this year. I have no doubt at all as to its great utility. Speaking for myself, it was not that one discovered anything startlingly new or unforeseen, but it enabled one to identify with the region, and to visualize its features in a way that only actual looking and seeing can ensure. May I once again thank our kind hosts, on both sides, for affording us this opportunity.

VII

And now I am approaching the end of my task for this morning. In connexion with the oral hearing, in which the Parties will begin their statements tomorrow, the only procedural problem that arose was as to which of them should start. Where the written pleadings have been delivered successively, the normal course is for the side that deposited the first such pleading also to speak first at the oral hearing, in answer to the last of the written pleadings, which will have been delivered by the other side. But where the written pleadings have been simultaneous, not successive, no such automatic solution is possible. Fortunately, in the present case the Parties have been able to agree amongst themselves, and the Court has concurred, that the Republic of Chile shall start—but this is on the clear understanding that Chile shall not on that account be regarded as being in the position either of plaintiff or defendant in the case—and nor will Argentina either; —and it is equally understood that the order of speaking will not in any way prejudice any question of the burden of proof that may arise in this case, should such a question come up. The task of the Court in these proceedings is to decide—on the basis of the requests of the Parties as respectively formulated in Article I of the *Compromiso*—what is the boundary-line in the disputed areas and, as required by Article XII of this instrument, to draw that line on a chart. These tasks the Court will carry out objectively, and to the best of its ability, without preconceptions.

For our working meetings we have been fortunate in securing premises in the new buildings of the International Labour Organization, whose administrative authorities, represented here today by the Deputy Director General, Mr. Valticos, I have much pleasure in thanking. A provisional time-table for these meetings, subject to adjustments and all necessary flexibility, has been agreed between the Court and the Parties with a view to terminating the hearing by about the last week in October. The Court thereafter will hope to produce its report by about the end of November, but there again there must be flexibility. This concludes my remarks, and I will now give the floor to the Agents of the Parties.

No. 2

Valedictory speech of the President at the end of the oral hearings 23 October 1976

My friends, for I know I speak on behalf of all my colleagues here when I say we believe that we can call you that, on both sides. The time has come to bring this part of the case to a close—these oral proceedings in which we have been engaged here for some weeks. This is always rather a solemn and even rather a melancholy moment in the history of an international litigation, especially for those on either side who have laboured so long and so faithfully, for months and even for years on the preparation and presentation of the case, and who now see it pass out of their hands to rest in those of the Court. There is also some sadness for the Court itself. The Court is now left to take difficult decisions on its own without the help and—if I may say so—support so unstintingly given to it by the Parties and by all those who have worked for them, and from most of whom we must now part.

Therefore, may I take this opportunity of thanking all those concerned on both sides, and not only those who have written so well and spoken so elegantly, but also those who—in the background—the backroom boys and girls—have carried out the researches and prepared the documentation and the maps, diagrams, tables and other compilations without which this case would have been hard to assimilate, and which have been of such great

* Page xiii in this publication.

assistance to the Court. The role of those who appear as counsel or advocates in these cases is an especially difficult one, for they have always to bear in mind that they have a duty not only to the Party they represent but also to the Court and to the law itself. And these duties may sometimes conflict. In the present case they have been carried out with exemplary fidelity, and highly complex arguments have been presented persuasively but also honestly. The Court is grateful to all those concerned for that.

It has indeed been a complex case, but it has also had the compensating advantage of being an intensely interesting one. Few cases—in the experience of my colleagues and myself as international judges—have exceeded it in that respect. We have learned much and have taken pleasure in much. And, may I say, not least in hearing the sonorities and terms of speech of the noble Spanish language.

The Court now remains here to reach its decision and this will take time. The arguments on both sides are powerful, and the choice between them will be far from easy. The Court will act as conscientiously as it can, bearing in mind the great importance which the outcome will have for both Parties. But here may I, in conclusion, add this: it is one of the more sombre aspects of litigation, and the Court is fully aware of it, that a decision given according to law is in principle bound, unless the circumstances are very exceptional, to disappoint one or other of the Parties. This is a risk they take in advance, together with the obligation of honour as well as of law to abide by the result, whatever it may be.

Now, to end up, I will ask the Agents of the Parties to remain available for consultation by the Court during the coming weeks and possibly even—I do not know—months. And subject to this request and to the delivery to the Registrar of the written statements which I mentioned earlier and regarding which I can give time-limits, if the Parties so desire—that can be done afterwards—subject to all that, I declare these oral proceedings closed. And I say to you, one and all: " Vayan con Dios ".

Printed in England by Her Majesty's Stationery Office

3177571 Dd 586676 K4 9/77

